ONE SIGNAL
PUBLISHERS

ATRIA

GUILTY CREATURES

SEX, GOD, AND MURDER
IN TALLAHASSEE, FLORIDA

MIKITA BROTTMAN

ONE SIGNAL
PUBLISHERS

ATRIA
New York   London   Toronto   Sydney   New Delhi

ONE SIGNAL
PUBLISHERS

ATRIA

An Imprint of Simon & Schuster, LLC
1230 Avenue of the Americas
New York, NY 10020

First One Signal Publishers/Atria Books hardcover edition July 2024

ONE SIGNAL PUBLISHERS / ATRIA BOOKS and colophon are
trademarks of Simon & Schuster, LLC.

Simon & Schuster: Celebrating 100 Years of Publishing in 2024

For information about special discounts for bulk purchases, please contact Simon &
Schuster Special Sales at 1-866-506-1949 or business@simonandschuster.com.

The Simon & Schuster Speakers Bureau can bring authors to your live event. For more
information or to book an event, contact the Simon & Schuster Speakers Bureau at
1-866-248-3049 or visit our website at www.simonspeakers.com.

Interior design by Jill Putorti

Manufactured in the United States of America

1 3 5 7 9 10 8 6 4 2

Library of Congress Cataloging-in-Publication Data
Names: Brottman, Mikita, 1966– author.
Title: Guilty creatures : sex, God, and murder in Tallahassee, Florida /
Mikita Brottman.
Description: New York : Simon & Schuster, 2024. | Includes bibliographical references.
Identifiers: LCCN 2023037692 (print) | LCCN 2023037693 (ebook) |
ISBN 9781668020531 (hardcover) | ISBN 9781668020548 (paperback) |
ISBN 9781668020555 (ebook)
Subjects: LCSH: Murder—Florida—Tallahassee.
Classification: LCC HV6534.T34 B76 2024 (print) | LCC HV6534.T34 (ebook) |
DDC 364.152/30975988—dc23/eng/20240313
LC record available at https://lccn.loc.gov/2023037692
LC ebook record available at https://lccn.loc.gov/2023037693

ISBN 978-1-6680-2053-1
ISBN 978-1-6680-2055-5 (ebook)

. . . I have heard

That guilty creatures sitting at a play

Have, by the very cunning of the scene,

Been struck so to the soul that presently

They have proclaimed their malefactions.

For murder, though it have no tongue, will speak

With most miraculous organ.

WILLIAM SHAKESPEARE, *HAMLET*, ACT II, SCENE II, 583–89

Contents

CONTENTS

ACT IV

Author's Note

This is a work of nonfiction. In addition to personal interviews with those involved in the case, my research in this book is drawn from the Florida Department of Law Enforcement homicide file (FDLE case number TL-1-0102 Jerry Michael Williams); the transcript of *State vs. Denise Williams*, Circuit Court of the Second Judicial Court, Leon County, Florida, volumes 1–7 (12/11/2018–12/14/2018); associated depositions and other court proceedings; the *Tallahassee Democrat*; trial footage posted online by the *Tallahassee Democrat* and the Law and Crime Network; the Record on Appeal *Denise Williams vs. State of Florida* (District Court of Appeal Case No. 2018 CF 1592 A), among other documents. No individuals other than Denise Williams and Brian Winchester have been charged. Some events and dialogue have been re-created.

– ACT I –

The Four of Us

"I am now in the hot gardens of the sun, where the palm meets the pine, longed and prayed for and often visited in dreams . . . though lonely to-night amid this multitude of strangers, strange plants, strange winds blowing gently, whispering, cooing, in a language I never learned."

JOHN MUIR, *A THOUSAND-MILE WALK TO THE GULF*

They say that hell is hot and dry. Tallahassee has hellish heat, but it's wet, not dry, which may be worse. There's no ocean breeze to cool things down, only thundershowers that come out of the blue, last for two minutes or six hours, then stop abruptly, moving to a different part of town. The humidity is stifling. Mold creeps into bathrooms and kitchens. Roaches grow fat. Snakes and lizards breed in crawl spaces.

With a population of fewer than 200,000, Tallahassee is less than half the size of Tampa, Miami, and Jacksonville, and less crowded than Orlando, St. Petersburg, and Hialeah. Visiting in the winter of 1827, Ralph Waldo Emerson described it as "a grotesque place . . .

rapidly settled by public officers, land speculators and desperadoes." Locals today call it "a small town with big pants on." In fact, Tallahassee became the capital almost by accident—it was conveniently equidistant from St. Augustine and Pensacola, the state's two largest cities at the time.

The public officers are still there—around a fifth of the city's population works for the state—but the desperadoes are long gone. Most of today's locals find the city pleasantly quiet—even boring, in a good way. Residents, for the most part, live ordinary, suburban, middle-class lives. But although the city in general may not be characteristic of the rest of the state, it shares the sense of the signature Floridian lassitude fostered by intense, humid heat. The journalist Edward King, writing in 1873, called it "slumbrous, voluptuous." Early visitors had a general foreboding that, although Florida was rich in beauty, its torpid atmosphere could lead to inertia, moral complacency, weakness, and sin.

Make no mistake: Tallahassee is a city of great beauty, full of lush, glossy greenery, moss-draped oaks, pine, hickory, and magnolias. In summer, the sky is full of stars. The sun sets over red clay hills. Strawberry trees and crepe myrtles shade old plantation homes, their lawns brightened by beds of azaleas and hydrangeas. For the most part, the city is safe and clean. As the slogans say, it's a "great place to raise a family."

Beneath the civil façade, however, things aren't so pretty. In the nineteenth century, this was the heart of Florida's slave trade; the legacy of injustice remains, defining the city's residential patterns and lingering in its place-names. Dreadful things have happened in these genteel suburbs. In 2018, in Glendale, a misogynistic gunman went on a shooting spree at a hot-yoga studio, shooting six women, two of them fatally. In 2010 in Beacon Hill, Henry Segura butchered his ex-girlfriend and her three children over child support payments. In 2014 in Betton Hills, the law professor Dan Markel was murdered by a pair of inept assassins hired by his ex-wife's periodontist brother. That same year, in the tony suburb of Golden Eagle, the high-profile podiatrist Adam Frasch bludgeoned his fashion model wife to death with a golf club and then dumped her body in the couple's swimming pool. Tallahassee was also the place where, in 1978, Ted Bundy went on a murder spree in a Florida State University (FSU) sorority house, attacking four women and killing two.

This underbelly is what haters call "Tallanasty." Not the Florida of beaches, golf carts, and retirement villages, but rather the slice of state that slips underneath Georgia and Alabama, like the nation's baseboard, or the gap beneath a badly fitting door. It has a higher per-capita crime rate than most other cities in the state. Trailer parks outnumber gated communities. In these low-income neighborhoods, billboards advertise home loans, mortgage refinancing, accident attorneys, Cash-4-Gold. Apart from the dollar stores, the strip malls are vacant: Retail Space Available. Rusting cars sit on blocks outside tumbledown ranch houses. A third of the city's population lives below the poverty line. You can sense the creeping swamp life.

———

In the 1988 North Florida Christian High School yearbook, the girls sport feathered bangs; the guys have shadows of facial hair. The cornerback Jerry Michael Williams, always known as Mike, grins openly at the camera. His girlfriend, Denise Merrell, three rows above him, smiles warily. To his left is his best buddy, Brian Winchester, looking self-conscious and hard to read. Brian's sweetheart, the curly-haired cheerleader Kathy Aldredge, wears a faux-pearl necklace. Leaf through the pages, and you'll spot Mike posing proudly in his football uniform, helmet under his arm; Brian, down on one knee, clutching his hunting rifle; Kathy waving her pom-poms; Denise, praised for her "bubbling personality," framed by pink and white balloons.

North Florida Christian High, formerly a segregation academy and still almost entirely white, is a private Baptist school. Set back from a quiet, oak-lined street, it shares a campus with the North Florida Baptist Church, and it is large—in 1988, there were more than 1,600 students. Teachers are required to be church members and attend services; a portion of their salaries is automatically taken by the church as a tithe. For students, Bible class is mandatory—every semester of every grade. The dress code is strict. Biology lessons include teachings on creationism. The school emphasizes sports, especially football; the campus has its own stadium. The school's parent-student handbook outlines its undergirding principles: "homosexuality, lesbianism, bisexuality, adultery, and pornography" are considered "perversions of God's will regarding sexual intimacy" and, when weeded out, are "subject to corrective action."

By consensus, for kids in the 1980s, Tallahassee was dead. You could hang out at Sears, or JC Penney, or the drugstore in the Northwood Mall. You could go to the library or the public swimming pool. There were two roller rinks, Skate Inn East and West. Slumber parties were a big thing, and mini golf. Those who'd grown out of such juvenile amusements spent their teenage years in their bedrooms, playing video games or Dungeons & Dragons.

But for children of churchgoing families, the city was a thrill. Mission trips, choir practice, summer camps, bowling nights, dodgeball games, potlucks, parties. Church-endorsed leisure pursuits were positive, friendly, and uplifting. If you'd never been exposed to Nintendo or D&D, you couldn't know what you were missing. Of course, sex was out of the question; even dating was discouraged. But sacrifice, some say, helps cement belief.

Although North Florida Christian was private, tuition in 1988 was affordable (around $5,000 a year), and the students didn't necessarily come from wealthy families. Brian Winchester came from a comfortable background—his father had worked hard to establish an insurance and investment firm, Winchester Financial—but his three friends came from more humble means. Mike's dad, J.J., was a bus driver; his mom, Cheryl, ran a daycare from the family's doublewide in Bradfordville, a suburb just north of the city. Kathy's folks ran the local print shop. Denise's dad, Warren, was an engineer with the Florida Department of Transportation. Her mom, Sylvia, known as Johnnie, stayed home to raise their four well-dressed daughters, Denise, Deborah, Deanna, and Darla.

Unlike the others, Mike Williams wasn't raised in a strict Baptist home. His mother, Cheryl, would cite the family's "very strong" belief in God but they rarely attended services, in deference to J.J.'s work schedule. Still, Mike was pretty straightlaced. At school, he was a standout athlete, council president, and active in student politics. He was social and gregarious, popular with girls, star of the high school football team. He wasn't a straight-A student, but he stayed on top of things, juggling a busy schedule. He didn't drink or smoke. For a teenager, he was disciplined and restrained, but he wasn't perfect. By the time he graduated from high school, he'd developed a few bad habits that became worse as he got older: He was untidy, tight with money, and never on time.

Among the four friends, Brian and Denise had known each other the longest. They first met at Holy Comforter middle school. Denise's father was a church deacon, and Johnnie, her mother, was a full-time wife and homemaker, devoting herself to raising, dressing, and disciplining the children. Like most Baptist wives of her generation, she was emotionally and financially dependent on her husband, and with only one wage earner in the family, money was tight. Nevertheless, Johnnie ensured her four girls were always immaculately dressed and groomed and taught them to be righteous, God-fearing, and submissive.

Denise was a cheerleader like Kathy and a finalist for homecoming queen. A slim brunette, she was voted "best dressed" in her senior year. She was also smart (she was student council president) and a compassionate Christian. She belonged to the Civinettes—an all-female high school service organization that visited the sick and elderly in nursing homes. Mike was her first real boyfriend. The moment she saw him, she wanted to be with him.

Brian, Kathy, Mike, and Denise made a tight foursome: all hardworking, responsible young people from close-knit, conservative families. There were no keg parties, no drug binges, no one-night stands. The boys played football; the girls cheered them on.

According to Church doctrine, God's plan for sexual intimacy was a lifetime relationship between one man and one woman. Extramarital sex was taboo, along with alcohol, abortion, and "alternative lifestyles." After high school, the four friends all went to FSU, commuting to class, and after graduating, they stayed at home with their families, saving up to get married while they settled into their careers.

———

Southern Baptists split from the Baptists who'd settled in the American colonies in the seventeenth century following a rift with their northern counterparts over the issue of slavery. The churches affiliated with the Southern Baptist Convention (SBC) generally identify themselves as independent, autonomous congregations that have voluntarily joined together for mutual support; nonetheless, the vast majority are conservative and evangelical. Even today, congregations are predominantly white. Most prominent Southern Baptists are outspoken Republicans, and many have political influence.

In a literal sense, all it takes for a church to be "Baptist" is for congregants to practice baptism by full immersion at the time they accept Christ as their personal savior (rather than at birth, as a matter of course). However, Baptist congregations, like those of most traditional churches, tend to be homogeneous and self-resembling, with an attachment to autocratic leadership and centralized forms of power. As a result, they adhere to the doctrine laid out by the SBC: the Bible contains no errors; personal acceptance of Jesus Christ is the only way to salvation; abortion and homosexuality should be discouraged; same-sex marriage is not respected; and those who are not baptized will go to hell ("an eternal, conscious punishment"). Many endorse the laying on of hands. And although such practices are not sanctioned by the SBC, some also speak in tongues and cast out demons.

North Florida Baptist Church was affiliated with the SBC, the largest Protestant denomination in the United States, which experienced a huge upheaval known as the "conservative resurgence" in the 1980s. Theologically liberal pastors were removed and replaced with traditionalists; churches, colleges, seminaries, and other Baptist institutions were likewise purged of moderates, who decried the atmosphere of dogmatism and intolerance. Pastors adhered to traditional interpretations of the gospel, anxious not to fall foul of the Convention authorities; congregants, too, were caught up in the widespread paranoia.

Still, although beleaguered internally, most Baptists kept their theological anxieties to themselves, putting up a united front and practicing their own beliefs as they saw fit. Most Baptists are unfailingly generous, kind, thoughtful people who treat others with respect, whatever their lifestyle or politics. Although to the outside world, the Church's regulation of sexual desire might seem uncompromising, for the most part, Baptists endorse the doctrine of "love the sinner, hate the sin."

Perhaps ironically, a 2019 investigation by the *Houston Chronicle* and the *San Antonio Express-News* revealed that a disturbing number of Southern Baptist leaders—pastors, deacons, and youth ministers— had been caught engaging in sexual misconduct since the latter years of the twentieth century. The investigation named 218 people who, since 1998, have either worked or volunteered in Southern Baptist churches and have been convicted of or pleaded guilty to sex crimes.

Many more have been accused, and more than 700 victims have come forward. Several esteemed figures of the Southern Baptist Convention were investigated by the U.S. Department of Justice for their role in covering up the abuse.

This religious and sexual catastrophe led to a torrent of scandalous revelations and expensive lawsuits, and, to some degree, the erosion of the deference traditionally shown to the formal heads of the Baptist church by its followers. By allegedly concealing wrongdoing and handling the abuse quietly, as an internal matter, the Church caused even further harm to victims. Like the similar scandal in the Catholic Church, these revelations showed how religious organizations can become perverse and pathological.

In short, all-powerful institutions left to their own devices breed secrets, and in their shadow, terrible crimes can be hidden for years.

———

Denise planned to marry and have children, in the Baptist tradition, but she also wanted to work. Like her mother, she had a good head for figures. She qualified as a certified public accountant (CPA)—a safe, stable job—and began working for the state. Her husband-to-be, Mike, appraised real estate. Kathy and Brian both found work in their respective family businesses—she at the Copy Shop, he, a political science major at FSU, selling insurance for his father's firm.

The two couples fit comfortably into their allotted roles, their lives absorbed by work, church, and family life. Mike stayed late at the office. Denise, too, worked hard. Kathy was committed to her parents and the family business. Compared with the others, Brian had a more leisurely schedule—his dad gave him a free hand, allowing him to work at his own pace. Nonetheless, although they now had less time together, the foursome stayed tight. They saw one another on weekends, spending time outdoors whenever they got the chance. Mike and Brian had learned to hunt and fish as kids. They'd be out in the woods or on the lake when hunting season came around. Sometimes Kathy and Denise would go with them. Occasionally, the two couples would go quail hunting on a plantation in Thomasville, just over the state line in Georgia. Sometimes they went fishing, scalloping, or bowling. It felt like things would go on that way forever—the four of them hanging out together on weekends, going to the park, going to restaurants, and eventually raising their kids alongside one another as well. Both couples married in 1994. Church weddings. Cake and lemonade.

————

"We are just totally overwhelmed!"

It's May 9, 1999, Mother's Day, and the lucky timing of their daughter's birth has earned Mike and Denise a fleeting appearance on a local television station, WCTV Tallahassee. A camera crew visits the maternity ward and films a brief interview with the proud parents. Denise, in a floral nightdress and dressing gown, is glowing. Her thick, shoulder-length hair is now blond, as it will be for the next twenty years, and with her pale complexion, she looks like an elfin version of Alice in Wonderland. The baby, named Anslee, has arrived early. "She was due Tuesday, and she would have made me wait a whole 'nother whole year for Mother's Day, but she came yesterday so I could enjoy this day and spend the day with her," says Denise, smiling bashfully. Mike, by her side, is wearing a black polo shirt and baseball cap. He's boyishly hand-some, with blue eyes and a dimpled chin. Like his wife, he speaks with a southern drawl. "It was unbelievable," he says, glancing at Denise. "I have a whole new respect for my wife, and women in general, and what they go through in order to bring new life into the world."

The couple wanted two more children, at least—and they could afford it. Mike was making good money. In August 1999, with their growing family in mind, the couple moved into a two-story, three-bedroom home at Midyette Plantation, a gated community. The sub-division was about five miles east of the beltway, just off picturesque Miccosukee Road, with its dense, dark canopy of overhanging Spanish moss. The house was airy and modern, with a large backyard sheltered by basswood, Scotch pine, and magnolia trees. It was an upward move for the couple, who both came from families that struggled financially.

Mike, with his working-class background, grew up wanting a better style of life. During high school, he worked hard to save for college: shelving cans at the Food Lion, serving customers at the Circle K, roll-ing coins at the bank. It's in childhood that we first learn the magic of money; we pick up on our parents' feelings about spending, saving, and owing, their regard for its importance, their ways of handling it. It's how we recognize power. Like many, his parents' financial struggles shaped Mike's feelings toward wealth.

As a student, he was hired by a small, family-owned company, Ketcham Appraisals, and began learning about the real estate busi-ness. He worked hard and discovered how it felt to start accumulat-ing cash. It was addictive. He graduated from college free of debt and continued working for Ketcham Appraisals, taking on more and more responsibility. He was ambitious and competitive, driven to improve and accumulate. The more he earned, the harder he worked. Making money was his only goal.

Ketcham Appraisals was a warm, welcoming family firm. When things were going well financially, the boss, Clay Ketcham, would take the entire office and their families to Disney World or Panama City. Mike made friends with some of the other young real estate agents, and he went deep-sea fishing with a couple of them. Most of the other employees were more prosperous than Mike, who was younger, and he looked up to them. "He thought people who had money were in a different strata from him. And he finds himself up in this different strata," recalled Clay Ketcham. "He's just got to work extremely hard to make the money that these guys were making, which meant he didn't spend much time at home."

At first, Mike shared space with two other real estate agents, but soon graduated to an office of his own. "He worked almost twenty-four hours a day," said Clay. Mike was always thinking about the future. He aspired to make partner at Ketcham Appraisals, or start his own company. He joined the Rotary Club to make local connections that might help him in business and planned to run for a seat on the city council or the county commission. Not yet thirty, he was already making nearly $180,000 a year. He planned to retire at fifty. He had it all figured out.

Denise adored their daughter, but the first year of motherhood was a struggle. She suffered from postpartum depression, and the baby's crying set her nerves on edge. Mike was frustrated; Denise stayed home from work until she felt more stable; her unhappiness put the couple's sex life on hold. They hired a maid to keep house. Mike would get back from work at 7 p.m. most days to cook supper, or he'd pick up something on the way home. He'd feed and play with the baby, give her a bath, put her to bed, then go back to the office and work until 2 or 3 a.m. If his daughter wouldn't settle, he'd take her along. "It wasn't uncommon to see Anslee in a little car seat sitting by Mike's desk, and him rocking her with one foot while he got on with his work," his boss recalled.

Mike's insecurities around money made him nosy about other people's income. He idolized Brian's security, partly because Brian seemed to have plenty of cash without ever having to work too hard. That was the kind of life Mike wanted to have one day. Instead, he was constantly fretting about how much he made compared with his colleagues. Clay described him as having a "shifty eye" when paychecks and income statements were lying around his desk. "He never had access to our accounting or anything, but you could tell he'd love to know how much was coming in and going out," said Clay.

His boss grew worried about him. One day, Clay insisted Mike hand over his office key and spend some time at home with his family. Mike tried, but he couldn't do it. "When Mike got upset, his mouth would break out in fever blisters . . . he was just coming unglued," Clay would recall. "Mike lived his life as if there was something haunting him."

Over Thanksgiving weekend in 2000, Brian and Mike drove out to Stuttgart, Arkansas, the "Duck Hunting Capital of the World," for the annual Duck Calling World Championship and Hunting Expo. Just the guys, with Brian's dog, Maggie, in a crate in the back. The hunting competition was a bust—Mike fell overboard and later caught pneumonia as a result. Too sick to work, he took a whole week off for the first time in his life. The moment he recovered, he made plans for another trip, this time with Denise. December 16, 2000, would be the couple's sixth wedding anniversary. Mike booked them a suite at the Gibson Inn, a ninety-minute drive south, in the quiet coastal town of Apalachicola. Denise's sister would take the baby. This would be a special, romantic trip designed to recharge their marriage. Adults only.

Alligators in the Winter

"This is the law of the beasts, and of the fowl, and of every living creature that moveth in the waters, and of every creature that creepeth upon the earth."

LEVITICUS 11:46

The security alarm at 5017 Centennial Oak Circle was disengaged at 4:30 a.m. on Saturday, December 16, 2000, the morning of Mike and Denise's sixth wedding anniversary. Mike set out early that morning to go duck hunting alone, which wasn't unusual. On the way, he dropped into Ketcham Appraisals for five minutes to pick up his gun, which, as the responsible dad of a curious toddler, he kept locked up in his office closet.

Around 12:30 p.m., Denise called her sister and said she would be late—Mike was still at the lake and wasn't answering his phone. It wasn't a big deal. Losing track of time was one of her husband's bad habits. When there was still no sign of him an hour later, Deanna drove to Denise's house to wait with her. Once before, while duck hunting on

Lake Seminole, Mike and Brian got stranded on an island and had to be rescued by Fish and Wildlife officers. Deanna assumed something of the kind had happened again.

When Mike still hadn't returned by 2 p.m., Denise called her father, Warren, and asked if he'd mind going to look for him. It was a tall order. Lake Seminole, an hour northwest of Tallahassee, sprawls across north Florida and south Georgia for sixty square miles. It was formed in 1958 by the deliberate flooding of large areas of land, much of which was heavily forested. The trees died, leaving an unsettling landscape of leafless, blackened stumps which—much to the annoyance of hunters and fishermen—protrude from the water, jamming up motors and damaging propellors. The reservoir is also known for its thick beds of hydrilla (aggressively growing tangled weeds with stems up to twenty feet long) and its sizable alligators.

To help with the search, Warren took along Mike's protégé, a young college student named Damon Jasper, who also worked at Ketcham Appraisals. Damon had been hunting with Mike the previous weekend and knew the boat ramps he liked to use. When Mike went to Lake Seminole, Damon said, he drove to the small town of Sneads then headed north, up River Road, launching his boat from a ramp on the lake's southwest side. The men thought he'd probably hit a stump, knocking out his motor. He still wasn't answering his phone.

It was 3:30 p.m. by the time Warren and Damon got to Sneads. They started by checking out some of the concrete boat ramps at the lake's edge. It didn't take them long to find Mike's green-and-tan Ford Bronco, which was parked in a grassy area by the road, but there was no sign of the boat, which made it even more likely that Mike was still out on the lake. Warren called the local Fish and Wildlife Commission office to let them know what was happening, and an officer named Greg Morris came to meet them. The three men drove around the lake for the next hour until the sun went down, pulling up at different vantage points to scan the water. They focused on the area near where Mike's car was found, known to locals as Stump Field, but there was no sign of either the hunter or his boat.

North Florida has a subtropical climate, with dry springs and mild winters, but summer and fall bring the threat of extreme weather: hurricanes, tornadoes, and floods. December is usually mild, and in keeping with the season, the day had been warm but overcast, with temperatures in the 70s. But as dusk fell, a heavy storm front moved in, and it started to rain. The temperature dropped from 80 degrees to 45, and a 50-mile-per-hour wind gusted through the trees. Fish and Wildlife officers wanted to start a full-scale search-and-rescue effort, but they had to wait another five hours until the storm had cleared. Warren Merrell and Damon Jasper drove back to Tallahassee for the night, returning early the following day, by which time the news of Mike's disappearance had begun to spread. Mike was popular and well-loved; everyone was desperately worried.

The next morning, dozens of friends and family members turned up at the lake, along with sheriff's deputies from Jackson County, the north Florida jurisdiction that includes Lake Seminole. The search went on all day and continued after dark, but nothing was found. Around midnight, law enforcement deployed a helicopter with a thermal-imaging radar device. Still, no one found anything until Brian Winchester and his father, Marcus, came across Mike's boat in a sawgrass-covered cove 75 yards south of the lake's western shore, not far from Stump Field. The boat, a 13-foot Gheenoe (a cross between a motorboat and a canoe), was full of hunting equipment (duck decoys, lifejackets, an ammunition box, and a 12-gauge shotgun, still zipped up in its case), but significantly, there were no waders. Mike's flashlight was also missing, and so were the keys to his truck. The boat's engine was in the "on" position, the fuel tank almost full, the motor undamaged.

Until then, everyone had assumed something must have happened to the boat, but now it looked as though something had happened to Mike, and the search took on a new urgency. People had conflicting opinions about his hunting skill. Some said he was careful and safety-conscious; others remembered him taking unreasonable risks. If he'd stood up in the boat to take a shot, some said, he could easily have lost his balance, fallen overboard, hit his head on a stump, and knocked himself out. If he'd managed to reach dry land, he might be lying on an island unconscious or suffering from hypothermia, given the recent cold snap.

There were a few clues, although no one knew what to make of them. A man told law enforcement officers he'd been hunting on the lake early on Saturday morning with his son. They'd seen Mike's truck and trailer, he said, and they'd heard shots out on the lake. On their way back, around 8:30 a.m., they'd seen Mike's boat floating in the sawgrass, not far from his truck. Another hunter said he'd seen three young men out on the lake that morning engaged in what appeared to be "a friendly conversation." He said one of them looked exactly like Mike, but they were farther up the road from where Mike's truck was found. Also, an elderly couple said they'd seen a young man dressed in camouflage jogging along River Road on Saturday morning at day-break, with no hat, no gun, and no flashlight.

Scott Dungey was a friend of Mike's from North Florida Christian High who'd spent a lot of time with him, fishing and hunting—in fact, he kept Mike's offshore boat in his garage. As soon as Scott learned that Mike was missing, he called his father-in-law, whose brother was head of the Florida Game and Fresh Water Commission, and the three of them drove up to the lake together. Years later, Scott recalled the temperature. "It was bitterly cold." Scott and his friend Kip Bembry were out searching for Mike until February. According to Dungey, for the first two weeks, there were "no less than twenty to twenty-five people out there every day."

Alton Ranew, a Florida Fish and Wildlife officer, had been patrolling the state lands and waters of Jackson County for almost twenty-five years. He was off duty on Saturday, December 16, the day Mike went missing, but the following morning, Sunday, he got a call from his supervisor telling him they needed him at the lake. To help with the search, Ranew took out a Fish and Wildlife boat with an outboard motor on the back, but there were so many stumps in the area he ended up exchanging the boat for a borrowed Go-Devil with an engine at the end of a long shaft that you could lift out of the water.

In the first days and weeks of the search, several colleagues from Fish and Wildlife joined Ranew, along with divers and deputies from the Jackson County Sheriff's Office. Helicopters and small airplanes conducted surveillance overhead (this was before drones were commonplace). They set up a temporary command post where Mike's boat had been found at the landing. Howard Drew, a family friend who'd taught Mike to hunt, kept a barrel fire burning. Local businesses in Sneads donated coffee, food, and blankets to the searchers, who, in addition to law enforcement officers, included Mike's family and friends, neighbors, business associates, old high school buddies, and strangers who just wanted to help. The search focused on the vicinity of Stump Field; everyone worked with painstaking vigilance.

In this eerie inlet, the water, for the most part, is no more than four to five feet in depth—not deep enough to conceal a dead body—but there is a murky slough to the west where it reaches up to fourteen feet, and this is where the search team focused. Alton Ranew went to the hardware store in Sneads and purchased some inch-and-a-half white PVC pipe, which he cut into sections of fourteen to sixteen feet, inserting a bamboo cane inside each section of pipe to keep it firm. He divided the area into a grid of six-foot squares; after thoroughly searching each square, he planted a cane in the mud at the bottom of the lake.

In addition, Ranew attached infrared cameras to the bases of two poles. As the men worked them through the mud, officers on the shoreline watched the camera feed on a monitor, looking for anything of interest and indicating by two-way radio where the searchers should focus. Progress was slow and frustrating due to obstructions on the lakebed. Nine days later, there was nothing to report except roots, stumps, and the tops of flooded trees.

On the tenth day, Mike's hunting hat turned up, floating in the water.

Missing Since: *December 16, 2000, from Tallahassee, Florida*
Classification: *Endangered Missing Adult*
Date Of Birth: *October 16, 1969*

Age: 31

Height: 70 inches

Weight: 170 lbs

Hair Color: Brown

Eye Color: Blue

Race: White

Gender: Male

Distinguishing Characteristics: Chicken pox scar on left cheek, previously wore braces on teeth and corrective shoes.

Clothing: Possibly wearing camouflage hunting clothes.

Jewelry: Possibly wearing a "St. Christopher" medal on a gold chain, a watch, and a wedding band on left ring finger.

Case Number: 00-121624

Details of Disappearance

Unknown. Jerry, also known as Mike, was last seen leaving his residence in the vicinity of the 5000 block of Centennial Oak Cir. in Tallahassee, FL. He allegedly was going duck hunting at Lake Seminole. His boat and vehicle, described as a green and tan 1994 Ford Bronco, were later found at the lake as well.

Investigating Agency

If you have any information concerning this case, please contact:

Jackson County Sheriff's Office

(850) 482-9624

During the following weeks, while deploying fewer law enforcement officers, the Florida Department of Law Enforcement (FDLE) commissioned more sophisticated technological equipment, including giant magnets, sonar scanning devices, and a high-powered underwater camera on loan from the National Geographic Society. It brought in a dive team from Montgomery County, Alabama, just north of Lake Seminole, and another from the Army Corps of Engineers. Cadaver dogs from Northwest Florida Search and Rescue were taken to Stump Field and given items of Mike's clothing to smell. There was a northeast wind that day, and even though the dogs indicated here and there, no solid evidence was found.

Officer Ranew continued to search, but more and more often, he did so alone. As the weeks turned into months, it became obvious: Mike Williams was dead. Law enforcement officials called off the search on February 10, 2001, after forty-four days.

Later that month, Mike's family and friends held a memorial service at Thomasville Road Baptist Church. The gallery was packed. A slideshow of photographs chronicled special moments in his life. Mike's friends and family shared their favorite memories, although many were too distraught to attend.

No one found any further trace of Mike until early June 2001, when Alton Ranew got a call from a local fisherman, Joe Sheffield, who'd found a set of waders floating close to shore on the southwest side of the lake, not far from Stump Field. Wrapped around the waders was a fanny pack containing fifteen unspent shotgun shells. Scott Dungey learned of the discovery through his father-in-law at the Game and Fresh Water Commission. That same day, he and Kip Bembry drove out to Lake Seminole with a seasoned cave diver named Charles Lamar English, an expert in deep-water body recovery.

It was summer now, the hydrilla thicker than ever. English didn't even bother with his dive mask—with all the weeds, he knew he wouldn't be able to see. He descended where Joe Sheffield had found the waders then pulled himself along the lakebed using the PVC poles still planted in the mud. Within five minutes, he emerged with a Maglite flashlight (still working) and a camouflage hunting jacket whose sleeves were inside out, suggesting that somebody had struggled to remove it. In one of the pockets was a laminated hunting license in the name of Jerry Michael Williams.

On June 29, 2001, Denise's attorney filed a petition for a presumptive death certificate. The same day, Judge John E. Crusoe of the Leon County Circuit signed the certificate. A victim of "presumed accidental drowning," Jerry Michael Williams was pronounced legally dead.

But still, no body had surfaced.

———

Lake Seminole always had its share of fatalities. Swimmers get cramps, duck hunters fall overboard, teenagers take risks. Boats flip, slam into rocks, spring leaks, collide, capsize. Hurricanes come out of nowhere. In June 2011, a thirty-four-year-old duck hunter in an inflatable chair was caught in a powerful current and dragged to death over the dam's edge. In May 2017, a fifty-six-year-old fisherman drowned after falling out of his canoe and getting tangled up in hydrilla and fishing line.

A dead body in a lake may not surface immediately, but it will undoubtedly surface in the end. In warm, shallow water, decomposition happens fast, and the release of putrefying gases can cause a body to emerge in two or three days. But the colder waters of winter slow decay, and may conceal a corpse for weeks or longer. When it does emerge, there may not be much left. Aquatic predators (fish and turtles) act quickly, and in the southern states, there's another threat. Alligators.

As far as anyone was aware, alligators had never killed anybody at Lake Seminole, although in June 2000, a man walking in three feet of water on the Georgia side of the lake had a chunk bitten out of his thigh by one. But during the search for Mike Williams, it was impossible to miss them. "They were swimming around, even though it was cold, all around the boats," recalled Scott Dungey. Fish and Wildlife officers noticed two fourteen-footers, and when handlers brought in cadaver dogs, they kept them on the leash. "Search personnel were routinely entertained at night by the sounds and eyes of numerous alligators inhabiting the area," reported Captain Debra Goebels of the Montgomery County Search and Rescue Team. "Two divers had physical encounters; once when an alligator brushed against a diver's leg and another when a diver actually stepped on a submerged alligator." Captain Gary Perdew, the dive team leader, noted that cadaver dogs picked up the scent of human remains all over the lake, just as they'd done at the scene of a recent airplane crash—another clear indication of "alligator involvement."

By late summer, when Mike's body still hadn't surfaced, rescue officers reached a morbid conclusion: "alligator involvement." They concluded Mike's body must have become tangled in the vast underground beds of hydrilla, where it was discovered and consumed by the lake's largest and most fearsome inhabitants, with turtles and catfish polishing off the remains.

But for some people, the alligator element didn't add up. How, for example, had alligators removed Mike's waders and jacket? If he'd had the strength to undress while in the water, why wasn't he capable of swimming to land? Lamar English, the diver who discovered the jacket, noticed it was in strikingly pristine condition, given the presumption Mike had been torn apart by aquatic beasts. "At the time, I thought, well, you know, alligators, they don't eat by . . . taking a bite, and nibble, or whatever," he said. "They grab ahold. They tear off a hunk and swallow it whole." English also pointed out that "gators don't have opposable thumbs. They're not going to very gently pull a set of waders off a body or take a hunting jacket off somebody."

FDLE officers talked to alligator experts, who said the scenario was impossible—not only because alligators wouldn't know how to remove waterproof outerwear, but because they don't eat during the winter. Some suggested that even if that was true, alligators might have taken Mike's dismembered remains to a den or a cave, stowing them away until the weather warmed up. Some pointed out that the morning Mike went missing was unseasonably warm until the storm front moved in. There was also a theory that northern Florida alligators had different eating habits from southern Florida alligators. Others thought alligators behaved differently according to whether they lived in a shallow pond or canal, where the water rarely chilled, or a large body of water like Lake Seminole, where the water temperature got much colder. Suddenly, everyone was a gator expert.

Confusion reigned. An investigator asked Denise's sister, "Has anybody in your family done any research about . . . the actual habits of alligators in the winter months, especially north Florida alligators, because they're different than south Florida alligators?" Deanna replied, "You know my dad was told, alligators—and I'll get this mixed up, but—feed when it's cold or don't feed when it's cold. He was told a lot of information by people out there."

Most herpetologists agree that between November and late February, alligators, even in Florida, go into a state called brumation—a kind of semi-hibernation in which their metabolism slows down to conserve body temperature, and they no longer need to eat. But everyone involved in the search at Lake Seminole noticed active alligators in the lake, and they didn't appear to be semi-hibernating. People pointed out that hunters' dogs were taken by alligators all year round. And not only dogs. Of the thirty-four fatal gator attacks in the United States in the last fifty years, two happened in November; nonfatal attacks have occurred in December and January. Perhaps some alligators don't realize they're supposed to be brumating. Either that or they just don't care.

– 3 –

Your Son Is in the Lake

"Almost without exception, a corpse lying on the bottom of a lake or river eventually will surface because of the gas formed in its tissues as a result of decay and the action of internal bacteria . . . Witnesses to this event have described corpses breaking the surface of the water with force, like the popping of a cork."

GARY HAUPT, "DROWNING INVESTIGATIONS,"
FBI LAW ENFORCEMENT BULLETIN (2006)

"Mike did not drown. He did not get eaten by alligators. You have to bring him home."

This was the revelation received by Mike's mother, Cheryl Ann Williams, as she stood gazing out over the calm waters of Lake Seminole on Christmas Eve 2000, eight days after Mike disappeared. God, she believed, was speaking to her.

The pronouncement reinforced what Cheryl already felt. Mike had been hunting since elementary school. Their friend Howard Drew had given him lessons, spending hours on safety techniques. Howard had often made Mike practice getting out of his waders in the family's ten-foot-deep backyard swimming pool. "Mike knew Lake Seminole by heart, every stump and every hole," recalled Cheryl. If he wasn't dead something terrible must have happened to him.

Cheryl was fifty-six when her son went missing, but her bright blue eyes and cherub's face read younger. She dressed in bright colors and wore her gray hair in pigtails. For twenty years, she'd run a small daycare facility from her double-wide trailer in Bradfordville, north of Tallahassee. Children loved Ms. Cheryl, but adults sometimes found her naïve and a bit eccentric. She was deeply spiritual, believing in dreams, omens, portents, and messages from God. When something mattered to her, she didn't let go.

Two years earlier, her husband, Jerry Jerome, known as J.J., had died unexpectedly at age sixty after undergoing emergency surgery for injuries he'd sustained in a motorcycle accident. Cheryl believed that medical negligence had caused J.J.'s death—he'd developed pneumonia and an undiagnosed bleeding stomach ulcer after the surgery but was sent home from the hospital anyway and died five days later. Cheryl had filed a lawsuit against the hospital. About six weeks before Mike went missing, he'd called her late one night and asked whether, if she won the case, he could have $50,000. Cheryl wondered why he needed it. "Momma, I just want to take a year off from everything," he told her. Cheryl realized Mike had been working too hard. He needed a break. "If I win, you got it," she said.

Recalling what Mike had told her about working too hard and needing to take "a year off from everything," Cheryl started to wonder whether he might have had a nervous breakdown. Maybe he'd fallen and hit his head. Perhaps he'd lost his memory. Or maybe he'd decided to take a year off without telling anyone. Stress could lead people to do strange things. In March 2001, she went to court in the medical negligence case. Nothing came of the lawsuit, but it didn't matter by then. All she cared about was finding Mike and bringing him home.

In her journal, Cheryl wrote down everything she saw and heard that might help her make sense of her son's disappearance: tips from TV crime shows, dreams, suspicious conversations, memories, speculations, rumors, gossip, newspaper headlines, and mystical visions. Whenever they had time, Cheryl and Nick, Mike's older brother, would drive out to Sneads and other small towns around Lake Seminole to distribute the flyers and missing posters they'd made showing Mike's picture. Cheryl wrote letters to the *Tallahassee Democrat*, begging it to bring attention to Mike's case. Someone must surely have seen him if he was still alive, as she believed.

One thing she felt sure of: Her son hadn't been eaten by alligators. She'd heard they hibernate during the cold weather and knew duck hunters took their hunting dogs on the lake in winter, which they'd never do if there were a chance of losing them to gators. Following her intuition, she wrote to a biology professor at FSU to ask him about the habits of alligators. Matt Aresco specialized in turtles, not alligators, but as he told Cheryl, wherever you find turtles, you find alligators. "Professor Aresco has studied the behavior of alligators at Lake Seminole," wrote Cheryl in her journal. "He told me *alligators don't eat in cold weather*. . . . He said, 'Alligators did not eat your son!'" The professor, she wrote, respected her tenacity and devotion. "I offered to pay him for his research. He said, 'No way! I have a mother too!'" Aresco told Cheryl that alligators are dormant once the temperature drops. "It is impossible physiologically for an alligator to eat in cold water," she noted. "It would kill the alligator."

Seven months after her son disappeared, Cheryl got a call from Tony Bridges, a *Tallahassee Democrat* staff writer researching a short piece on local people who'd gone missing. He asked for permission to quote from Cheryl's letters to the newspaper, and he also asked for a photo of Mike. The article, "Missing People Not Lost Causes," appeared on August 5, 2001. The timing wasn't good—four days earlier, a tiger had killed a man at Savage Kingdom in Ocala—but this was Florida. There was always something.

According to the article, of the fifty-seven local people who'd been reported missing since January, Mike was one of only three still unaccounted for. Bridges quoted Cheryl's speculation that Mike might have suffered an injury and could be "wandering, not knowing who he is or where he is."

––––––––––

When Mike went missing, it felt like time slowed down. Some people, such as Cheryl, still couldn't believe he was dead. Those who did mourned in silence. His absence broke up the longtime foursome, and everything felt unbalanced. Kathy was broken by the loss; Brian, whose grief was less palpable, began to distance himself from her. Kathy thought he was cold and unfeeling; she couldn't believe he was going on with his life as though nothing had happened. As for Denise, she locked herself in her room and wouldn't see anybody except her family. For months, she was in a terrible state. By all accounts, Mike's disappearance left her utterly devastated. "She seemed truly heartbroken, like her world had ended," her mother-in-law would write in her journal.

On September 10, 2001, Cheryl and her oldest son, Nick, were about to go over to Centennial Oak Drive for their weekly visit with Anslee when they got a call from Denise telling them not to come. Instead, she said, she'd bring Anslee over to their place. Two hours later, she hadn't shown up. Cheryl, concerned her daughter-in-law might have gotten into a wreck, was pacing up and down in her driveway when Denise's father drove up. There was no sign of the baby.

"Warren was livid," Cheryl wrote later. "He was screaming at me. I was shocked. This was not the Warren I knew." She invited him inside, but he wouldn't come. "You're crazy; you need psychiatric help. Your son is dead in the lake," he insisted, castigating Cheryl for believing in signs and omens. "If you were a Christian and in the church, you would believe your son was in the lake," he said. When he'd gone, Cheryl could only wonder if Warren knew something she didn't. She found his certainty suspicious. Of Warren, she wrote in her journal, "I believe he knows where my son is and what happened to him." She added, "Denise has never been to the lake because her daddy told her not to go."

Two years after Mike's death, his widow was starting to socialize again. In her journal, Cheryl jotted down the local gossip. "Denise has joined the gym by the Miracle Five Theater. She goes three times a week and has a personal trainer." Karen Lamb, Deanna's sister-in-law, passed along some mysterious news. "Karen told me that Denise has been meeting people in parking lots. . . . The grapevine has it that she is dating."

In October 2002, a friend of Cheryl's named Elizabeth Triquet had a dream about Mike. Said Elizabeth: "I went to the woods and the woods were silent. He's been there the whole time and he has been watching us, he knows what is going on." Three days later, Cheryl and Nick visited "our friend who has the gift of prayer," a woman named Edith Crisp. "She had the feeling that Mike was close and he was watching us."

––––––––––

Notes from Cheryl's Journal:

> *February 5, 2003. Mike Klaas on NBC Laci Peterson Case—* "Spouse of missing person doesn't normally sell loved one's belongings."
> *August 6, 2003. New York Times headline: "Most murders committed by family or friends."*

In October 2002, Cheryl discovered that what she'd heard on the grapevine was true—Denise was dating. She was going out with Jimmy Martin, a close friend of Mike's from North Florida Christian High School. Everyone was baffled by the match. Jimmy was reputedly a loner with little apparent interest in women. By all accounts, Denise had never cared for him. Everyone wondered why she'd changed her mind. Was she dating Jimmy because he reminded her of Mike, or was he simply close to hand? "Has she lowered her standards just to have a date?" wondered Cheryl. The romance was perplexing, but she was pleased that Denise was preoccupied—dating, shopping, getting her hair and nails done. Her daughter-in-law's distractions meant Cheryl got to spend more time with Anslee. The child brightened her life, but being around her could be heartbreaking. One night in February, Cheryl noted in her journal, "Anslee asked me, 'Grandma Cheryl, do you know my daddy's telephone number? My mommy lost it.' I told her, 'Anslee, they don't have telephones in heaven.' It depressed me terribly."

Cheryl often mentioned Brian Winchester in her journal but wrote about Kathy less and less as time went by. She knew Kathy had been terribly shaken by Mike's disappearance; in their grief, Kathy and Brian had drifted apart, and Kathy had moved back in with her parents. By April 2003, the couple had officially separated and shared custody of Stafford, their young son. By then, Denise's feelings for Jimmy had gone cold. Cheryl suspected a new guy had pulled her away, but she couldn't be sure.

Brian took the separation in his stride. He didn't seem jealous when Kathy started dating an old family friend, Rex "Rocky" Thomas, Jr. Cheryl ran into Brian at Anslee's fourth birthday party on May 8, 2003, and he seemed to be doing just fine. "Brian Winchester and I talked at length," she noted. "He asked about girls at the party. He said he was single and could look legally." Later that same day, Clay Ketcham would catch her ear. "He said a day never goes by that he doesn't think of Mike."

Cheryl continued to do practical things to help find her missing son. She put up more missing posters, handed out more flyers, and wrote more letters to the *Tallahassee Democrat*. She also wrote to the Florida Department of Law Enforcement, imploring it to reject easy explanations about Mike's disappearance. "I don't believe that he walked off," she wrote, "I believe there was something he found out about someone he knew. PLEASE HELP ME FIND MY SON. THANK YOU."

Since Mike's disappearance, to Cheryl's confusion, she'd been receiving catalogs from companies that sold duck-hunting equipment and accessories, such as Cabela's and Mack's Prairie Wings. They were addressed to both her and Mike. This was strange because Mike hadn't lived at her address for many years before his disappearance, and it wasn't as if she'd suddenly decided to take up duck hunting in middle age. Why had they started filling her mailbox?

She called both companies, pretending she wanted to place an order, and gave them the customer number from the catalogs. The representative from Cabela's told her she'd last placed an order in her name eleven years ago, and they had no idea why she'd started getting the catalogs again. Mike, she learned, had last placed an order in March 2000, nine months before his disappearance.

Mack's Prairie Wings was a store in Stuttgart, Arkansas, where Mike and Brian had traveled for the hunting competition a few months before Mike's disappearance. When she called the store, the representative told Cheryl customers received catalogs only by request, and the company kept no record of when and who made the order. They were a small business, too small to advertise nationally, and they didn't buy or exchange customer lists.

The night of September 12, 2003, marked the fifth anniversary of J.J.'s death. Cheryl dreamed Mike was home, and everything was fine. The following evening, she had a more disturbing dream. J.J. was telling her to "look at the pictures." When she woke up, she made a note in her journal. "'Cheryl, look at the pictures,' he said. I looked everywhere—nothing." Two days later, sitting in her living room armchair, she noticed the catalog from Mack's Prairie Wings. For the first time, she saw the picture on the back, and it gave her chills. It showed three Labrador retrievers—one black, one choco-late, and one yellow—all wearing bandanas and posing in front of a stars-and-stripes flag.

Was this the picture J.J. had been telling her to look at in her dream? The chocolate Lab looked just like Hershey, the dog Brian had given Cheryl for protection after J.J. died. In her journal, she asked: "Is it possible that Mike saw the catalog in the store and requested it to be sent to me (as a message) knowing that Stuttgart, the black lab and the chocolate lab would signal to me that he's okay?" If the catalog was a message from Mike, what did it mean? And why couldn't he simply call her on the phone or write her a letter?

Around this time, Cheryl discovered that Denise was dating a forty-three-year-old coworker. One Saturday night, her new admirer invited Denise to an Eagles concert in Panama City. Cheryl took care of Anslee while her daughter-in-law was out of town. It must have been a long date—uncharacteristically, Denise was two hours late picking Anslee up the next morning, and they missed church. The shadowy romance ended—badly—in mid-August. Marcus Win-chester, Brian's father, apparently went to speak to the inspector general at the Department of State to stop the man from bothering Denise at work.

It wasn't unusual for Brian to protect and defend Denise, but this upsetting episode seemed to bring them together in a different way, almost as if he were guarding his territory. After fighting off Denise's alleged stalker, he rarely left her side. Some wondered whether Brian's concern for his best friend's widow might have developed into something deeper. Were Brian and Denise a couple? If so, they kept quiet about it. But people were starting to talk.

Persons of Interest

"'Had a husband once. Looked like a bad one to me. He
died.' She paused and thought. 'I guess he died natural,'
she added. 'I never heard different.'"

RAYMOND CHANDLER, *FAREWELL, MY LOVELY* (1940)

Almost overnight, it seemed, Denise had become devotedly, even
ostentatiously religious. She'd joined a women's prison ministry
run by Henree Martin, Jimmy's mother, and had started going into the
prison to give Bible classes. Her car got rear-ended because, allegedly,
she was reading her Bible at a stoplight. On January 23 and 24, 2004,
Cheryl took Anslee while Denise went to preach in prison. The same
thing happened in February and again in March. "Does she want to
know what prison is like?" Cheryl wondered.

Still consumed by her son's disappearance, Cheryl felt uneasy about
the budding romance between Mike's widow and his closest friend. In
the past, she'd never doubted that Mike and Denise were in love. Their
marriage, she believed, was solid and stable. But after her son went

missing, Cheryl realized she'd been naïve. Others who knew the couple, including Denise's sisters, had seen red flags. "Everybody in Denise's family knew there were problems," Cheryl learned. "Even Mike's boss knew there were problems because Mike had talked to him." According to Clay, Mike's co-workers all hated Denise. She had him under her thumb, they said. They'd heard her on the phone with Mike, nagging and bullying, withholding sex until she got what she wanted. Clay himself thought Mike's marriage had taken a "strange" turn on Anslee's first birthday, when instead of spending time with her baby daughter, Denise decided she needed to "take a breather" and spent the weekend alone in a fancy hotel. People found it hard to fathom. Gossip spread.

For the first time, Cheryl started to see things clearly: When Mike went missing, his marriage was on the rocks. Was Denise having an affair? If so, she would surely have kept it secret. "Denise's whole life was built on appearances," said Patti Ketcham. What if Denise's new relationship with Brian wasn't as new as it seemed? Could Brian and Denise have been involved in Mike's disappearance? Had they forced him to leave town? If so, why? And where had he gone?

"Ms. Williams, now's your chance. Tell me what you want me to know."

It was February 6, 2004. Four years and two months since Mike went missing. Cheryl was sitting at her kitchen table talking to John Stevens, a Florida Department of Law Enforcement investigator who had reached out a week prior. For almost two hours, Stevens listened gravely, taking notes while Cheryl told him everything she knew about the strange events surrounding Mike's disappearance. Before he left,

Stevens made a promise. "You are not crazy," he reassured her. She'd be hearing from the FDLE again very soon.

Cheryl was exhilarated. Four years of pressure were finally paying off. She still didn't believe Mike was dead, but at the same time, she knew he'd never walk away without saying a word, leaving behind friends, family, and his cherished baby daughter. She knew something had happened to make him leave town—she thought maybe he was being blackmailed—but until now, whenever she'd approached law enforcement, she'd been patronized and dismissed, treated as naïve, eccentric, and emotional.

But John Stevens was true to his word. Ten days later, two more investigators came by: Ronnie Austin, a seasoned cop in his forties from the State Attorney's Office in Tallahassee, and Derrick Wester, also an experienced officer, from the Jackson County Sheriff's Office. Cheryl told them what she'd told Stevens—about Mike's habits and personality, her dreams and premonitions, and her feeling that Brian and Denise, now undeniably a couple, were somehow involved in his disappearance.

Austin and Wester listened closely. Working the case wasn't going to be easy, they warned her. Mike's truck, boat, and trailer hadn't been processed for fingerprints, inventoried, or impounded as evidence. Nobody had sent the waders and jacket to the crime lab. All this was old news to Cheryl. But there was one thing she hadn't known—that before his disappearance, Mike had taken out three separate life insurance policies. "Anyone who had this file in front of them would know something is majorly wrong," Ronnie Austin told her as the pair pored over the documents. Cheryl was encouraged by the officers' sympathy and understanding. Austin impressed her with his sincerity.

"He doesn't think I'm crazy. He wishes I'd said something earlier," she wrote in her journal. But while she welcomed the attention from law enforcement, she didn't want Denise to know she'd been talking to the cops. Their relationship was already frayed, and Cheryl was worried about losing access to her granddaughter. To avoid trouble, the officers promised they'd keep their investigation hush-hush.

All summer, Denise seemed off-kilter, unstable. She'd always been lithe and slight, but now she seemed frail and malnourished. Her blond hair hung limply to her shoulders. Frankly, she looked ill. In July 2004, in her journal, Cheryl wrote, "Everyone is shocked by Denise's appearance. She's lost a lot of weight. She's too thin!" Her daughter-in-law seemed to be under some terrible pressure, observed Cheryl. On October 6, she asked Denise's sister Deanna if she could intervene. "Get Denise to eat," she implored. On October 14, she reached out to Denise's mom, Johnnie Merrell. "[She] knows Denise is in trouble," noted Cheryl, after their conversation, adding that Johnnie had said something very strange. "Brian Winchester is holding something over Denise. When it comes out the family might not be able to survive it."

Cheryl was extremely busy: running her daycare, babysitting her granddaughter, and feeding twenty feral cats. Nevertheless, she was devoted to finding her son. She put missing-person flyers on utility poles and in the lobbies of grocery stores. She saved up to pay for a billboard display on Thomasville Road showing Mike's picture and details about his disappearance. She made a handheld picket sign containing a photo of her son under the word "MISSING" and carried it around the FSU football stadium before home games, hoping it might jog someone's memory. On Sundays, she'd walk up and down holding her sign outside the Four Oaks Community church, where Brian and Denise attended service. Some of the congregants felt sorry for her. Others felt she was purposely disrupting the Sabbath and yelled at her to go home.

But Cheryl wasn't the only one who thought Brian and Denise were behind Mike's disappearance. Others in the community were sharing their suspicions in whispers. Nobody believed Mike had drowned in Lake Seminole. Cheryl thought he was still alive, but others had darker misgivings. Some suggested Brian and Denise might have been "involved" in Mike's disappearance or that they "knew something." Clay and Patti Ketcham both surmised that after coming into the office to get his gun on the morning of December 16, Mike had changed his mind about going duck hunting. Maybe he didn't feel well. Maybe he thought better of spending his wedding anniversary away from his wife. Returning home unexpectedly, did he find Anslee on her own? Worse, did he find Brian and Denise in bed together? Was there a terrible confrontation? Or perhaps Mike had learned some shocking news. Did he discover he wasn't Anslee's biological father? Did he decide to walk away from his life and start over somewhere new? It was easier to think up hypothetical scenarios than to face the possibility that either Denise or Brian had committed cold-blooded murder.

Letter to Florida Department of Law Enforcement from Cheryl Williams:

Dear Investigator Wester,

If my son were living or hunting in or around Stuttgart, Arkansas, I believe he would be in disguise. Mike would know that people from

*Tallahassee go there to hunt. He would know that someone might rec-
ognize him. He might be wearing glasses. He might have a full beard.
He might have long hair.*

Thank you again,
Ms. Cheryl Ann Williams (Mike's Mom)

———

On December 16 every year, the anniversary of Mike's disappearance,
Cheryl paid for a picture of her son to be published in the *Tallahassee
Democrat*, along with a reminder that he was still missing. Every time
the photograph appeared Denise got a little more upset. In 2001, after
seeing Mike's photo in the paper, she told Cheryl she didn't ever want
to see Mike's picture in the newspaper again. She didn't want to hear
his name or anything more about him. She and Anslee needed to go
on with their lives without constantly being reminded of their loss.
Cheryl found this baffling.

"Imagine it was Anslee that had gone missing, and you believed she
was still alive," she asked her daughter-in-law. "Would you just stop
searching?"

"I'd take the advice of the experts," retorted Denise.

It didn't take long for word to spread that law enforcement officers
had been visiting Cheryl's house. One day, she and her son Nick were
at a Chili's eating lunch when they got a call from Denise asking if
she could come over to talk. When they finished their meal and drove
back home, Cheryl told investigators, Denise and Brian had beaten
them to the punch—they'd set up shop and were waiting for them at
Cheryl's house, ready to tamp down any thought of wrongdoing, do-

mestic or otherwise. Denise coldly informed her mother-in-law that if she continued cooperating with law enforcement, she'd never see Anslee again. Cheryl tried to object, but, as she later noted, "Brian told Denise they weren't getting anywhere and they got up and left."

Cheryl never saw her granddaughter again.

Hoping for a breakthrough in the case, Ronnie Austin and Derrick Wester started following up Cheryl's leads. They talked to alligator experts. They examined climate data for Lake Seminole. They analyzed tips from the Crime Stoppers hotline. They filed Mike's description with the National Center for Missing Adults. They talked to people who thought they recognized his photo from the flyers and posters Cheryl was still distributing. They interviewed Mike's family, friends, and colleagues. Everybody wanted to help, but nothing panned out. It was one dead end after another.

But something curious emerged from the interviews. When it came to the day Mike went missing, there were discrepancies in people's accounts. Denise's sister Deanna mentioned that when she drove to Denise's house in the early afternoon, expecting to pick up Anslee and free the couple for their anniversary celebration, "there were no bags packed . . . Not even Denise's makeup kit was packed." After Mike disappeared, Brian told Cheryl that he and Mike had planned to go duck hunting that morning, but he'd called Mike at 3 a.m. to cancel. This was Denise's story, too. Mike and Brian had planned to go duck hunting, but Brian had called at 3 a.m. to cancel, so Mike went to the lake alone.

But if Brian had made plans to go hunting at Lake Seminole with

Mike—plans that he didn't cancel until a couple of hours before they were supposed to meet—then why did his father-in-law, Jimmy Aldredge, tell investigators that Brian had called him at 9 p.m. the day before Mike went missing to invite him to go duck hunting the following day at Lake Seminole? They'd planned to meet in the T.J.Maxx parking lot on Thomasville Road, where Mr. Aldredge would later state he'd waited for over two hours as Brian failed to show up. Brian called afterward to apologize, saying he'd overslept and misplaced the keys to the boat they were going to use, which belonged to a friend.

Later that day, the Aldredge family got together for their annual Christmas party at the home of Kathy's grandparents in Cairo, Georgia, thirty miles north of Tallahassee. Kathy and Brian were supposed to drive up together with their son, but Kathy told investigators Brian was out on the lake all day, and she and Stafford had to set off without him. He wouldn't answer his phone, and she was very annoyed. He finally showed up in Cairo mumbling something about losing the keys to a friend's boat.

To confuse matters further, Mike's friend Damon Jasper told investigators that he, too, was supposed to go hunting with Mike the morning he went missing, but went out drinking the night before and overslept. Damon's story was a curveball—he was mistaken, he later confessed. He'd gotten the days confused. Perhaps he truly believed he was supposed to be meeting Mike that morning, or perhaps he felt the need to insert himself into the catastrophe. A loose connection to a tragic event can seem solid and sure in hindsight, turning a vague plan into a lucky escape or a blessing from God.

One more thing caught the investigators' attention. Apparently, not long before he vanished, Mike had complained about Denise taking money from their account without explanation. Denise's sister Deanna told Ronnie Austin that a few weeks before she last saw him, Mike had told her, "I've given Denise six months to straighten up." Austin was confused by the phrasing. Did he want Denise to spend more time cooking, or cleaning the house? "None of my sisters do that," laughed Deanna. "We're very spoiled." No, what Mike meant, she said, was for Denise to stop taking cash from their bank account without telling him.

Another morning, Mike called Deanna to ask her whether Denise had paid her a $500 advance for babysitting Anslee. He was shocked when Deanna said she knew nothing about it—so upset he made her swear to her claim on the Bible. When Deanna reached out to him later that day to find out what was happening, he wouldn't take her call. All she could think was that perhaps he was embarrassed to have it known that Denise had lied to him. "I have no idea," she said. "We never spoke of it again."

Clay Ketcham described a conversation he had with Mike not long before he went missing. They were outside the Winn-Dixie on Magnolia Drive, recalled Clay, when Mike confided that his wife had used her credit card to make a $3,000 cash withdrawal. When he'd confronted her, Denise told him she'd spent it on marijuana, which she'd baked into cookies. Clay didn't say so at the time, but he found the story unconvincing. Denise was "as big as a pencil" and surely wasn't capable of eating $3,000 worth of marijuana cookies. He wondered if she might have been using another drug, maybe cocaine.

Having money taken out of his account would have been especially bothersome to Mike because he was notoriously frugal—so frugal, according to Clay, that when he went on a weekend trip to visit relatives with their new baby, he bought a crib from Walmart on Friday then returned it on Monday to get the money back. Clay thought it was possible Denise had been unfaithful to Mike, but he knew Mike's legendary tightfistedness made it unlikely he would carry on an affair. Even going for a quick bite to eat after a meeting made him uneasy. He would "look nervous" and ask, only half-jokingly, if anyone could spot him for lunch. After Mike went missing, the Ketchams would sometimes say that he was probably picking up coins at the bottom of the lake with a metal detector. A light comment at a time of heartrending tension. Years later, in the homicide file, the quip reads differently—as inappropriate, almost sacrilegious. Absence had cast its spell. Mike had become a martyr: suffering, betrayed, beloved.

———

Notes from Cheryl's Journal:

May 7, 2004. Did anyone ever check to see if Mike and Denise had reservations for the night of December 16th at the Gibson Inn in Apalachicola? Denise said she called and cancelled on Saturday afternoon.

May 8, 2004. Anslee's 5th birthday out Black's Pony Farm . . . Denise and Brian were hanging on to each other. Brian looks as bad as Denise. Is it drugs or her conscience?

October 6 or 7, 2004. . . . Deanna believes Brian and Denise could have killed Mike for insurance. All of the Merrells hate the Winchesters. I don't know why.

———

If Mike had "walked off," as Cheryl believed, he must have done so on the spur of the moment. The Monday after he went missing, Patti Ketcham went to his office and looked through his desk for clues. What she found—an open bank statement, a stash of chewing tobacco, and a bird gun missing from his office closet—convinced her that Mike hadn't planned to leave town. In public, like everyone else, she held out hope, but privately she knew: Mike was dead.

When someone disappears out of the blue, all kinds of emotions are stirred up. Usually, the confusion is temporary: Most missing-person cases are resolved within forty-eight hours. This doesn't always mean the person is found alive and well, but if they're not, information about their death can be gleaned from the state of the body and the circumstances in which it's found. Loved ones can be buried and mourned, lives resumed. But when there's no body, the normal process of grief is disrupted. The missing person is gone, but our bonds with them are alive and intact, as though they're living among us invisibly, like ghosts. Psychologists call this "ambiguous loss," and it can cause lasting emotional trauma. As when people die in floods, bombings, or plane crashes, the grieving process can be fraught and prolonged. If a disaster is significant enough, efforts to find the victims' remains are driven by emotion (or, more cynically, by public relations) rather than finances or practical concerns; law enforcement will persist in recovery efforts even when the search for survivors is clearly futile.

When Mike went missing, most of his friends and family returned to Lake Seminole again and again even though it was increasingly clear he was dead. Patti Ketcham felt an irresistible urge to visit the place where he was last seen. "I'd always wondered, when there's an accident and there's no survivors, why families would go to the place where it happened. I remember seeing news stories and it just made no sense to me," she said. "But when we got the call that Mike disappeared, we couldn't get out there fast enough. It was like an overwhelming compulsion."

Denise, on the other hand, had the opposite reaction; after a seemly interval, she started going about her business, erasing all evidence of Mike from her life. This, too, is a normal reaction to ambiguous loss. Still, it made people think twice.

————

By November 2004, four years after Mike's disappearance, investigators had begun to tighten their grip on the case—which, although not yet reclassified as a homicide, was starting to be considered that way. On the ninth of that month, Brian got a call from Derrick Wester asking him to come down to the FDLE office in Tallahassee to account for his whereabouts on the day of Mike's disappearance. Contradicting what Kathy had told them, he said he'd spent the day driving thirty miles or so up to Cairo, Florida, with his wife and son. As for his relationship with Denise, Brian said they were no more than very close friends.

Denise's turn came a month later, on December 21. During the interview, she was polite but noncommittal and unforthcoming. She answered Donnie Wester's questions about her marriage briefly, without offering any substantiative information. The only time she bristled was when Wester asked her about Cheryl. "She's been psycho from the beginning," said Denise. "I feel sorry for her."

In the file, Mike's disappearance was reclassified. "Missing person" became "suspicious missing person." Officially, Brian Winchester and Denise Williams were now "persons of interest."

− ACT II −

David and Bathsheba

"Hell could have opened for me then, and it wouldn't have
made any difference. I had to have her, if I hung for it."

JAMES M. CAIN, *THE POSTMAN ALWAYS RINGS TWICE* (1934)

"How I would describe it is, we had grown up," said Kathy, of the
years after the two couples married in 1994. They were sheltered
and naïve. None of them had lived away from home before. But after
they married, free from parental constraints, they began to unfasten
their lives, button by button. They started to explore and experiment,
discovering things in adulthood that most people enjoyed earlier in life.
They started hanging out at Tallahassee nightclubs: the Moon, Brothers,
Floyd's Music Store. They drank and danced. They got into industrial
rock, going to see bands like Creed, Econoline Crush, and Sinomatic,
finding new friends outside their parents' Baptist community. They took
a ski trip to Colorado together. They skipped church, tried drugs, went
to strip clubs. Denise even had a "party name"—"Meridian," after the

road she lived on. One night the four friends went to a concert at the Moon; Denise bought a CD from the band and asked the musicians to sign it: "To Meridian."

A couple of times, Brian suggested they take a trip out of town for some "adult fun." Mike wasn't interested—hangovers stopped him from getting to work on time—so Brian, Kathy, and Denise went without him. They'd drink all day in strip clubs; when they were drunk, Brian would get Kathy and Denise to take their clothes off and fool around while he took Polaroids. He kept these risqué photographs as mementos.

"Growing up" is one way of putting it. Less generous people might say the four had regressed. But for these two couples, North Florida Christian High wasn't a transitory phase in their lives but a perpetual present. However hard they tried, they couldn't escape its influence. Same people, same gossip, same drama.

Kathy's rebellion was short-lived, a moment of kicking up her heels before she settled down. She assumed Brian, too, would get over the drinking and partying once they were married. She thought he'd start taking his responsibilities more seriously, but she was disappointed. "The four of us would talk about it," said Kathy. "I didn't want to wait until my thirties to start having kids. And Mike didn't want to wait either. . . . Mike and I were kind of, like, this is fun or whatever, but we were ready to have kids."

But for Brian, the exploring didn't go far enough. His parents had raised him to believe that sex was shameful—girlfriends had broken up with him because he wouldn't even kiss—but he thought about little else. Even though it went against God's plan for marriage, he looked at porn daily. Then, after so many years of fantasy and anticipation, when he finally got married, sex was a big letdown. He'd imagined adventures and experiments, but his wife wasn't interested. To Kathy, the strip clubs and threesomes were just for show. She didn't really get into it. According to Brian, his wife "didn't live up to my standards of what sex should've been."

A couple of years into his marriage, he found a note in his wife's purse from a high school friend. Brian wondered: What if Kathy was getting her sexual needs fulfilled elsewhere? He had no proof she'd been cheating, but he was competitive; it hurt his ego to imagine he'd been bested by an old rival. At the same time, he knew that if Kathy was unhappy, it was partly his fault. He hadn't been a great husband. His wife was a homebody. Brian, tough and energetic, loved the outdoors; domestic life smothered him. Whenever he could, he escaped from home to go duck hunting out on the lake or to train his dogs in the woods.

Things between the couple got tense. Brian started to wonder whether he'd married the wrong girl. He found himself looking at Denise differently. The feeling, it seemed, was mutual. He described how their flirtation began. "My wife and I, and Denise and Mike . . . we started going out to bars and concerts, and drinking . . . a lot of drinking," he said. "And I remember one night in particular . . . we started talking about sex a lot. . . . I think that's when the spark kind of started between the two of us."

———

In the crowd, Brian and Denise pressed against each other. They kissed and made out in the dark. October 13, 1997, became their secret anniversary. The two couples had gone to see the rock band Sister Hazel at Floyd's Music Store, a concert venue in downtown Tallahassee. The lights were low, the music loud, and Brian and Denise disappeared into the crowd. The need for secrecy amped the tension to fever pitch. After the concert, they stayed up all night talking on the phone. "We really connected, like nobody else," said Brian. "We met up the next day during her lunch break at work, and that's just what started the whole ball rolling with her and I."

They'd both been taught that abstaining from sex before marriage would lead to spiritual, physical, and emotional satisfaction. All their lives, they'd struggled to follow the Bible, and when the time came for them to reap their reward, it wasn't there. They felt cheated.

Now a door had opened. Forbidden sex, it turned out, was a lot more exciting than anything that happened at home. At the same time, they couldn't set aside what they'd learned in church—that adultery was a terrible sin. They could go to hell for what they were doing—which made it even hotter. Denise, in Brian's words, was "off the charts in bed," although they hooked up more often out of bed than in it. Like teenagers, they did it in the car, getting to know places they wouldn't be disturbed. Church parking lots were good for that, ironically. They'd sometimes meet outside Home Depot or at the back of Keiser University, leave one of their vehicles there, and drive off in the other.

Logistically, it was easier for Brian than Denise—he didn't have to clock in and out. Mostly, they met during her lunch break; she had an hour off work but often took longer. If they had time, they'd get a room at the Ramada or the Hilton or go to Denise's house since Mike was always at work. "There was a church in the woods off of Meridian," Brian recalled. "I would park at that church. And there was a drainage ditch that ran from the church through the woods into her neighborhood and I would walk down the drainage ditch."

When he hooked up with Denise, Brian found everything that had been missing in his marriage—and more. He was spellbound. "I told her all my dirty secrets. . . . She shared her secrets with me about the same things," he said. ". . . I had found a woman who shared my enthusiasm for forbidden sexual activities." They urged each other on, exploring fetishes and fantasies, plotting schemes, taking risks. It was intense. Sometimes they had sex in public places. They once did it on a roof of the state capitol building.

They also managed to meet up out of town when one or the other of them was on a business trip. They hooked up at the Plaza Hotel in New York, in South Beach, Orlando, Destin, and—more than once—in a hotel at Panama City Beach. Just two hours from Tallahassee and a popular destination for college students on spring break, the town was a place to cut loose. Parts of the beachfront had a debauched atmosphere, with adult movie theaters, massage parlors, and swingers' bars. Brian liked the strip clubs, especially the Show N Tail, with its low lights, padded booths, and mirrored ceiling. He loved going there with Denise, who didn't get jealous when he looked at the dancers and sometimes even joined him in a threesome with a stripper.

The only time Mike traveled was for business, and Denise often went along. If the trip was local, she'd arrange with Brian to hook up at their hotel when Mike was busy at work. Despite the risks, they didn't get caught—although there were some awkward moments and a couple of close calls. They ran into one of Denise's sisters in a Tallahassee shopping mall, and once, when leaving a strip club in Panama City, they met a buddy of Brian's who was on his way in.

The affair was supercharged, the sex darkly obsessive and intense. They did it up to fifteen times a week. The boldness of their transgression reinforced their mutual admiration, their sense that they were special, smarter than others. After years of obedience and good behavior, they got a big kick out of outwitting their spouses and their families, behaving recklessly, taking perilous chances. Drawn to the edge, they took dangerous risks, gambling on their cleverness and nerve. Their audacity paid off. "We were pretty good at getting away with things," Brian would recall.

To grow and thrive, an extramarital affair needs isolation from society and the external world. Brian and Denise began to retreat into a private dyad, apart from the wider community. The sex got more intense, and still they didn't get caught—probably because the affair was so shocking, no one could ever conceive of such a thing. (Psychologists call this "inattention blindness"—we don't notice things that we're not expecting to see, even if they're right in front of our eyes.)

It's been shown that sexual experiences, even if they're only fantasies, cause a slackening of religious aspirations and moral behavior, possibly due to their release of self-control. Accordingly, Brian and Denise's secret connection drew them away from the church. Those around them suddenly seemed narrow-minded and obtuse. Religion, duty, and family faded into the background, along with concern for the welfare of others.

"I had a good wife. . . . And I had Denise on the side . . . in my mind, I had it pretty good." Why make waves? Brian was happy with the status quo. Denise was less blasé, especially after she got pregnant in 1997 (with Kathy following suit in 1998). In public, everyone was thrilled, but in private, Denise was anxious. She'd tried to use protection with Brian, but they'd been reckless, and she couldn't be 100 percent sure the baby was Mike's. On top of that, the timing was awkward—the child came just as she was starting to feel most ambivalent about her marriage. "When we were out at their house for parties or whatever, there was no outward affection between [Mike and Denise]," observed Clay Ketcham's wife, Patti. To Denise, Brian made Mike seem dull and ordinary. Being pregnant was a good excuse for her to stop having sex with him. And Brian "kept her juices flowing."

After the baby was born, sex became a problem. Denise had been making excuses to Mike for almost a year, using her postpartum depression as an alibi. When it lifted, she told Mike she was still sore from giving birth. Having a baby made her stop and think carefully about what she was doing, and she realized she was in love with Brian. He felt the same way. "The more we were together, the more we wanted to be together," he said. "It just snowballed. It got worse and worse." Now that both couples had young children at home, however, the lovers couldn't hook up as easily as they used to. Everybody was getting frustrated.

As their relationship became deeper and more serious, Denise and Brian were drawn back into their faith. They started going to church more regularly, justifying their adulterous relationship by telling themselves God sanctioned their love. Why else would he have led them to each other? At the same time, they began, in Brian's elusive phrasing, "talking about options and ways that we could be together."

Divorce was the obvious solution, but it would have been devastating to their families. When Denise's younger sister Deborah had decided she wanted to get married right out of school without going to college, Cheryl remembered a time when her parents had thrown her out of the house. "Warren took all Deborah's belongings, clothes and everything, and threw them out in the front yard," recalled Cheryl. "Johnnie and Warren were members of Parkwood Baptist Church. . . . Half of the church sided with Deborah and David over the fact that Warren shouldn't have thrown her out, and the other half sided with Warren and Johnnie." Cheryl recalled Deborah's parents didn't speak to her for years.

To Denise in particular, divorce was out of the question. She'd been raised to believe divorce was against the Bible, and she couldn't get over it. "Denise, because of the way she was raised, because of her pride, I guess I can't say all the reasons, but she did not want to get divorced," said Brian. She was too self-righteous, too concerned about family and appearances. Social status, money, and her daughter's interests all spoke against it. More significantly, she didn't want to share custody of Anslee with Mike. "Better to be a rich widow than a poor divorcée."

It's difficult to believe anybody could find murder more palatable than divorce. Morality aside, the risks are enormous. But undue reflection can weigh heavily on the brain, and if a desire is strong enough, cognitive distortions will find a way around moral inhibition. A couple torn apart by the conflicting demands of family, church, and community might begin to convince themselves that murder is the only way out. In the United States, annual FBI statistics (for those that are solved) suggest that a high proportion of murders are committed by someone known to the victim, usually their spouse or intimate partner, often to avoid the consequences of divorce. For men, it's primarily financial loss they fear—men, more often than women, end up working to support a family they no longer have. For women, the greatest anxiety is losing custody of their children. Although the murder may be carried out so a couple can be together, these aren't crimes of passion but deeds that are carefully planned, sometimes for years. They are "cold" rather than "hot" acts, transgressions with forethought. Not the heat of the moment, but premeditated murder.

When and in what circumstances does someone bring up the possibility of killing another? Brian couldn't remember who mentioned it first. All he could recall was the mounting pressure. Denise and Mike were at each other's throats. Plus, Mike was getting suspicious. The couple had a rule: They'd discuss all purchases over fifty dollars. Mike kept a close eye on their bank account. During the early months of 2000, according to Brian, Denise had broken their agreement more than once. She had to withdraw large sums of cash to finance her secret trips. Brian would tell investigators that Mike knew something was up. "He went to Denise's mom, Johnnie Merrell, and was . . . concerned about money, cash, that was disappearing from their accounts," said Brian. "He didn't know if she was having an affair, or was using it for drugs, or what was going on." Denise was afraid that things were going to blow up. The lovers had to be very careful. They still got together when they could, but now, as often as not, they met just to spend time together. They fantasized about the future. They imagined what things would be like if they were both single. "The subject of Mike's death started coming up in conversations. . . . There were scenarios that were discussed," said Brian. They talked about boating accidents and people falling overboard. At first, their talk was just speculation and hypothesis. It wasn't serious. And then it was.

In April 2000, Brian sold Mike a million-dollar insurance policy. Mike already had two insurance policies. Brian had sold him the first in 1995—a $250,000 policy with Kansas City Life—but wasn't involved with the second policy, which Mike had purchased on his own a couple of years later. This second policy, with Cotton States, was for $500,000. The million-dollar policy he bought from Brian in April was supposed to replace the Cotton States policy, which Mike intended to let lapse. It was paid in quarterly installments; the next was due in the fall. However, in the Williams household, Denise took care of the family's finances.

Come fall, without Mike's knowledge, instead of canceling the Cotton States policy, she paid the quarterly installment. The next one was due at the end of December.

The clock was ticking.

———

The seed of the crime was planted in the late summer of that year when Mike and Brian were out duck hunting together at Lake Miccosukee. They were walking through a swampy field when Mike inadvertently stepped into an alligator hole. It looked like solid ground but gave way suddenly beneath him, sucking him down. He was floundering, falling. At the last minute, he made a lifesaving, split-second decision to drop his shotgun and grab Brian's hand. Brian told Denise about the incident later. "If I hadn't been there, if I hadn't helped him out, he very likely would have disappeared, and nobody would have known what happened to him." The episode sparked a plan. The lovers decided that Mike would die in a "duck-hunting accident." With some assistance from Brian, he'd fall into the lake while wearing his full-body waders. It was common knowledge among duck hunters that if your waders filled up with water, you didn't stand a chance. When people found Mike's body, they'd assume he'd fallen out of his boat and drowned.

Most religious people are tempted, at some time or another, to transgress the rules of their church; for the most part, they overcome the desire through confession, self-reckoning, and prayer. Those who sin, in order to assuage their guilt, will sometimes try stretching their religion to cover their sin. Rather than acknowledging that what they want is wrong, they tell themselves that God, in his omniscience, understands the irresistible power of the temptation, and will forgive them their trespasses. In other words, they see God as a sidekick who'll help them to work out the details. Sometimes they even tell themselves that God *wants* them to be led astray—it's all part of His mysterious plan. Sinning and gaining God's forgiveness, they tell themselves, are necessary stages in spiritual growth, taking sinners closer to heaven than those who haven't broken the rules. "There will be more joy in heaven over one sinner who repents than over ninety-nine just persons who need no repentance."

It was the word "accident" that turned the key for Denise, opening the door to the crime. In her mind, making the murder into an "accident" conceded a slight possibility that Mike might survive. It eased the couple's guilt to pretend they were putting him through a "test." They rationalized the crime the same way they justified the affair—by telling themselves that this was what God wanted. The "test" would determine if God meant for them to be together, as they believed He did. "It will be up to God what happens, and not us," Brian testified. Their relationship, they told themselves, wasn't driven by lust or sin—it was holy love, sanctioned by the Lord. They were committing the murder in the service of a greater good. "We were like David and Bathsheba." After all, David committed adultery and murder, and God forgave him. David and Bathsheba's son Solomon became a wise and respected king. Brian and Denise used the biblical narrative to reassure themselves that what might look sinful to others often turned out to be part of God's holy plan (conveniently overlooking that God struck down an earlier son as punishment for David's sins). "God was going to forgive us," concluded Brian.

Every act of violence involves a hardening of the heart. In this case, there was no sit-down meeting, no written agreement, but according to Brian, he and Denise were equal partners in planning the murder. They talked about it hundreds of times, but once they'd agreed on a general plan, Denise didn't want to discuss the details. She left all that to Brian. Mostly, they talked about what they'd do if the police questioned either of them. "We promised each other neither one of us would ever say anything. We knew the only way they'd get anything is if one of us talked," said Brian. "The agreement was that neither one of us would say anything no matter what happened, no matter how much pressure we were put under." They were best friends, Bonnie and Clyde, partners in crime. The "accident" would be a sacrificial act, binding them together for life.

———

The means of Mike's death had been decided, along with the alibi. All that remained was the act itself—and the window of opportunity was closing. The next payment on the Cotton States policy was due in the middle of December. Duck-hunting season lasted from Thanksgiving to January. They set a date: Saturday, December 10. The weekend before Mike and Denise's anniversary trip.

As planned, late in the evening of Friday, December 9, Brian called Mike and invited him to go duck hunting early the next morning at Lake Seminole. He called late to be sure Mike wouldn't have the chance to tell anyone about his plans. As expected, Mike said yes. But shortly before midnight, he called Brian back and said he had to cancel. Denise didn't want him to go.

Brian was pissed. He got together with Denise the following day in the parking lot at Rhoden Cove Landing, an isolated boat ramp on the edge of Lake Jackson. Curtains of Spanish moss hung from the utility wires overhead. It was a chilly day, and the sky was overcast. As he suspected, Denise had got cold feet.

He laid down an ultimatum. "Either we're going through with this or we're not," he told her. "Either we're going to be together, or we're not. . . . This isn't something to be wishy-washy about." Even if she made it through the dreaded anniversary trip, he reminded her, the

Cotton States policy was about to lapse, then duck-hunting season would be over. It was now or never.

Denise agreed. She wanted to be with him, she said.

They made plans for the following Saturday—Denise and Mike's sixth wedding anniversary.

This time, she didn't back down.

– 2 –

Double Indemnity

'

"When a man takes out . . . an insurance policy that's worth $50,000 if he's killed in a railroad accident, and then three months later he *is* killed in a railroad accident, it's not on the up-and-up. It can't be."

JAMES M. CAIN, *DOUBLE INDEMNITY* (1943)

In Billy Wilder's 1944 movie version of James M. Cain's *Double Indemnity*, the insurance salesman Walter Neff (Fred MacMurray) is smitten by a sexy housewife who lures him into killing her unsuspecting husband. Neff has been in the insurance business for some time; he's developed a sixth sense about what types of inquiry bode trouble. When sultry Phyllis Dietrichson (Barbara Stanwyck) starts asking him about accident insurance for her husband, Neff knows he should walk away, but his better judgment is overthrown by a moment of self-destructive perversity.

According to Cain, the seed for Neff's character was planted by a story he once heard from a newspaperman about a printer's error that turned an innocent pun into a dirty joke. An ad for ladies' underwear in the Louisville Courier-Journal was typeset to read: IF THESE SIZES ARE TOO BIG, TAKE A TUCK IN THEM. But when the paper hit the street, the "T" in "tuck" had been changed to an "F." After two days of questioning, the guilty typesetter finally confessed. He'd done it deliberately—he couldn't resist. "You do nothing your whole life but watch for something like that happening, so as to head it off," he admitted, "and then you catch yourself watching for chances to do it." In the same way, Walter Neff prides himself on knowing all the angles on insurance fraud. He lies awake at night thinking of tricks people might play, so he'll be ready for them when they come at him. But his superior knowledge, combined with the boredom of his job, twists his thinking. Instead of preventing the perfect crime, he starts to imagine pulling it off.

James M. Cain was a former insurance man himself—he worked for the General Accident Company—and he knew the business had its poetry, as well as its prose. He was fascinated by how insurance companies, with their complex analyses of contingency and probability, come up against the irrationalities of human behavior. And in the long term—as we learn from Walter Neff—placing bets on human life can lead to a kind of moral indifference. Cain said he started writing *Double Indemnity* after talking to some insurance men in Los Angeles. One of them told him: "All the big crime mysteries in this country are locked up in insurance company files, and the writer that gets wise to that . . . is going to make himself rich."

This may have been true in 1943, but these days, murder for life insurance happens more often in the movies than in real life. Insurance companies have become increasingly difficult to outsmart, and for the most part, a life insurance policy won't pay out if it appears the policy was procured with the intent to kill the insured. If it does pay out, the proceeds will go to an "innocent contingent beneficiary," usually the victim's child or children, or their estate.

Underwriters know all the schemes and loopholes. Unnatural deaths are always investigated closely. Once you get past the age of twenty-four, your chances of dying unexpectedly (in an accident or a murder) start to decrease (although your chances of dying from disease or illness start to go up and keep on going until you reach the grave). Other circumstances that raise red flags: people who buy cheap, short-term contracts for large amounts of life insurance, especially when it's bought from mail-order companies; claims within the first one or two of years of the policy; and healthy people who die in distant places or from unusual causes like accidental poisoning, drowning, and death by fire.

Even suicide is difficult to get away with when it's committed for reasons connected to life insurance (to be sure family members are provided for, most often). In the past, insurance companies didn't pay out to the beneficiaries of suicide, but after realizing this made them look chintzy, most now have a two-year exclusion period to prevent people killing themselves as a favor, to profit a pal. Two years is usually enough time for potential suicides to start having second thoughts (or for the pal to fall out of grace). If the impulse remains, the payout will probably go uncontested.

Insurance companies themselves are sometimes investigated and held responsible in cases where it can be proved they "unreasonably imperil the lives of the insured" by insuring them, either by issuing a policy on someone without their consent, or to a beneficiary with no interest in the continuation of the life of the insured, or, on occasion, by being informed of a plot to murder someone but failing to cancel their policy. Some have even argued that the insurance industry itself is detrimental to society because its benefits are offset by the way it induces people to engage in antisocial, illegal, and unethical activities. These can range from minor deceptions like "slip and sue" scams to more serious crimes (it's been proved that buying kidnap-and-ransom insurance increases the possibility you'll be kidnapped and held for ransom).

Things are more complicated, of course, when the murderer is an insurance man himself, like Walter Neff. Or, for that matter, like Brian Winchester, who seemed to share Neff's perversity in the face of risk. For Brian, as with Neff, the payout was a bonus; it was the woman he wanted first. When he was asked by a member of the jury whether the money was his primary motive in killing Mike Williams, he considered the question, but not for long. "It was more like the icing on the cake," he said. His honesty may have worked against him: When a person attributes their criminal behavior to money, rather than their own wickedness, it can diminish their moral failings in the eyes of others. Many people unconsciously believe money, a potent and perilous force in our lives, provides a compelling external justification for wrongdoing.

Still, even if it wasn't the object of the crime, the money was crucial to the case. To guarantee the insurance paid out, Brian had to ensure the murder looked like an accident rather than, say, the result of an interrupted robbery. The two insurance policies Brian sold to Mike both had double indemnity clauses. In a deposition, Brian's father, Marcus Winchester, who helped get the wheels rolling on Denise's insurance claim, was asked to clarify how double indemnity works. "Double indemnity simply states if the death is accidental or violent in nature, that the policy face amount will be doubled," Marcus explained.

An indemnity is compensation for a loss. Most people die from natural causes rather than accidents. In fact, a double indemnity policy is a good deal for the insurance company—a bit of flimflam to entice buyers by making the policy seem worth twice as much.

———

Typically, in the absence of a body, it takes seven years for a missing person to be declared dead. After her husband went missing, Denise had no regular source of income. She'd left her full-time CPA job at the State Board of Administration when Anslee was born. Now, as a widow with a child to raise, she had a hefty mortgage payment to meet. In the short term, things were manageable because Mike was owed a little over $20,000 for appraisal projects he'd already completed, and there was also money in the couple's savings and stock market accounts. Still, Denise wasn't sure when she'd be able to go back to work. Fortunately, Marcus Winchester, who'd loved Mike like a son, stepped in and took control of things. He was worried about Denise. He could tell she was in a fragile state of mind and he didn't want her to be struggling with her finances. Eleven days after Mike went missing, Marcus filed a "notice of death" with Kansas City Life.

Three weeks later, he helped Denise file a claim, listing Mike's cause of death as "accidental drowning."

This made sense: Initially, no one suspected foul play. The police hadn't treated the search like a crime scene—no evidence had been kept or processed. There was no investigation. When Mike's body failed to turn up, people were surprised, but everyone assumed it was just a matter of time. Denise filed early for a death certificate, true, but on the face of it, everything was aboveboard. Insurance companies emphasize that a claim should be filed as soon as possible after a death, as the procedure can be long and complicated. In this case, with the help of Marcus Winchester's business connections, things were fast-tracked, and the court issued a Certificate of Presumptive Death on June 29, 2001.

As soon as Denise received the certificate, she applied to Kansas City Life for Mike's death benefits. Notably, when she filed the claim, she didn't mention the policy with Cotton States. She even wrote another quarterly check to Cotton States on April 16, 2001, months after Mike had been declared dead. She was in no rush to collect. Neither Brian nor Denise wanted to push the money issue. "I felt that we needed to kind of lay low," recalled Brian. He didn't want Denise to seem like "the eager widow ready to cash in on her life insurance." Accrued interest was an added benefit: The longer they waited, the bigger the payout.

Whenever she met with the insurance company representatives, Denise went with her attorney, her father, or Marcus Winchester. The men would do the talking while the grieving widow sat mutely, head lowered, eyes downcast. A representative from Kansas City Life who spoke to Denise on the phone noted that although she gave them the

information they needed, she appeared to be "very tense and upset."
Neither company had any reason to delay writing the checks. In sum,
Denise received almost $1.8 million.

RESEARCH SERVICE BUREAU, INC.

P.O. BOX 837 NAPERVILLE, IL 60566

(630) 961-4890

Acct: 8174X

February 2, 2001

RE: Williams, Jerry M

*On 1/03/01, we received your request to conduct a Contestable
Death Claim investigation. Date of issue 4/15/00, date of disappearance 12/16/00. We were to handle as per your specific instructions.*

*. . . The insured was an avid duck hunter and had planned to go
duck hunting early in the morning of 12/16/00. He had planned to be
home in time for him and his wife to leave for a "get away" that night to
celebrate their 6th anniversary. They planned to go to the Gibson Inn
in Apalachicola, Fl for an overnight stay.*

*. . . He would hunt with a friend or if no one was available he would
go alone. That was not unusual for him. That morning he left so that
he would be at his hunting spot by dawn. He normally hunted on Lake
Seminole near Sneads, FL. He owned a "duck boat" and a motor for
the boat. The wife did not know much about the boat or motor other
than to say it was small. More of a trolling motor. It did not drive the
boat fast. He did not have a hunting dog.*

. . . There were no marital problems and no infidelity on the part of either. They had no money problems and no problems with the law.

. . . When they found the boat on 10/17/00 it had life jackets on the bottom of the boat and they were wet. On top of them they found his gun in the case and on top of that, duck decoys. There was no indication he was wearing a life jacket, normal for him. With what he was wearing and the fact that his waders would rapidly fill with water if he went over, it is not at all likely that he could have swum or stayed above water.

. . . Brian Winchester said that because of the shape of the boat and what was in it, the insured could have easily lost his balance, if he were standing, and fallen out of the boat had he hit a stump or a log. He confirmed the weather conditions, as did the wife. He said the thunderstorms and tornadoes started late in the afternoon. The Fish and Game Department is handling the search and used a wide variety of equipment in the search. As far as this source knows, the search continues.

This source says there is a wide variety of wildlife in this lake which includes some very large alligators. He also says it had been colder than normal and they are hoping warm weather will bring the insured to the surface.

Mike's death caused problems at Ketcham Appraisals. The company was in a tricky position for a while. He'd been the hardest worker in the office, and then one morning, he just walked out the door and didn't come back. Patti Ketcham had to take on the administrative duties while Clay tried to pick up the pieces of Mike's workload. But the more time he spent going over Mike's accounts, the stranger it seemed to Clay that Mike had spent so much money on something as unnecessary as life insurance. This was a man so tight he'd drink from a gas station hosepipe rather than pay for a can of soda. He was thirty-one years old and in perfect health. Why was he so heavily insured?

One in three families in the United States have no life insurance at all, and it's fair to say that most people, even if they have life insurance, don't give it much thought. But Mike was different. As Brian pointed out, he and Mike talked about life insurance all the time, and Mike understood most people are significantly underinsured. Brian had told him that, according to the guidelines, you should be insured for between seven and twelve times your annual income, and Mike earned, on average, around $180,000 a year. During depositions, Brian and Marcus told investigators there was nothing unusual about the amount of insurance Mike had. "He was below the guidelines as a matter of fact," said Brian. "If he had two million dollars, he would still be under the guidelines . . ."

Marcus Winchester had helped Denise file and receive her payment, and it was only natural that she should turn to him for financial advice—after all, that was his business. Following his suggestions, she invested several hundred thousand dollars in mutual funds, which Marcus would manage. She bought two pieces of land: three acres at Miller Landing on Lake Jackson for $125,000, and an eight-acre tract on Duck Cove Road on Lake McBride for $275,000. Even if she didn't build on them, the two waterfront properties would still be profitable investments. Otherwise, if Denise changed her lifestyle after Mike's death, it was to cut back. She fired her maid and her yard man. The car she drove was so old that her sister Deanna considered it "unsafe," although it was surely an exaggeration to claim, as Deanna did, that Denise lived "like a pauper." It was true, however, that now she was a millionaire, Denise seemed determined to exhibit a high degree of self-restraint.

Some people wondered if her guardedness with money suggested a guilty conscience. Others pointed out that, while $1.8 million was a lot of money in the grand scheme of things, it wasn't excessive for a lifetime's income. The annual interest would come to around $50,000, far less than Mike had been earning. Even considering the fact that Anslee would receive survivor's benefits from social security until she was eighteen, Denise couldn't live comfortably without breaking into the principal unless she went back to work.

And that's precisely what she did. She returned to the State Board of Administration and later took a CPA position at Image API, an information technology company. When the company downsized and laid Denise off, she drew unemployment ("the only millionaire I know that was on unemployment," commented Brian sardonically). Later, she settled into a long-term position in the finance department at FSU.

It was the insurance money that first made people stop and wonder whether there might be more to Mike's death than a horrible accident. Until then, everyone except Cheryl assumed he'd drowned. The fact that his body hadn't materialized was unusual, sure, but not necessarily suspicious. No one found the situation shady until word got out about the cash. When people learned how much Mike was worth and that Denise had filed an insurance claim only three weeks after he went missing, whispers began to spread.

Clay Ketcham, like Mike, belonged to the local Rotary Club, and he recalled talking the situation over with three other members who had experience with drowning deaths. One was a retired state marshal, one was a medical examiner, and the third was a funeral director. Independently, they all told him the corpse was sure to surface when the water warmed up in April. But April came, and there was no sign of Mike's body. When Ketcham mentioned the fact to the three men, "they all kind of looked off distantly, and said 'that's most unusual.' They all used the same phrase." At this point, people started to pay more attention to what Ketcham described as "the fragmented puzzle . . . little bits here and there." A vague picture was forming, but the pieces weren't coming together.

In Ancient Greek, as in modern German, the word for "debt" is the same as the word for "guilt." In the Bible, too, debt and guilt are closely linked. "Vengeance *is* mine; I will repay, saith the Lord" (Romans 12:19). Sin and transgression are described in terms of dues and balance. Christianity is in some ways a form of theological economics, in which good and bad deeds are weighed and counted.

The Baptist Church has a complicated relationship with money. On the one hand, congregants are encouraged to avoid secular, commercial environments polluted by material temptations and selfish desires. With biblical and community guidelines to keep you on the straight and narrow, it's easier to avoid struggles with self-control and the temptation to overspend or get into debt, even to cheat or steal (although cheating and stealing happen in the church, too). On the other hand, many Baptists believe there's nothing wrong with being rich. Financial advancement, they trust, is God's way of telling them they're on the right track. Tithing and charity are encouraged not only for spiritual reasons but because they will surely increase the giver's prosperity in the long run. We reap what we sow.

Denise lived by a value system heavily inflected by the church. Among her social circle and fellow congregants, no one would have frowned on a display of wealth; nonetheless, for many years Denise was restrained and withdrawn. Her tastes remained moderate, her lifestyle middle-class. She drove an older Suburban SUV, went to the gym, baked and iced her own cakes, volunteered at the church nursery, and stayed close to her friends and sisters. She liked fashion but sought bargains and wasn't ashamed to shop at Goodwill. Her only indulgence was her collection of Lladró porcelain figurines, which cost around a hundred dollars apiece.

Brian and Denise both worked in the financial industry, Denise as a CPA and Brian as a financial adviser and insurance salesman, but they had different attitudes toward wealth.

People's beliefs and behaviors around money reflect their personality structure; for example, those who withhold money, like Denise, may also tend to harbor secrets and keep information to themselves. The insurance money was paid to her alone, not to Brian, and from the way she hoarded it, she clearly associated it emotionally with Mike. It may also have given her a greater sense of security, along with feelings of power and freedom, but if so, she kept these feelings to herself.

If Denise was a hoarder, Brian was the opposite. He knew how to amass money, but he also liked to spend it, and when it came to investments, he didn't mind taking risks. Denise may have let her hair down in private, but she was conservative by nature, where Brian was more impulsive.

Their finances were separate, but not their fates. Like the lovers in *Double Indemnity*, the two had tied themselves together so that, if either one turned on the other, both would be destroyed. Their situation is summed up by the insurance claims adjuster Barton Keyes, played in the movie by Edward G. Robinson: "They may think it's twice as safe because there's two of them, but it isn't twice as safe. It's ten times twice as dangerous. They've committed a murder. And it's not like taking a trolley ride together where they can get off at different stops. They're stuck with each other and they got to ride all the way to the end of the line, and it's a one-way trip, and the last stop is the cemetery."

As one law enforcement investigator observed of Brian and Denise, "unless they turn on each other, nothing will happen." This proved to be an astute prediction. When things finally went wrong, the impact was explosive—and irreversible.

– 3 –

Spiritual Awakening

"... all the time I was trying to pull away from it, there was
something in me that kept edging a little closer, trying to
get a better look."

JAMES M. CAIN, *DOUBLE INDEMNITY* (1943)

*M*eridian.

That was the name on the necklace, in cursive script. Name necklaces were all the rage in 2001. According to the receipt Kathy Winchester found in a desk drawer among a pile of bills, Brian bought the memento at the Gold Center in Governor's Square Mall for eighty dollars. Not a pricey gift, but a token of shared secrets. The receipt was dated July 28, 2001, just two months before Kathy found it. Five months before Mike's death.

Kathy was no longer the sweet, naïve cheerleader from North Florida Christian High. Although petite and demure, she was smart, independent, and perceptive. Many times, she'd suspected Brian and Denise were having an affair. She couldn't prove it, but she'd sensed there was something between them. The necklace confirmed her suspicions, but she kept the secret to herself, continuing to monitor the situation from a distance. Best Brian didn't know she'd been snooping around.

After Mike's disappearance, Kathy and Brian spent a lot of time with Denise, but eventually, to Kathy, things started to feel weird. The foursome was now a threesome, and three was a crowd—only the odd one out wasn't Denise, it was Kathy. When the three of them socialized or took trips, Kathy was always in the back seat. She was sick and tired of feeling neglected. She told Brian she wanted to separate. The following year, she moved out.

———

"It's you and me," says Frank to Cora in *The Postman Always Rings Twice*, another James M. Cain novel about insurance fraud. The pair have just murdered Cora's husband. "There's nobody else. I love you, Cora," Frank tells her. "But love, when you get fear in it, it's not love anymore. It's hate." In its self-destructive passion, Frank and Cora's relationship resembles that of Brian and Denise: The intensity of their affair fed on their struggle to be together at all costs. But without obstacles, there was no excitement, nothing to fight for. As soon as Denise was widowed and Brian separated, their relationship lost its buoyancy. Perhaps they needed the friction of secrecy; in the absence of external constraints, they created their own. For the next three years, they stalled, struggled, fought, lied, cheated, made each other jealous, started fights, and sought revenge.

At first, they kept things on the down-low. It was too early for them to be seen together, and although Brian and Kathy were separated, they were still married. To show she was open to dating again, Denise had been going out with Jimmy Martin, but the relationship wasn't serious, and it soon petered out. Next, she began dating Charles Bunker, her boss at the Florida State Board of Administration. "She kind of had a crush on him," said Kathy. Even before Mike's disappearance, Denise used to talk about Mr. Bunker and how cute he was. "I think they were flirty at work," Kathy recalled.

Charles Bunker, known as Chuck, was ten years older than Denise, recently divorced, and, like her, a single parent. In June 2003, Brian learned from one of her sisters that Denise had gone to Atlanta with Bunker, and he was furious. He did some sleuthing and discovered the couple were staying in a hotel in Buckhead, a chic Atlanta suburb. Denise was treating him monstrously, he thought. "I wanted to confront her," he admitted. ". . . I killed her husband to be with her."

Not for the first or last time, Brian forced an altercation. "I was determined to get her back or kill myself," he said later. He drove to Buckhead, found the hotel, and sat waiting in the lobby. The longer he sat there, the angrier he grew. Finally, "she came prancing by holding his hand." An unpleasant scene ensued. Denise was upset, Brian enraged. Bunker, confused, persuaded Brian to step out into the street, where the argument continued. Brian was so distraught that at one point he even considered throwing himself into traffic. Eventually, Denise intervened, juggling her two lovers in an expert display of double-dealing. Taking Chuck aside, she said she needed to speak to Brian privately for a moment. Alone with Brian, she apologized and promised she'd send Bunker away, then instructed him to meet her back at the hotel in an hour. When he'd left, she told Chuck he should go back to Tallahassee without her—Brian was hysterical, she said, and she ought to stay with him until he calmed down. When Brian returned, Denise told him she was glad to get rid of Chuck. It was all a big mistake, she said—a workplace flirtation that had gone too far. "Denise has this thing where she gets people to do stuff for her and she minimizes her . . . guilt, her conscience . . ." Brian would explain. "She's unbelievably good at lying, manipulating, having things go her way, not just with me but other men." The lovers spent the night together in the Buckhead hotel, then Brian drove back to Tallahassee, arriving home in a state of emotional exhaustion. "I was just done, spent," he said. The following day, Sunday, June 29, he attended church. "And I had—I guess you would call it a spiritual awakening or conversion."

In anticipation of the upcoming holiday, the pastor gave a sermon about the "true" meaning of independence. It was cheesy, but for Brian, it hit home. "I felt like I was a slave to all that I had been living for . . . in my relationship with Denise." He knew Denise was his soulmate, but he also realized their relationship had been forged in sin, and he wanted God's forgiveness. He started attending church regularly, reading the Bible, and trying to follow the holy word. It was at this time that Denise, too, immersed herself in religion, joining the women's ministry and going to preach in prison.

Notes from Cheryl's Journal:

February 6, 2004: . . . *There is possible insurance fraud. FOLLOW THE MONEY!*

February 19, 2004: Johnnie and McLin came to pick up Parker for Deborah. Johnnie was friendly. Warren, 64, will retire the last day of June. . . . Money is tight for Denise.

February 22: Anslee got "student of the day." I got a call from Denise's cell phone.

February 28: Denise called. I missed it. I was helping Nick move.

March 1: Nothing.

———

There's no question that both Denise and Brian were serious about their spiritual awakening, but they were also trying to distance themselves from the murder, still a dangerous presence in their lives. As well as being Baptists, they were both professional bookkeepers, and despite Denise's huge insurance payout, they may have felt, perhaps unconsciously, that the murder had put them in grave spiritual debt. In terms of profit and loss, their biblical credit balance was in negative figures; they had to build it back up through religious devotion, as well as monetary tithes. Their recommitment to the church was also a symbolic attempt at moral cleanliness, a desire to sanitize themselves, to rewrite their story. It was a kind of hand washing or exorcism, a cleansing of the self after encountering a contagious force of evil. Never mind that the force was their own.

To the faithful, transgression has a special force and valency that's absent from secular life. Among the laity, things like masturbation, pornography, and casual sex can be take-it-or-leave-it affairs; a person might dabble, indulge now and then, get bored, try something else, or grow out of the habit. But to the devout, these are carnal sins whose indulgence leads directly to hell. A source of endless guilt and shame, they never lose their gloss. The atheist can just pull the plug; to the devout, sin never loses its charge.

———

Despite re-embracing the church, Denise was still juggling her two lovers, Brian and Chuck, who were circling her like predators competing for a mate. According to Bunker, Brian began to stalk and harass him after the encounter in Atlanta, trying to get him to break up with Denise. He found out where Chuck lived, stole his mail, threatened to burn down his house. Bunker said he dismissed Brian as a blowhard. "I thought he was just a guy that ran his mouth," he said. "He threatened to do this; he threatened to do that. . . . I think he would tell Denise stuff just to show that he was a big guy in town and that he was in charge."

But this, too, was a display of bravado. The incident in Atlanta left Chuck shaken and hurt. Until then, he'd assumed he was Denise's boyfriend. They'd even talked about marriage. Now he discovered he was playing a minor, walk-on role in a sordid drama with a long history and multiple layers of lies and secrets. It's not clear whether Chuck realized Denise had been lying to him about her relationship with Brian or whether the Atlanta episode had simply bruised his ego, but he launched a campaign to damage and defame her, threatening to tell everyone about her private life. Brian warned Kathy that she was going to get an anonymous letter that was "going to say a bunch of crazy stuff in it, and you are going to get all upset." She should give him the letter without opening it, he told her. Instead, when the letter arrived, Kathy read it, made a copy, and gave it to her attorney to keep on file. It was unsigned. "Ms. Kathy Winchester," it began. "I am sorry that I find myself writing this letter to you about one of your best friends Denise Williams and your ex-husband Brian Winchester."

The letter-writer claimed, among other things, that Denise had cheated on Mike, "so it was easy for her after her husband's death to start a bizarre affair with your then husband Brian." He asserted that Brian and Denise had been leading a double life, and "this affair was not a normal affair. It involved decadent sexual behavior with various people, strippers and other sordid acts." He mentioned that Brian owned "pictures and film of Denise performing in sexually explicit circumstances on different occasions" and had threatened to send these images to her parents and post them online. "These are just the brief highlights," he concluded. "Denise and your ex-husband . . . are both extremely malicious, self-serving and scheming." He pointed out, "This situation should not be taken lightly. Decadent sexual behavior, death threats, and threatening arson are not normal behavior." He added, "Who knows when the next blow up will occur. Hopefully no children will be around when this happens."

Kathy knew the letter was from Chuck Bunker. She didn't believe he was writing to "warn" her because he was "concerned for the children," as he claimed. She thought he was angry with Denise and wanted to get back at her. He'd been stalking her, apparently. Denise said he was obsessed with her. She'd had to file a restraining order against him. Kathy didn't necessarily believe everything Chuck had written in the letter. Still, ever since she'd found the "Meridian" necklace receipt, she'd realized that, during their marriage, Brian had been cheating on her with Denise, and she suspected the affair was still going on. She'd been planning to file divorce papers for a long time, but the task was unpleasant, and she'd been putting it off. Now, however, she and Rocky wanted to get engaged, and she needed to make her split from Brian official.

Throughout their marriage, Brian had treated Kathy badly; he either browbeat her or ignored her completely. She was surprised, then, when he refused to go along with the divorce. Brian admitted it "sounds screwy," but after a long discussion, he and Denise had concluded, absurdly, that it would be healthier and more appropriate if he tried to "save" his long-dead marriage to Kathy. Divorce, after all, was not sanctioned by the Bible.

When Kathy told Denise she was planning to marry Rocky, instead of congratulating her, Denise told her she was being cruel to Brian and treating him horribly. In the eyes of God, Denise reminded Kathy, she was still Brian's wife, and she should try to save her marriage. Kathy thought her friend had to be crazy. She couldn't understand it. If Denise was romantically involved with Brian, as Kathy suspected, why wouldn't she want him to be single? Why did she want Kathy to go back to a useless, bullying husband instead of marrying a man she really loved? Denise had no response other than that "being divorced is trashy" and getting divorced was a "white trash" thing to do.

They had a huge fight about it. Denise told Kathy they couldn't be friends because of how she was treating Brian. For a while, they didn't speak other than to say hello in passing while picking up their children from school, but the fight didn't last long. Kathy and Denise had a pattern of getting close, arguing, falling out, then reconnecting. They made up their differences, but Kathy insisted on going through with the divorce. She was baffled by the fact that her husband, who'd barely noticed when she'd moved out of the marital home, now kept calling to inform her that divorce was "against the Bible." He said that if she were a faithful Christian, she'd stay in the marriage even though it made her unhappy. He said it was hypocritical of her to go to church on Sunday and then file for divorce. Kathy ignored him, filing the papers in January 2003. At this point, to her surprise, Brian became very emotional, begging her to change her mind. The divorce hearing was held in March. Brian sat on the courthouse bench behind Kathy, sobbing uncontrollably. Kathy, embarrassed, turned around and told him to be quiet.

In a satirical essay, the author Thomas De Quincey makes light of the fact that some people think of murder as a kind of art, failing to consider its implications. "If once a man indulges himself in murder," writes De Quincey, "very soon he comes to think little of robbing; and from robbing he next comes to drinking and Sabbath-breaking, and from that to incivility and procrastination." He concludes, "Many a man has dated his ruin from some murder or other that perhaps he thought little of at the time." The essay is a spoof, but as is often the case with jokes, it contains a bud of truth. Brian and Denise had committed murder with little forethought; now they struggled long and hard against Brian's divorce, doing everything possible to prevent it, just as they fought against lesser vices. If, after all their persuasion, Kathy insisted on going through with it, then the sin would be hers, they told themselves, and not theirs. Just like the fantasy that Mike could "escape" from the hunting "accident," this delusion was a means of dispensing guilt, allowing the lovers to persuade themselves their relationship was ordained by God.

————

Letter from Denise to Brian, December 2003

. . . I want you to know how thankful to God I am for you and your new life. I am <u>so</u> proud of you—following God like this. It is so incredible to me that you have come so far in such a short amount of time. We both have. Our hearts are completely different & I am so thankful for that. Remember how in the past I was always telling you I was not happy & that something was wrong with me. I tried (we tried) to come up with hobbies for me & I felt so bad that I did not have a passion for hobbies the way that you did. I would also tell you how I wanted to volunteer & do "good deeds"—of course I never did—but in my mind I thought it would make me be happy. I was <u>so</u> <u>so</u> lost. This Purpose Driven Life *stuff has bought me focus in my new Christian life that I needed so badly & by doing these purposes that God created for me I will (& do) have joy & peace (not just being happy but <u>real</u> joy) & for the first time in my life I got to feel real joy in that prison (when Dana became a Christian). I am telling you—it is an addictive feeling & I want to feel it again. . . . It is a passion that I have—isn't that great?!? I finally found <u>peace</u> (living <u>one</u> life following God daily), <u>joy</u> (sharing Jesus with unbelievers), and <u>passion</u> (inmates & other lost people).*

————

Kathy and Rocky's wedding was planned for January 2004. Even then, Brian wouldn't let it go. The divorce was final; now her ex-husband began a righteous campaign to get Kathy to call off her wedding. As the date got closer, he continued to assail her, imploring her not to go through with the ceremony. "Brian starts these systematic letters, phone calls, emails to me and Rocky," said Kathy. "Please don't get married. Please don't get married. Please don't get married." She said he stood on her front porch waiting for her to come outside so he could harangue her. "We can get back together. We can make this work. God can heal this marriage. Blah, blah, blah." She had to take out an injunction to get him to stay away. She knew he didn't care about her; she suspected he didn't want her to get married simply because he didn't want another man raising his son. Brian had always liked to be in charge. His heart was with Denise, Kathy felt, but at the same time, he didn't want to lose the hold he had over his ex-wife.

Brian and Denise's resistance to Kathy's divorce and remarriage highlights the emotional complexity of this case. To say that they were "faking" or "lying" about their feelings would overlook the complications and paradoxes of desire. By all accounts, divorce was against their Christian principles. Their parents had raised them to believe that, in the eyes of God, marriage was for life. None of their parents or siblings were divorced. If Kathy could get divorced from Brian readily, with no social stigma, it made these deeply held principles seem outdated and absurd. If divorce was just a simple matter of paperwork, what did that imply about Denise's decision to have her husband killed?

Despite his "spiritual awakening," Brian was still drinking and partying. One night, in the summer of 2004, he ran into Denise when she was out with her friend Angela. Brian, Denise, and Angela made plans to get together later that night to go drinking, but right before Brian came by to pick them up, Denise's babysitter called to cancel. The three friends hung out at Denise's place while she tried to get another sitter, but she was out of luck. To Denise's annoyance, Brian and Angela went partying together. After a few hours of bar hopping, they ended up at a gay club called Brothers, then went back to Brian's place to hook up.

When questioned by investigators, Angela testified that she and Brian were "in the middle of intimacy" when someone entered the house and walked straight into Brian's bedroom. It was Denise. Angela panicked, froze. Denise looked at them, "made a sarcastic comment," turned, and walked out. "Brian got up and put a pair of pants on and ran out after her," Angela recalled, but it was too late—Denise had already gone. Brian returned to the bedroom. He gave Angela the lame excuse that the intruder must have been his estranged wife, Kathy, who still had a key to the house, but Angela wasn't stupid. She didn't buy it.

Denise was beside herself with rage. She made a pile of Brian's love letters in her backyard and burned them in a sacrificial fire. Brian kept calling, trying to calm her down by reminding her that she'd cheated on him first. He insisted he had no genuine interest in Angela—he just wanted to even the score after her affair with Chuck Bunker. Eventually, Denise softened. Once again, rather than breaking up the romance, their jealous anger brought the lovers even closer. By fall, they were back together—and ready to go public.

Everyone knew the pair had been close since high school, and they wouldn't be the first two longtime pals who'd reconnected after finding themselves single again. Their first official date—in fact, a double date with Brian's hunting buddy Roman Fontenot and his girlfriend, Erin—showed how seriously they were taking their new commitment to God. Instead of choosing a romantic comedy, they elected to sit through the harrowing ordeal of Mel Gibson's *The Passion of the Christ.*

One day in Spring 2004, Brian turned up at Kathy's house in need of first aid for their son, Stafford. He'd been stung by a bee while father and son were picking blackberries with Denise and Anslee. Anyone who didn't know them would think it was sweet, Kathy thought to herself: the widow and divorcee out picking blackberries with their two children. But she had a different perspective. By now, she knew, as Chuck Bunker had written in his "anonymous letter," that "Denise and Brian have been leading a double life."

In fact, by the time the couple were officially "dating," they'd already been through a murder and its aftermath, a seven-year-long extramarital affair, and a series of tangled infidelities and reconciliations.

Now, however, they were starting afresh. The past was past. Their relationship was sanctioned by God. They were no longer sinners—they were blessed.

− 4 −

Good Christian People

"The wicked who are happy—a species about whom moralists are silent."

FRIEDRICH NIETZSCHE, *BEYOND GOOD AND EVIL* (1886)

Cutting off Cheryl's contact with her granddaughter seems like a callous act of vengeance and cruelty on Denise's part. But look at it from a different perspective: It could be seen as the protective conduct of a conscientious mother worried about her daughter's psychological well-being. If Anslee continued to visit her grandmother, she'd surely hear people talking about Mike, how he was still alive, how they had to bring him home. Anslee was at a tender age; she was recovering from the loss of her daddy, and perhaps Denise didn't want the child to get confused and upset. Still, to many, her treatment of Cheryl seemed cold and suspicious. "Cheryl had to make a decision between her grandchild and her soul," said Clay Ketcham. "And I think that was the defining moment in Cheryl's mind because she thought, 'Why would my son's wife not join me in trying to find out what happened to him?'"

By December 2003, Brian and Denise had gone public with their relationship and were engaged to be married. They no longer attended Thomasville Road Baptist Church and were now congregants at Four Oaks Community Church, seven miles north of Midyette Plantation. Even in a conservative community like Tallahassee, people were starting to regard Baptists as legalistic, puritanical, and out-of-touch; some congregants were looking to distance themselves from traditional forms of the religion. Four Oaks was nominally more liberal than established Baptist churches and pronounced itself to be "a non-denominational Bible church," but this is new wine in old bottles. Although not part of the Florida Baptist Association, Four Oaks described itself as "Baptistic"; it endorsed the Gospel Coalition Confessional Statement, which affirmed most traditional Baptist doctrines.

It's impossible not to wonder what went through Brian's and Denise's minds every Sunday in church when they listened to sermons, read the Bible, lowered their heads in prayer. Did either struggle with the temptation to confess, or had they repressed their memory of the crime so deeply that they really believed Mike had been eaten by alligators?

People often refer to repression and denial interchangeably, but they're different things. Repression is adaptive; we couldn't have civilization without it. At an early age, we learn to repress sexual and aggressive feelings that are inappropriate or taboo. It's an instinctive bodily reaction, a response to internal stimuli. Even animals can repress their hunger, hostility, or sex drive when necessary. Denial, in contrast, is a reaction to something outside the self. As a defense mechanism, it can be helpful, encouraging us not to dwell in the past. But the term is more often used to refer to a maladaptive process covering a wide range of mental states. On one end of the spectrum, a person can be in denial about a painful event because, either consciously or unconsciously, they've blocked it out of memory. At the other end of the spectrum, a person can be perfectly aware of something but unwilling to speak openly about it. At its heart, denial is an affirmation of guilt; all denial contains a shadow of its opposite.

One common form of denial is reaction-formation, which happens when a person unconsciously replaces an unacceptable impulse with its opposite. The preacher who rails against sexual immorality may be secretly defending against his own adultery. The churchgoer devoted to good deeds might have a terrible wrongdoing in her recent past. Those who are unfaithful are the first to suspect infidelity in others. Criminals trust no one.

The month she got engaged—the same month she cut off Cheryl's contact with Anslee—Denise wrote a seventeen-page love letter to "My dear, sweet, adorable, beautiful Brian." The couple were spending the holidays apart, abstaining from sex as part of a forty-day premarital Christian counseling program. Along with the letter, Denise sent Brian some cake frosting she'd made for him. "I remember that real frosting was something you really wanted so I made it for you," she wrote. "I hope you like it . . . Keep it in the refrigerator and if it gets a little hard put a little milk in it . . ."

It's unsettling to read these intimate letters; they break through the surface of our preconceptions, showing Brian and Denise to be loving, affectionate people. Whatever might have happened in the past, to them, it was all over. They didn't see themselves as cold-blooded murderers. They saw themselves the way we all see ourselves: as good people doing our best to live decent lives. From time to time we may get a glimpse of a darker and more complex truth, but swiftly retreat into the shell of our imagined integrity.

A single act, however dreadful, does not define and circumscribe a life. As Georges Simenon's Inspector Maigret points out, "there is no such thing as 'a murderer.' Until the moment of the crime he is a man like any other." A family-focused, churchgoing mom can conspire to kill her husband, and the fact does not make her less of a loving mother. Similarly, a man can murder his best friend and still be good, kind, and loyal. The act of killing, to put it another way, doesn't require a particular kind of psychological makeup. Anyone who's loved intensely and passionately is capable of murder. Most of us know—or can easily imagine—how it feels to be desperately jealous, obsessively in love, or burdened by overbearing emotional ties. A crime like this comes not from our propensity for hatred and violence but from our propensity for love. Murder, so it is said, comes from the heart.

———

From an undated letter from Brian to Denise:

> *I love her beautiful hair.*
> *I love the way she makes lists and checks off boxes . . .*

I love that she will sit on a cooler and help me gut scallops.

She is the most beautiful woman in the world to me.

She had a heart for children and babies . . .

She is funny and has made me laugh more than anyone.

She could be a professional makeup artist—she is good!

She can cook the best cake with icing in the world . . .

She is like a model who can wear anything and make it look

good . . .

I love it when she does her "white girl" dance.

She is the best kisser in the world.

———

Now that she was remarried and no longer beholden to Brian, Kathy did something she'd been wanting to do ever since Mike disappeared— she paid a visit to Cheryl. "Brian . . . made sure that I was separated from Cheryl. . . . I would want to go see her, and he would say no . . . and it would just be this understanding that, you know, Cheryl was, quote unquote, 'crazy' about all of this and you just don't need to talk to her," recalled Kathy. After Mike's memorial service, she'd wanted to go up to Cheryl and offer her condolences, but Brian wouldn't let her. Kathy obeyed, but she didn't like it and didn't think it was right. As soon as they were separated, she visited Cheryl, which is how she learned about the police investigation. Cheryl gave her the name of Derrick Wester, the officer in charge.

When Brian asked Kathy whether she, too, had been called in to give a deposition, she told him no, the police hadn't called her in, but if they did, she'd cooperate. This made him anxious. He kept telling her that if the cops started looking at her past, things would become very embarrassing.

Kathy was telling the truth: The police hadn't called her. She'd gone to them.

On February 1, 2005, she met with Derrick Wester at the Jackson County Sheriff's Office and, at Wester's request, agreed to enlist as a confidential informant. Kathy wanted to help, but she was wary. She'd seen what Denise had done to Cheryl and was worried that if Brian found out she'd been talking to the cops, he'd do the same thing— take her child away from her. Brian's family was wealthy and well-connected, and she was afraid the distance between them would make it easier for him to pull off an underhanded move. Her life was moving in a different direction from Brian's, especially after January 2004, when she remarried. Kathy and her ex saw each other only when picking up or dropping off their son. Other than issues related to Stafford, they had nothing to discuss.

Still, whenever Kathy learned anything she thought might be helpful, she gave the information to the police. In October 2005, she forwarded to Officer Ronnie Austin a threatening email she'd received from Brian. She'd asked him if they could switch Stafford's schedule so she and Rocky could take a trip in December. Brian was still annoyed with Kathy for saying that, if necessary, she'd cooperate with the investigation; his reply was classically passive-aggressive. "Based on what you have told me my time in Stafford's life may be over soon so I am not real eager to give it up," he wrote. He also hinted that investigators might dig up evidence of the two couples' sexual adventures, and if that happened, Kathy had as much to lose as any of them. "We all—

you, me, Denise and Mike—made a lot of bad decisions and committed a lot of sins but NONE of us ever committed murder," he wrote. "I do not know what happened or where Mike is but I know he would not want our kids to suffer and pay the price in this hunt for 'justice.' If this continues down the path that is being created ALL of us and everyone close to us will be devastated regardless of the outcome."

———

Notes from Cheryl's Journal:

April 10, 2004. My brother . . . talked with a friend in insurance and a forensic psychologist. They say Denise acts exactly like someone who has something to hide.

April 11. Easter. . . . Denise is thinking about leaving Thomasville Road Baptist Church.

April 13. My brother returns my call. He's had hernia surgery and been at home. I told him more about life insurance. It tends to make him think Mike is dead.

April 14. Sally called. She had questions about insurance. Do you have to pay premiums on the policy until a person is declared dead or if there is no body? If so, this means Denise knew about the insurance policies. Was the life insurance convertible? Meaning did Mike expect to live to change from term to whole life? Good questions!

———

On Saturday, December 3, 2005, Brian Winchester and Denise Williams were married at Four Oaks Community Church. Pointedly, they did not invite Cheryl. Some were scandalized by this; others could understand: The eccentric grandmother could be a loaded gun. She'd been known to speak unpalatable truths, like the child who points out that the emperor has no clothes.

Denise and six-year-old Anslee arrived in a horse-drawn carriage. After the wedding, the couple danced to "Indescribable," sung by the contemporary Christian musician Chris Tomlin. One or two members of Denise's extended family disapproved of remarriage after divorce. Still, most of those present—even those like the Ketchams, who believed the rumors about Mike's death—gave the couple their blessings. After the wedding, Denise took Brian's name, keeping her assets, stocks, and property, including the insurance money. Brian moved into the house on Centennial Oak Drive, where Denise lived with her daughter. Stafford, too, lived with them part-time.

Perhaps the couple had visions of themselves as elderly retirees, living in harmony till-death-do-us-part, their bond sealed by a long-ago secret. This thought may have given them comfort in the aftermath of the crime: Their pledge was unbreakable because there was no way out. Their prenup was a murder.

––––––

It's tempting to see the relationship between Brian and Denise as primarily physical, forged in lust and shaped by greed. But this is simply inaccurate. The couple were together—first in secret, then as a respectable married couple—for fifteen years, from 1997 until 2012, and stayed married for another four years after separating. It's a fact: Their marriage lasted twice as long as most. Lust and greed don't sustain a relationship for fifteen years. That Brian and Denise loved each other intensely for a long time is indisputable. To their family, friends, and neighbors, the marriage appeared to be stable and solid, built on God's genuine and abiding love.

In different ways, the two were both outspoken about their faith, and it wasn't a false front. They were closely involved with Four Oaks Community Church. They studied the Bible, followed the lessons outlined in *The Purpose Driven Life*, donated to charity, and participated in Christian counseling. To their pastor and fellow congregants, they were worshipful, generous, and polite. Denise continued to volunteer with the women's prison ministry; Brian led family devotionals and led a group prayer before hunting. He reminded his fellow hunters to observe ethical sporting behavior and "always made sure that any live wounded ducks were promptly removed from the pond after a hunt, ensuring a merciful ending."

That the couple went to church isn't surprising. After all, they were Tallahassee-born, raised in Baptist homes, and attended a Baptist school. But after their marriage, Brian and Denise acquired the zeal of converts, an overcertainty that, in retrospect, seems dangerously complacent. Throwing yourself into the church is one way to whitewash past sins, making a spiritual virtue out of denial. Beyond this, adhering to biblical doctrine removed the possibility of divorce. Whatever difficulties they might face in the future, their union was sacred. The lovers had buried the past, and as long as their bond stayed tight, the vault would remain sealed.

Murder had brought them together, but in other respects, the Winchesters were an ordinary family. By 2006, the police investigation, while still ongoing, had lost its momentum, and as the pressure lifted, the couple's day-to-day life stabilized. Together, they developed a supple range of psychological defense mechanisms to keep their self-perception intact. At first, Brian was confident and blasé; Denise, fearful and shaken. Over time, isolated and confined, they started to support each other's delusions—to believe, along with their friends and neighbors, that they were decent, law-abiding members of the community.

Judging by the evidence in the homicide file, they were no different from any other hardworking, close-knit, churchgoing couple. They lived a quiet, conservative life, attending their children's school events, eating at local restaurants, taking family vacations. Denise worked full-time as a CPA while Brian built his portfolio as a financial adviser and property manager. Winchester Financial specialized in wealth management, insurance policies, and estate planning. Many of Brian's clients were personal friends, mostly older people in overlapping church and social circles. They, in turn, would recommend Brian's business to colleagues and acquaintances. This is how he made a living: from discreet recommendations, considered advice, and quiet encouragement. He coached Cub and Little League baseball, played racquetball, participated in water ski tournaments, went mountain biking and duck hunting with his son. Denise baked cakes, took Anslee shopping, volunteered at the church nursery, and spent time with her grandparents. The banality of their life safeguarded their secret.

On December 1, 2006, on behalf of the police, Kathy recorded a telephone conversation she had with Brian. This piece of evidence shows how, when adequately repressed, an act of homicide can neatly coexist with ordinary life: concerns about a child's car seat, trick-or-treating, foot cream, homework, and which people can be trusted (dark whispers of murder are in the air at Cheryl's house). We also get a sense of Brian and Kathy's relationship: It's easy to see the couple slipping into what was clearly a familiar dynamic. During the first part of the conversation—Kathy describes it sarcastically as "a parenting lesson"—Brian's tone is condescending, belittling, sometimes even bullying. He nags and lectures, repeating anecdotes and quoting statistics. Kathy is impatient and irritable, agreeing just to get him to move on. "What do you want me to say?" she asks, more than once. "I can't undo it, so next topic."

Brian tells Kathy he's called to discuss some concerns about their son. Kathy has recently given birth to a daughter, and Brian is worried that, with the stress of caring for a newborn, she may be neglecting Stafford, who's just turned six. His first concern is that when Kathy drops Stafford off at school, she doesn't wait until he's reached his classroom safely. "I mean, it would be so easy to kidnap a kid," Brian reprimands her. "It's scary how easy it would be."

Next he complains about Kathy letting Stafford spend time at a neighbor's house. "I just think you need to be extremely, extremely careful about who you let him play with," says Brian. Kathy tells him the neighbors are "good, Christian people," but Brian isn't reassured. "I'm just saying, you don't know people, Kathy. No matter how nice they are to you, you don't know them."

Coming from a man who killed his best friend, such reprimands seem, on the face of it, hypocritical. But murderers rarely think of themselves as murderers; even if they do, it's in fleeting moments. There's no reason to believe that Brian isn't genuinely concerned about his son's well-being; his moralizing may be an attempt to balance the discordances in his character, making places for the parts that don't fit. The fact that a man has committed a terrible crime does not preclude him from wanting to protect his child. But to tell himself a story he can live with—that he's a cautious and responsible parent—Brian has to repress the painful truth: That nothing could threaten Stafford's safety more than having a murderer for a dad.

Later in the call, when Brian takes Kathy to task for talking to the cops, the conversation develops a different rhythm. Kathy stops acquiescing and starts asking questions of her own. "There's not a day that goes by that I don't hear things," she tells him ominously. Brian wants to know what kinds of things she's heard. "I've heard that you and Denise are not letting Anslee see Cheryl," she says. This sets Brian off on a rant. "I feel horrible for her," he says of Cheryl. "If she dies, she's burning in hell . . . She's reading books about communicating with the dead. . . . She's talking with Indian chiefs over in Jackson County. I don't think she's a Christian, Kathy."

———

Brian and Denise had never talked about the details of Mike's death, but during the early years of their marriage, when the investigation was still in progress, they often talked about what would happen if the police arrested either of them. As things remained quiet, however, they began to relax. Even their contingency plans "kind of tapered off over time," as Brian would put it. The couple no longer saw themselves as partners in crime. As they grew older, like most people, they became less egocentric, more levelheaded, more family-focused. Their self-perception had changed. In their mid-thirties now, the Winchesters had become stable and conventional. They'd grown complacent. Brian was handsome, muscular, and athletic. Denise, still a fashionable dresser, was slim and lithe, with glossy blond hair. As a couple, they were popular and charismatic; they acted as though they'd achieved the American Dream in matters of both money and the heart.

As time passed, they started to believe the investigation had faded away. No more articles appeared in the *Democrat* or anywhere else. The couple went on with their busy lives, raising their kids, spending time with friends, attending church. In 2010, planning their retirement, they bought an office building and created a property management business together as an investment. They also began looking for a new home they could retire to—a large, modern house with plenty of land, preferably by the water.

But whenever they started to think the murder was behind them, Mike's specter would rise up from the lake, summoned, as Brian would recall, by "something in the newspaper, or online, or something one of Denise's sisters said." Each time it happened, they'd get paranoid and go over their alibis.

They wouldn't talk at home. Ever since Cheryl had gone to law enforcement with her suspicions, Brian and Denise had been worried the police had bugged their phones; they'd worked out a series of gestures to use when they wanted to discuss anything to do with the murder. One was to trace the letter "C" for Cheryl, and another was to mime a pair of hands gripping the bars of a prison cell. If either of them made one of these gestures, they'd get in the car and drive to one of the benches on the Miccosukee Canopy Road Greenway, an expansive park with walking trails and hills in the distance, where they'd sit and talk. Occasionally, if the weather was bad, they'd stay in the car, but they wouldn't start the conversation until they'd removed the batteries from their phones.

Brian was increasingly concerned that the two of them were being "watched or monitored," but Denise, in time, began to relax her vigilance. Once the police investigation was over, she appeared to have convinced herself that nothing would happen. She then went a step further. According to her husband, "she pretended she had nothing to do with it." Perhaps the shame was unbearable to her, or maybe she'd reached the stage where she couldn't think about what they'd done. "Denise has an uncanny ability to live in denial," observed Brian. "When you live a certain way over a time period, and you act like something is the truth . . . in the end, you begin to believe it."

But just as a drowned body will rise to the surface, whatever is repressed will always return.

– ACT III –

1

Venal Foul Play

"Foul whisperings are abroad: unnatural deeds
Do breed unnatural troubles; infected minds
To their deaf pillows will discharge their secrets."

WILLIAM SHAKESPEARE, *MACBETH*, ACT V, SCENE I, 75–77

Every year, on the anniversary of Mike's disappearance, a journalist named Jennifer Portman at the *Tallahassee Democrat* published an article reminding people he was still missing. She'd revealed that Brian had sold Mike two of his three life insurance policies and that Brian and Denise were now married. Her yearly articles kept Mike's case alive, although the pulse was often faint.

"Tomorrow Makes 2,556 Days He's Been Missing," read the *Democrat*'s headline on December 15, 2007, the seventh anniversary of Mike's disappearance. Some found it surprising the newspaper was giving significant coverage to this sad but relatively insignificant case when the city was hardly short of news: corrupt politicians, fraternity hazing deaths, football players charged with sexual battery, hurricanes, shooting sprees, bear attacks. In fact, as with the police investigation, it was Cheryl's stubborn persistence that had drawn Portman into Mike's story. She'd come to share Cheryl's suspicions and hoped that further attention might bring more facts to light. Brian and Denise Winchester were among the people she'd reached out to for a quote for her article; Brian had responded with a brief comment on the couple's behalf. "Nobody wants Mike to be found more than we do. We continue to love Mike and miss him every day. We ask again that our privacy be respected and that our family be allowed to live our lives in peace."

As Portman and the *Democrat* grew more suspicious about Mike's disappearance, law enforcement became less involved. While it was never officially closed, after 2007, the Williams case was cold. That year, Ronnie Austin left the Florida Department of Law Enforcement; thirty-four-year-old Tully Sparkman took over as lead investigator. Sparkman was chosen for the job partly because he'd formerly worked at the Florida Fish and Wildlife Commission and remembered the incident at Lake Seminole, although he hadn't participated in the search.

In August of that year, at Sparkman's request, divers from the auxiliary unit of FSU Panama City's Underwater Crime Scene Investigation program once again searched Lake Seminole for evidence of Mike's disappearance. They came up empty-handed, but the search stirred attention, making front-page news in the *Democrat* on August 8. Six months later, the case was in the news again. "Insurance Investigators Take a New Look at Disappearance," read the *Democrat*'s headline on February 27, 2008. In the article, Portman revealed that the Florida Division of Insurance Fraud was launching a new investigation into Mike's death.

On March 14, 2008, investigators from the Bureau of Alcohol, Tobacco, Firearms and Explosives contacted Carrie Cox, Ph.D., a forensic psychological profiler who used her intuitive powers to envisage what might have happened to Mike.

The medium described visions she'd had about Mike's murder. She told the officers that Mike was shot in a bedroom by a woman with "an older model revolver" that was "easy access, probably kept in a nightstand or dresser." The crime wasn't premeditated, Cox claimed. "The woman called a friend of Mike's to help her clean up the situation." The couple then drove past a lighthouse to an isolated place where they dug an "oval-shaped" hole in which they buried the body.

———————

Notes from Carrie D. Cox, Ph.D.:

Sent: Friday, March 14, 2008, 1:47 PM

There is a park . . . I see pine trees and power lines. The road is paved with black top . . . I believe the one in the google picture with the fork in it . . .

—I can see pine needles on the ground over it, so there must be pine trees nearby. (The landscape can change over time and I may be seeing a view now from six or seven years ago).

—The evidence in the lake was planted. I am drawn to boots and a jacket not being real evidence. There may have been other items too, but these I am drawn to.

—Pay attention to the latitude line 1924.

Tallahassee has plenty of parks, pine trees, power lines, and even a lighthouse (on the St. Mark's River), but when searchers followed the psychic's clues, they came up empty-handed. Yet while Cox may have been off target where the murder was concerned, when it came to Brian and Denise's relationship, her presentiments hit closer to home. She wrote of the man in the case, "He is the weakest link. He has conflicted feelings about the situation and would give the woman up if pushed hard enough, but I do not feel like you will get a conviction on her." The man "feels the most unstable," she emphasized, whereas "the female is able to pretend things away and convince herself of alternate truths."

"Eight Years Later, Still No Trace of Missing Hunter," read Jennifer Portman's annual reminder on December 16, 2008, now relegated to a small item at the bottom of the page. The article was resigned and downbeat. "Even though one investigator remains assigned to the cold case, and cadaver-sniffing dogs have been tromping in nearby woods, any hope that the Division of Insurance Fraud could break it open is gone." Spokesman Mark Schlein said they were "simply unable to develop enough evidence to proceed with the investigation." A sad coda to the year: The FDLE included Mike's picture in their annual "cold case deck," a set of playing cards distributed annually to inmates to generate tips. It was a last resort, and nothing came of it.

There were no further developments until December 2010, when the FDLE assigned a new detective to the case. Mike DeVaney was a heavy-set, sandy-haired gentleman with a walrus mustache. His first move was to sit down with investigators from the Tallahassee Police Department and the Leon County Sheriff's Office to conduct an "immense review" of the Mike Williams files with an eye to possible prosecution. Like others who'd worked on the case, DeVaney soon came to believe Brian and Denise were involved in Mike's disappearance, but he realized there was no evidence to prove it—just rumor, gossip, and hearsay. DeVaney and his team reached the same conclusion as earlier investigators. Unless Brian and Denise turned on each other, nothing would happen.

Cheryl was still listening carefully to what people were saying. She'd recently turned sixty-seven, and although she was still in good health, the struggle to find Mike was grinding her down. She'd lost all faith in the FDLE, which had spent eleven years doing nothing, or so it seemed. But she did have high hopes for the new governor, a tough-minded Republican named Rick Scott, who came into office on January 4, 2011. Cheryl began writing him a letter every day, begging him to either get a different agency to investigate Mike's case or to appoint a special prosecutor. She mailed more than two hundred letters without receiving so much as an acknowledgment, but rather than accepting defeat, she tried something more radical: paying for an ad in the *Democrat*—"An open letter to Governor Rick Scott," asking for his help with the case. Finally, she got an answer. The governor's office, she learned, had been forwarding her letters to the FDLE headquarters, where officers had placed them in the case file. Unopened. A punch in the face.

But Cheryl was no longer alone. Anyone who'd been following Jennifer Portman's coverage of the case in the *Tallahassee Democrat* would have to agree: The circumstances of Mike's disappearance were highly suspicious. Word began to spread. In 2011, news of the case reached the producers of *Disappeared*, an *Unsolved Mysteries*–type show on the Investigation Discovery Channel featuring interviews with the friends and families of missing people, testimony from law enforcement officers, and staged reenactments. Mike's story, the producers decided, would be perfect for the show. Episode 10 of Season 4, "Mystery on Lake Seminole," aired at 10 p.m. on Monday, November 28, 2011. The show begins with a narrator (the actor Christopher Crutchfield Walker) describing Mike's "duck-hunting accident" on the lake. "When his wife cashes in a large insurance policy and marries the man who sold her husband the insurance policy," he begins, ominously, "police suspect foul play." Mike, Denise, and Brian appear only in archival photographs. Cheryl Williams receives substantial screen time, as do Clay Ketcham, Mike's brother Nick, Jennifer Portman from the *Tallahassee Democrat*, and Derrick Wester from the Jackson County Sheriff's Office. Like most of the show's episodes, however, "Mystery at Lake Seminole" relies largely on clumsy "dramatic reenactments," with lookalike stand-ins playing a naïve Mike, a shameless Denise, and a weaselly Brian.

The search for Mike's body is described, and his alleged death by "alligator involvement." The timeline of subsequent events is flattened, repeated, and simplified: "Mike's widow receives all of Mike's assets and cashes in on life insurance worth at least one and a half million dollars. She later marries Mike's best friend, the insurance agent who sold Mike a million-dollar policy just six months before he went missing." Brian and Denise are the only suspects. "The Florida Department of Law Enforcement says they have persons of interest," reveals the voice-over, "but won't officially identify them." It doesn't need to. "If anyone should be questioning what happened to Mike, you'd think it would be his wife and best friend," says Jennifer Portman. "And they won't really comment on this."

The episode concludes with an email from Brian Winchester declining an interview and asking, once again, that the couple be left in peace.

Shakespeare's Hamlet, in order to prove his uncle Claudius is guilty of murder, asks a troupe of actors to reenact the crime. He believes that watching the performance will prick Claudius's conscience, and he's right: During the murder scene, Claudius stands up, calls for lights, and demands the play be stopped. On a different scale, while TV shows about unsolved crimes are popular for a variety of reasons, part of their appeal is that they might stir someone's guilt and prod them into revealing secrets, or even to confess (which sometimes happens). "Mystery on Lake Seminole" did not lead to a confession, but Brian and Denise couldn't avoid the fallout, and for Brian especially, it was a painful twist of the knife.

When Mike went missing in 2001, the internet barely existed. Google had only recently been launched. There was no Gmail, no Facebook, no Skype, no Twitter, no Instagram. Cell phones were common, but not smartphones. People didn't text. By 2010, however, things had changed significantly. Local news, once shared by word of mouth, had shifted to social media; those who made hints and accusations could remain anonymous if they so desired. Regional newspapers, while they still appeared in print, were also published online, allowing readers to comment publicly (although, like most national newspapers, the *Tallahassee Democrat* charges a subscription fee). In addition, forums like Websleuths, an internet discussion board devoted to unexplained deaths and missing people, let ordinary people speculate openly about unsolved crimes.

"Mystery at Lake Seminole" seemed heavy-handed and one-sided, but the implications were impossible to escape, and after it aired in November 2011, Tallahassee buzzed with gossip. People recalled seeing the billboard with Mike's picture and were shocked to hear the full story. A Websleuths discussion forum was set up for site members to discuss the Mike Williams case. Immediately after the show ended, people started to post. "This case SCREAMS of MURDER!" declared one. Others concurred. "My mom and I watched the show . . . At the end of the hour long episode, we both just sat there slack-jawed, in stunned silence." "I don't mean to prejudge people . . . but the circumstances of this really point to the wife and best friend IMO. I cannot believe that they haven't looked into them both in detail." But although everyone thought "*Disappeared* sure made it look like the wife and best friend did it," they also realized that "proving it will be nearly impossible."

"What I am puzzled about is why Denise and Brian continue to live in the same house as Denise and Mike did," speculated one armchair investigator. "With the whole town talking about them for 10 years, one would have thought Brian and Denise would have moved by now. Most people getting $1.5 million would buy a bigger, better house. There has to be a very good reason why she is staying where she is and the only reason I can think of is that there is some evidence at that house that Denise does not want anyone to find."

Another anonymous commenter claimed of Brian and Denise that "these are prominent families with connections to the state attorney (IMO a crook), a judge (IMO with questionable rulings) . . . it began in a rural county that was not capable of the investigation & has been bullied by the stronger agencies including a then deputy sheriff (IMO another corrupt official who is now Sheriff of Leon County & up for re-election . . .)." This Websleuths member seemed familiar with those involved; they commented again in January 2012. "I am so happy to see interest in Mike's case. If someone could pry open the good ol boys- school buddies- friends in high places—daddy's money buys protection & coverup, maybe Mrs Williams could finally have peace." A "forensic astrologer" discovered signs of "venal foul play" in Mike's horoscope. His moon was in late Sagittarius, implicating his wife, ruled by Mercury. "No doubt at all that Mike Williams was ambushed," concluded the self-assured mystic. "On this December 16 morning, Pluto blindsided him, a dead cert."

Post on Websleuths forum:

> *This case infuriates me! I actually lived in Tallahassee at the time and had never even heard about Mike . . . and for SOME REASON his disappearance was kept fairly quiet. . . .*

All I know is that if I had known about this at the time I would have tried to become involved in the search. Time was wasted, evidence handled incorrectly. I was shocked when I saw the Disappeared *episode—all of this happened in the city I was living in—and the fact that it was such a blatant and obvious case! I mean—you couldn't write this story and try to sell it . . . . it's too cliched to be believable. Man—my blood pressure rises every time I think of it. Need to go take a bubble bath to calm down!*

––––––––

For Brian, it was a bad winter. Guilt, the invader, pushed apart the cracked barriers of his conscience, and a siege of rumors and gossip forced their way inside. He'd kept his crime secret for more than ten years and must surely have struggled with temptation to confess. Still, he continued to resist the urge. There may even have been long stretches of time when he repressed thoughts of his fraudulent life so deeply that he, like Denise, came to believe the lies. But Brian was not as well defended as his wife. His armor was thinner, his capacity for repression less profound.

Denial allows a person to inflict harm on another; it also grows from that harm. And if the harm is ongoing, the denial continues. Brian and Denise might have managed to distance themselves from the murder, but they couldn't avoid seeing and hearing about Cheryl's pain. Nor could they help being aware of what the Bible has to say, in John 12:40, about those who refuse to believe the word of Christ: "He has blinded their eyes and hardened their hearts."

The *Disappeared* episode, along with Portman's articles in the *Tal-*

lahassee Democrat, had rattled Brian, and he began paying more attention to social media. The rumors made him edgy, suspicious, and paranoid. He suspected the cops had planted microphones in the house and his car. He became hypervigilant. He studied the *Democrat* every morning, reading the comments online. The gossip gnawed at him. Mistrust unbalanced his equilibrium. "Google my name—there are people all over the country who hate me," he wrote in his journal. "I get emails, voicemails, death threats, blogs, Facebook pages dedicated to hating me."

More than anything else, he needed to talk. But whenever he approached Denise, she would shut him out. "She didn't want to hear anything about it." With nowhere else to turn, Brian sought to repress his anxieties by returning to his old vice: alcohol. But drinking just made things worse; when relaxed, he let his guard down, which left him vulnerable. Repression, as Freud puts it, "proliferates in the dark," and to prevent it from breaking through to consciousness, the mind has to keep careful vigil (". . . I must set a permanent guard over the door which I have forbidden this guest to enter, since he would otherwise burst it open."). Like Shakespeare's Macbeth, who also conspires with his wife to commit murder, Brian had "a hell within him." A Baptist hell: "a place of eternal, conscious punishment."

No doubt Denise was equally assailed, but she expressed her anxiety in different ways. While Brian indulged in excess, Denise went in the opposite direction. She ignored the rumors and gossip, stayed away from social media, and blocked everything out, sinking further into denial. She became increasingly ascetic, devoting herself to biblical doctrine, immersing herself in the church. She lived by well-defined and tightly controlled rules. Financially, she remained frugal, making no change to her lifestyle, despite her vast windfall. Physically, she appeared to be restricting herself in a punitive way. She went to the gym as often as she went to church, if not more often, and ate very little. Friends and family continued to comment on her weight—they said she looked unhealthy, even anorexic. In photographs from this time, she appears angular and skeletal, as if the only thing she ever absorbed was her guilt.

Slowly and silently, it was eating her away.

2

You Will Answer to God

"I had killed a man to get a woman. I had put myself in her power, so there was one person in the world who could point a finger at me, and I would have to die. I had done all that for her, and I never wanted to see her again as long as I lived."

JAMES M. CAIN, *DOUBLE INDEMNITY* (1943)

For more than a year, Brian and Denise had been negotiating to buy a house they'd found on the banks of Lake Jackson, in a northeast suburb of Tallahassee. The Spanish-style 5,000-square-foot home, priced at $656,000, was three miles down Miller Landing Road, on the edge of the lake among picturesque canopy oaks. It was precisely what they'd been looking for—a waterfront property on three acres. The discreet, upscale house symbolized respectability and permanence, but its façade contrasted starkly with the desperate state of the couple's marriage. In August 2012, the purchase went through, and the Winchesters bought the property, but they never lived there. Brian later came to believe that, not long after the closing, Denise decided she was going to leave him. He thought, "She didn't want to uproot her life, her daughter, into that house."

As with most unhappy marriages, the couple's daily tedium turned minor frustrations into bitter fights. They were constantly on edge, rubbed raw by their shared secret. Their relationship, as they aged, was crumbling under accumulated years of anguish, argument, and the assorted debris of guilt. Unable to comfort each other, they began to drift in different directions. Denise sought solace in Anslee, now a feisty teenager with a startling resemblance to Mike. Brian found relief in alcohol, strip clubs, and porn. When his wife discovered what he'd been doing, she asked him to move out. Brian begged for another chance. They went to counseling. Things would stabilize temporarily, then something would happen, and the cycle would start again.

Finally, inevitably, the couple's relationship became unsustainable. Their complicity in the crime had left them isolated and confined, forced to rely on each other for support, but mutual reassurance was no longer possible. Their love had curdled into paranoia and mistrust. Under pressure, their marriage began to creak. The beams groaned and the walls crumbled, but it was six more years before the structure collapsed. When it finally gave way, the couple had been together for fifteen years. For twelve of those years, the crime had kept their bond sealed tight. Now they had nowhere to turn.

Denise was not compelled, like her husband, to put things down on paper. Her secrets stayed secret—even, perhaps, from herself. Brian's notes, journals, emails, and letters, on the other hand, recount a long, grueling dark night of the soul. His misery is palpable. Unlike Cheryl's concise and eclectic notes, Brian's journal entries from this time are detailed and verbose. At the behest of Ron Rickner, the couple's Christian counselor, Brian charted the course of his deteriorating marriage as part of a "training regime." In 2012, every Thursday night, he attended meetings of Sex Addicts Anonymous, also led by Rickner, noting his thoughts after each session.

> *May 1: Sin leads to death. I am blinded and in the dark because of my sin. Every little decision leads us closer to God or closer to Satan.*
>
> *May 10: I have to "weed" and "feed" my mind. I have to take the lies that the devil tells me and replace those thoughts with the truth.*
>
> *May 22: Kathy sent email asking what am I hiding—obviously someone saw me at SAA meeting—she thinks I am a child molester or something. Ron recommended telling her I have struggled with adult porn and I am seeking help with it. Tell her I am not proud or happy about it but I am seeking help.*

The couple's daily routine was that Denise would drop Anslee at school in the morning before going into the office; she always assumed that Brian was heading off to work too. But in the fall of 2012, Denise's employer, Image API, had to make cutbacks, and Denise lost her job. For a short time, she was at home all day, and she discovered that, as she later told Kathy, "Brian never worked." He wasn't going to the office every day and selling insurance, as he'd always claimed. It wasn't clear how much business he was undertaking, but Denise understood that he was drawing a salary from his father for "doing almost nothing." Kathy had observed the same pattern when she'd been married to Brian. "I think that caused a lot of tension between the two of them," said Kathy.

———

By 2012, the Winchesters' season of trouble had become a permanent state. Their marriage had imploded, but Brian was unable to call a truce and resign himself to cutting his losses. "Denise wants to separate," he wrote in his journal on October 25. "She agreed to give me two weeks to show her I could be nice and kind and not be mean. I blew it on the first day." His anger was becoming a serious problem. On November 11, Denise told him to leave the house after a loud argument, and Brian "lost it." He grabbed her by her wrists and pushed her up against a door. "I saw how she was scared so I let her go and she ran out," he wrote. To relieve his frustration, he kicked her exercise ball across the room, and unluckily, it hit her collection of porcelain figurines. A few of them broke. "It turned out they were some that Mike had given her (of course)," Brian noted. "She thinks I did it on purpose."

After that, Brian moved out. He had no choice. The obvious place for him to go would have been the house on Miller Landing Road, but Denise wouldn't let him. The pristine property had once been the couple's dream home; she didn't want Brian getting drunk and trashing the place or taking strippers or prostitutes back there. His second choice was his dad's hunting cabin, a small trailer on Lake Iamonia half an hour north of Midyette Plantation, but Denise didn't like that idea, either. She didn't want to have Anslee and Stafford visiting him there because, as she complained to Kathy, "it will be full of porn and hookers and everything else." In the end, Brian had no choice: At age forty-three, he moved back in with his parents. He and Denise continued to pay the Miller Landing mortgage for the next two years while it stood empty, ready for the family that no longer existed. Brian went by every week to mow the lawn and take care of general maintenance. It made no sense at all.

His journal was full of remorse. Still, for a repentant sex addict desperate to repair his marriage and get closer to God, Brian could be harshly critical of his wife. In his diaries, letters, and notes, different incarnations of Denise begin to solidify and merge, then break down and reappear in various forms, like a parade of ghosts. From Brian's perspective, his God-fearing Christian wife had turned into a lazy snob obsessed with name-brand fashion labels and reality television. He attributes her transformation to Anslee's growing up, almost as if Anslee has drawn Denise into the orbit of her teenage world.

In short, he'd been knocked off his throne by a child.

For many years after Mike's disappearance, Denise had been careful not to make a display of her wealth, but now that Anslee was a teenager, she began to spend more freely. She kept up her restrictive diet and gym sessions, but she finally loosened her belt when it came to money. It was almost as if, where Anslee was concerned, there was no reason for her to feel guilty. Perhaps Denise felt less conflicted about spending Mike's life insurance money on Anslee because she was his daughter, and it was what he would have wanted (although his notoriously frugal habits suggest otherwise). Whatever the reason, when it came to Anslee, Denise's generosity was unlimited. Through her daughter, Denise could finally drop her guard and live like the millionaire she had become.

Though Brian had moved out, a January 2013 letter shows his unhappiness with his wife's spendthrift habits. "Movies, parties, eating out, shopping . . .—it is constant," he complained. Then there was the traveling the couple had done together in the past. "We have been to Costa Rica, Belize, Chicago twice, Los Angeles twice, New York three times, Atlanta, Orlando, Jacksonville, Pensacola, West Palm Beach, Boca Grande, Colorado, North Carolina, Kiawah Island, Bahamas, Panama City, Destin . . . it's never enough. Now you are planning trips to Washington and a cruise to Europe?"

According to Brian's calculations, Denise had spent $8,000 over a three-month period on eating out at restaurants and shopping for "shoes, purses, knick-knacks, jewelry." He was particularly incensed by a "$900 poodle" she bought for her daughter. He lamented "the obsessions with Anslee, clothes, name brands, the hobbies, the eating out, the traveling, the wastefulness." He wondered when it would end. "I picture Anslee still expecting you to buy her lunches and dinners and take her clothes shopping forever," he wrote to Denise. "This is, of course, after her 'semesters abroad' and ridiculously over-priced wedding where you both fly to New York to get her Vera Wang dress made or consult with Randy at Kleinfeld's."

In James M. Cain's classic 1941 novel *Mildred Pierce*, a hardworking and ambitious divorcée becomes wealthy but is destroyed by her Achilles heel: pathological devotion to her selfish daughter, Veda. Mildred dotes on her daughter, Cain writes, "for her looks, her promise of talent, and her snobbery, which hinted at things superior to her own commonplace nature. . . . There was something unnatural, a little unhealthy, about the way she inhaled Veda's smell . . . This feeling she had about Veda . . . permeated every part of her, and colored everything she did."

Like Mildred's with Veda, Denise's relationship with Anslee—at least according to Brian—was "unhealthy" and "inappropriate." He complained about their "ongoing hugs" and "constant touching," the "holding hands," the "leaning and laying" on each other. "Even the way you talk to her in that little girl voice—she is way too casual in her relationship with you." Denise, he lamented, "fills her days and nights with TV, Anslee, shopping, eating out, and ANSLEE."

Another letter written in January 2013 begins by addressing the subject of Anslee taking part in the high school "Sweetheart Court," a type of beauty pageant. Brian disapproves. He brings up the couple's high school years, ever-present. He reminds Denise of something Mike once told him years ago: "He said there was no way he was going to let Anslee grow up to be 'another damn Merrell.'" Brian writes, "If we took a poll of people you all went to school with growing up and asked them to describe the Merrell girls in one word, what do you think people would say?" The question is rhetorical. Brian offers a few epithets for her to choose from: "snobs, stuck-up, bitches, selfish, narcissistic, mean, conceited, fake, spoiled."

Next, although he's moved back in with his parents, he complains about Denise's house being "a constant wreck," with "piles of boxes, letters, bills, packages, dishes, clothes, shoes" everywhere. He objects to the money she spends on Anslee's sports equipment: "multiple pairs of overpriced shoes, multiple athletic uniforms, practice uniforms, bags to carry them in, monogrammed drink cups and of course the high-performance sports drinks because water doesn't cut it for our 'athlete.'" Other things that spark his anger include Anslee "friending" reality TV stars on Facebook (including "a retarded woman" and "an HIV positive gay man"); Anslee "sleeping all afternoon and skipping church"; and, in short, Anslee turning into "a selfish, narcissistic, lazy spoiled brat."

———

Frustrated and angry as he was, Brian desperately wanted to heal the marriage, and for a while, it appeared, so did Denise. After everything they'd gone through to be together, the thought of divorce was terrifying. And dangerous.

Throughout 2013, Denise continued going to couples therapy with Brian. Both were also undergoing individual counseling, as well as a program of reading designed for them by Ron Rickner, which included *The Betrayal Bond: Breaking Free of Exploitive Relationships* by the sex addiction expert Patrick Carnes, *Recovering Redemption* by the Baptist pastor Matt Chandler, and *See Yourself as God Sees You* by the Christian evangelist Josh McDowell.

In addition, the couple embarked on a series of often costly workshops, classes, and residential retreats designed for Christian couples in crisis. In his journal, Brian refers to meetings of Sex Addicts Anonymous, Celebrate Recovery Fridays at Four Oaks Baptist Church, and the Bethesda Workshops in Nashville, Tennessee (for "Christian-based short-term therapy for sex and pornography addiction"). He also writes about Dr. Mark Laaser's "Men of Valor Faithful & True 3-day intensive sex addiction workshop" in Eden Prairie, Minnesota. He installed Covenant Eyes Screen Accountability software on his phone and laptop. Denise, too, attended workshops: the evangelist Beth Moore's Living Proof Live conferences, a Live the Life Hope Weekend, a Christian-based intensive marriage retreat, and a "Mending the Shattered Heart" clinic in Mississippi.

Phrases like "mending the shattered heart" and "recovering redemption" are reminiscent of biblical language, with its metaphors of stains and impurities that can be wiped out by the sacrificial blood of Christ, or burdens that can be lifted and cast aside. It's clear why these images would be appealing to Brian and Denise. They suggest guilt can disappear as if by magic.

Over the preceding fifteen years, the Baptist church in Tallahassee—as elsewhere—had been through some radical changes. It had become, according to detractors, overly consumed with marketing, fundraising, and establishing networks of donors. In some more progressive churches, Christian synth pop replaced traditional hymn-singing; instead of pastors reading sermons, motivational speakers paced the stage with clip-on mics. Partly, this was an attempt to attract younger people to the church. Baptist congregations had been shrinking and were losing their political influence. To regain strength, some Baptist churches had turned into family-friendly event centers that snuck in a little Gospel here and there. At Celebration Baptist Church, Brian's former place of worship, congregants eventually would pay tithes via a downloadable app. Prayers could be offered and requested by text. Services were streamed online. Worshippers could consult the Bible on their cell phones.

Despite their personal differences, when it came to the church, Brian and Denise stayed up-to-date, committing themselves to the church's new technology and the transformational, consciousness-raising aspects of their spiritual "training regime." Every day, Brian reprimanded and cajoled himself with a blend of scripture and thera-peutic advice, referring to "fear-based decision-making," "account-ability reports," "proof-texting," "liability or responsibility," "emotional dependency," and "surrendering to God."

In his journal, his stream of consciousness is, by turns, self-serving, defensive, and self-flagellating. Although he's writing solely for him-self, and despite his endorsement of soul-searching honesty, he never refers to the murder except in ways that place it at a distance: he calls it the "Mike Williams saga," and, in a limber feat of self-delusion, uses the "witch hunt" against him to excuse his sex addiction. "The Mike Williams investigation, accusations . . . shamed and isolated both of us," he wrote in his journal, "and I medicated all that shame and pain through sex."

Despite her purported desire to mend the marriage, Denise was eager to separate herself from Brian financially. The couple had sep-arate bank accounts, but Denise handled most of the expenses and she felt Brian wasn't pulling his weight. On June 6, she emailed him: "You know that I have wanted to separate the finances since before Christmas. You have taken full advantage of me in this area during our marriage." She added, unconvincingly, that this was "not a movement towards divorce but a movement towards health and healing." The fi-nancial separation occurred on July 1, 2013. The couple agreed to split the mortgage payments on their new house at Miller Landing, still standing empty. They would split therapy and counseling bills, utilities, and car insurance. Each would pay for their child's cell phone and orthodontic braces, and Brian would continue making child-support payments to Kathy.

It was gradually becoming clear to Brian that this was no temporary separation. He was starting to realize that, in her actions if not in her words, Denise was moving further away from him and had no genuine interest in repairing the marriage. By 2014, she'd found a new job at FSU, and despite Brian's many vows to abjure lies and secrecy, he started letting himself into the house on Centennial Oak Circle while she was at work. Not only did he read Denise's journal, but he also managed to access her emails and texts. To Brian, she seemed to be living in a daydream universe, paying not the slightest attention to his suffering. He made notes to remind him of what he read:

Jeff is worried for Denise—evil present.

Denise told neighbors to keep an eye on her.

Denise to Becky—I'm glad I didn't have a biological child with him.

Denise to Carla—I am going to tell him that I am going to get a divorce—I feel so free—it's awesome.

Denise to Kara: He is a dick with a capital D. And a capital I-C-K . . . I called the number that was on his phone . . . John's mother comes up as a Tallahassee prostitute.

Denise to Nancy—I feel like I am on drugs I am so happy and I cannot stop smiling AND I'm getting Krispy Kreme donuts to CELEBRATE!!! God is so good!!

Brian was not smiling. To him, it was clear: Denise was looking forward to the future because she'd forgotten the past. His prospects, on the other hand, looked bleak. At forty-three, he was facing his second divorce and living at home with his parents. "I am a sex addict," he wrote in his journal. "I struggle with fear and shame over the bad publicity and rumors about the Mike Williams saga. I feel lonely most of the time—and that's probably the hardest thing for me to deal with. I am lonely and I miss Denise." As usual, however, his self-recriminations quickly turn to anger. "I know you are afraid," he writes to his wife. "I know you would rather take the easy road. . . . The answer to everything is in the Bible. Where does it tell you to divorce me? You will answer to God for this decision."

– 3 –

Enjoy Your Riches
and Your Daughter

**"I had killed a man, for money and a woman. I didn't have
the money and I didn't have the woman."**

JAMES M. CAIN, *DOUBLE INDEMNITY* (1943)

"I couldn't even look at her," Brian wrote in his journal after a couples therapy session with Denise. "I was so ashamed." It was 2015. The couple had officially separated. In therapy, Denise was starting to characterize her relationship with Brian—especially in the early days of their marriage—as manipulative and abusive. He'd sexually victimized her, she told Ron Rickner. He'd made her get drunk. When she was barely conscious, he'd forced her to perform acts that were shameful and perverse. She'd been afraid to say no. In front of Rickner, she made Brian agree that their marriage had been "abnormal and abusive" and that she was a "trauma victim." In his journal, Brian described how she went into graphic detail about how he'd sexually exploited her.

Brian went along with Denise's version of the past, which he attributed to the influence of feminist group therapy and what he described as an "abused wives conference" in New York, even though he disagreed with it. Privately, he felt she was "attempting to falsely portray herself as a victim," but kept quiet because he still hoped to get her back. Even after reading the texts between Denise and her friends, Brian still deluded himself that with enough therapy and prayer, their marriage could be repaired. He'd even sign a postnuptial agreement, he told her. He'd wait however long. He'd take a polygraph—anything she wanted. He begged forgiveness for the way he'd treated her in the past.

August 2015 was a month of frustration, headaches, and anxiety; most days, the temperature was over 95 degrees. Denise finally agreed to let Brian move into the house at Miller Landing, which he interpreted as a sign that she was finally starting to forgive him and that the family would soon be back together. For this reason, he went along with her when, in front of fellow congregants, counselors, friends, and family members, she made him out to be a monster, establishing a narrative of their marriage in which she was the innocent, abused victim of a narcissistic sociopath. Brian, desperate to avoid divorce at all costs, felt he had no choice but to agree. "The more extreme she got," he said, "the more concerned I became about where it might lead." He suspected she was "manipulating" him. "I was in a position where I've got to agree to be the bad guy no matter what she said," he later explained. This rewriting of the couple's history made him very anxious. He couldn't help wondering: Was Denise trying to set him up?

Initially, whenever anyone had raised the subject of Mike's disappearance, the couple always stuck to the same story: Denise was at home with the baby, and Brian went to Cairo with Kathy. They'd discuss the murder only when they were alone together, out of the house, and away from their phones. Eventually, they grew so paranoid that they'd even pat each other down beforehand to be sure neither was wearing a wire.

During the separation, they hadn't discussed the murder at all. Now, even in private, when Brian brought up the subject of Mike's death, Denise would say she didn't know anything about it. It was baffling. After much thought, Brian came up with three possible explanations.

First: She'd concluded that "nothing would ever transpire from a law enforcement perspective." In other words, it was all over. They would never get caught; no one would ever question them. She didn't want to talk about it, so why should she?

Second: Her denial had gone so far that she'd repressed her involvement in Mike's death. Denise had a talent for compartmentalizing and blocking things out. Since passionately re-embracing Christianity, she'd wholly severed herself from her past. "I don't know what Denise's reality is," mused Brian in his journal. Perhaps, he wondered, "what she needed to believe, and tell her daughter, and tell herself, to be able to live with herself, was the story that we created for her, which was that she was at home with her baby."

The third possibility was even more chilling. Was it possible that his wife was secretly recording their conversations? Brian conducted a brief experiment. He told Denise he'd seen something about the investigation online—they might be called in for questioning, and he wanted them to go over their alibis. Denise said he was upsetting her, and she didn't want to discuss it. "It was very strange," noted Brian. "I almost felt like she was 'acting.'" He wondered whether she might be trying to get him on tape talking about the murder so that, if the police ever arrested them, she'd have an insurance policy, and she could pin it all on him. Maybe she was even planning to turn him in.

At that point, Brian realized the greatest threat to his safety wasn't the law enforcement investigation.

It was Denise.

―――――――

His accomplice had become his adversary. Brian was trapped. He felt as if he were behind a window, watching the world outside full of untroubled people going about their daily business. His suffering was impossible to communicate; his guilt left him alienated and alone. At first, like Denise, he'd refused to think about the murder, but as his wife sank more and more deeply into denial, Brian's understanding of his own culpability, once rudimentary, had grown and grown until it had become a terrible weight on his conscience. God knew his secret. But did God forgive him? He was no longer sure.

On August 7, 2015, Denise permanently dashed Brian's hopes of mending the relationship by filing for divorce, claiming the marriage was "irretrievably broken." She asked the court to restore her former name, Denise Merrell Williams, symbolically undoing her connection with Brian and reattaching herself to Mike. Brian begged her to change her mind, but she shut him out. By September, she'd stopped returning his texts and emails and wouldn't answer his calls. Brian grew angry, then despondent. "After it became clear to me that she was not interested in saving the marriage, that she wanted to take her money and her daughter and run, I did . . . stupid things," he confessed. When he received court papers concerning the divorce, he'd ignore them until the last minute, then request an extension. He wasn't going to let Denise walk away and leave him with nothing, especially after he'd spent the previous four years doing everything she'd asked of him.

"I did not handle the news well," Brian admitted. "I dealt with it by drinking and indulging in inappropriate relationships." Sex was his way of self-medicating, and when Brian fell, he fell hard. His job was giving financial advice to others, but when it came to money, like Denise, he lost all self-control and began spending selfishly and compulsively. He was unable to face an empty house: Most of his cash went to buy the company of strippers and prostitutes. He liked risky sex; his impulsive behavior fed on itself.

Although intensely unhappy, Brian didn't believe in taking antidepressants, because he didn't believe in depression. He accepted Christian counseling but kept his deepest inner conflicts to himself. His was not a religion that advocates confession. Like many Baptists, he saw mental illness as a spiritual rather than a medical issue—a reminder of man's brokenness from the Fall, which could be overcome with faith, charity, and prayer. He considered depression "a diagnosis created by greedy therapists and pharmaceutical companies for lazy people who couldn't suck it up when things got rough." Now, alone in the house he and Denise had chosen for their golden years, he drank himself unconscious and had trouble getting out of bed. He started spending more time at Winchester Financial.

When Stafford wasn't staying with him, Brian dreaded the end of the workday. He couldn't face the prospect of going back to an empty house, of being alone all night. Sometimes, at work, he'd lock his office door and lie on the floor in the dark, reluctant to leave. He spent a lot of time looking at family photographs and watching home videos. He was deeply concerned about the divorce, which, he believed, would bury him "financially and emotionally." During this time of crisis, his journals paint a picture of a man who is falling apart.

In February 2016, Stafford, then seventeen and a high school junior, went to look for something in his dad's bedroom in the Miller Landing house, which was full of boxes that Brian still hadn't unpacked. On the nightstand, he noticed a handgun in a holster, later identified as a Beretta. He was worried about his dad—Brian had been very emotional in the last few weeks, and Stafford had never seen a handgun in the house before, only hunting rifles. When asked about it, Brian said his friend Roman Fontenot had lent him the gun to use when duck hunting and to shoot pests on the property.

The following spring, the divorce—thanks to Brian's constant stalling and delays—was still in process, and Brian was increasingly anxious and depressed. He was still drinking, using drugs, and spending even more time with strippers and prostitutes. When Stafford was staying with him, Brian sometimes wondered what he knew. When his son was at school, Brian would read the boy's journal to be sure he hadn't seen anything compromising.

It was a low move, and in May, the snooping dad got a taste of his own medicine.

Stafford picked up Brian's phone and started scrolling through his pictures. The photographs weren't of fishing trips and soccer games but of girls posing sexually in the house at Miller Landing, along with sleazy texts planning late-night hookups. Stafford, shocked, wondered what else was going on. A quick search of the house uncovered alcohol in the freezer and pills on the bedroom vanity.

———

Stafford said nothing to his dad about what he'd found, but after he was back at his mom's, he told her everything. He'd taken photographs of what he'd seen and shared them with Kathy, who showed them to Denise and Anslee. Denise was livid. When she saw the sleazy pictures of women in the Miller Landing house, she sent Brian a huge box returning all the gifts he'd bought her (mainly lingerie), their framed wedding pictures, and an angry letter. But there was worse to come. A couple of days later, Brian got a phone call from his father telling him that Stafford wanted nothing more to do with him. The boy was moving in with Kathy full-time. "I was horrified," said Brian. "My first thoughts were to drive home and kill myself . . . my son was the main thing in my life tethering me to reality, and when I lost him I lost everything."

For all the years they'd been together, he and Denise had shared the guilt of Mike's murder between them, fifty-fifty. Now Denise wasn't only leaving her husband, she was leaving behind her complicity in the crime. She wanted to dump everything on Brian's shoulders, but he wouldn't let her. Denise might be able to break her marriage vows, he resolved, but she couldn't walk away from the bond of murder. Desperate, he played his last card—he tried to force her to talk to him by bringing up Mike's death. He planned to get her on tape talking about the crime. If she was going to cut off all contact with him, Brian wanted "an insurance policy" in case "anything came up." Still, even if the police called them in for questioning, he didn't believe Denise would turn on him. "She had no reason to talk," he told himself. "She had millions of dollars in the bank . . ."

One steaming hot day in July, he went to Denise's office at Doak S. Campbell Stadium, found her car in the parking lot, and left a note on her windshield. It was a blank envelope on which he'd written, "We need to talk about C." "C" had always been their code for Cheryl, and it meant something had come up about the murder. But Denise didn't take the bait, and she never called.

Next, Brian tried luring her with something more solid: money. Going through his financial assets in preparation for the divorce, he'd stumbled on $40,000 worth of savings bonds behind a sofa. They were in Denise's name, and she'd forgotten about them. "I could have burned the things and she would never have known they even existed," he realized. Instead, he used them as bait. He called Denise and left a message reminding her about the bonds. She called him back and told him to meet her in the stadium parking lot outside her office. When she came down, Brian turned on the recorder on his phone before handing over the bonds and tried to get her to talk about the murder. He said that people had told him "she was talking." It was a test. "I wanted to see what she would say if I brought up this scenario of her saying anything," said Brian. He asked her to get in the car so they could speak in confidence, but she refused. She told him, "Mike went hunting that day. I was at home with Anslee. I don't know what happened. We don't have anything to talk about." The rehearsed quality of her reply tipped Brian off: She knew he was recording. He couldn't get her to say anything else. He handed her the bonds. She took them and walked away without looking back.

———————

Love had turned to acrimony, threats, violence, and blackmail. In the second week of August 2016, the Winchesters had a court date for a preliminary hearing in the divorce case. Brian couldn't face it. "Mentally, I was a wreck," he said. He'd contemplated suicide for months; now, with nothing left to live for, he decided to shoot himself. On Thursday, August 5, he bought a pistol from a sporting goods store. He also bought a pair of sheets from Walmart to cover himself up when he shot himself so he wouldn't make too much of a mess. He put the gun and the sheets in his backpack, then wrote his will, leaving everything to Stafford to be doled out gradually over time. Next, he wrote a total of ten suicide notes: to his mother, his father, his sister, his son, his stepdaughter, his ex-wife, his pastor, his best friend, his cousin, and Denise. They all said the same thing: He was sorry for everything but couldn't face the upcoming divorce.

There's no doubt: Brian truly believed he was about to end it all. But anyone who writes ten suicide notes has their ego still profoundly invested in life. Moreover, although some of the notes mentioned remorse, there was nothing about Mike's murder. He could have told the truth, finally giving closure to Cheryl, but instead, he planned to go to the grave with his sins unconfessed. He even told his mother—who was dying of stomach cancer—that he'd see her in heaven. He repeated and contradicted himself. To Kathy, he wrote, "I'm sorry we got divorced. It never should have happened and I always regretted it. . . .

You were my first and I regret losing you." To Denise, "You were all I ever wanted. . . . I always loved you." Still, he couldn't resist a nasty dig. "Enjoy your riches and your daughter. I hope they make you happy."

Writing ten notes kept Brian occupied for a couple of hours. When he'd finished, instead of shooting himself, he fumed and brooded. In a final act of passive aggression, he decided to commit suicide in the gazebo where he'd proposed to Denise, near her home at Midyette Plantation. But first, he planned to confront her one last time. She wouldn't answer his texts or calls, so he devised a desperate plan: He'd kidnap her at gunpoint. He didn't care about the consequences. In fact, his plan was so perverse and self-destructive that it almost seemed as if he wanted to get caught.

That night, he ate a sad dinner at TGI Fridays, alone as usual, then got "plastered." When the bar closed, he drove blind drunk over to Midyette Plantation, arriving around 3 a.m. It was a hot night with just a sliver of moon. Brian parked his truck by the entrance to the subdivision and, too drunk to remember the access code, climbed over the gate. In his backpack were the gun, the sheets, and a large spray bottle of water. He knew Denise left her Suburban SUV unlocked; he got inside the Suburban, took the items out of his backpack, sprayed the windows with water so they'd mist up and she wouldn't see him hiding there, climbed into the cargo compartment at the back of the Suburban, turned on his side, and fell asleep.

———

Friday, August 5, 2016, was a blissfully temperate morning in Tallahassee, a moment of relief from the oppressive summer heat. At 9:10 a.m.,

Denise climbed into her SUV and pulled into Centennial Oak Circle. Her daily commute to FSU took anywhere from fifteen minutes to half an hour, depending on traffic. She wore a sleeveless black top, pink yoga pants, and a pair of casual flip-flops. Her shoulder-length blond hair was swept back over her head and tied behind in a tight braid.

She turned left onto Miccosukee Road; the morning sunshine glimmered behind her through the Spanish moss. On her morning commute, Denise usually chatted briefly with her younger sister, Deborah, and this morning was no exception. She placed her usual call, but the moment Deborah picked up, Denise saw a sudden movement in her rearview mirror and screamed. A second later, her estranged husband was climbing out of the cargo area into the seat behind her. He leaned into the gap beside the driver's seat, pulled the phone out of her hand, grabbed her head, and cursed at her. Denise cried out for help, hoping her sister would hear her.

"Shut up, or I'll kill you," Brian shouted. He tossed the phone away, then pressed something against her ribs. Denise glanced down. It was a gun.

Terrified, she tried to pull over, but Brian yelled at her to keep driving. Miccosukee Road, which she followed for two and a half miles, was broken up by roundabouts and traffic lights, and every time she slowed down, she considered swerving off the road and into the ditch. Right before they got to the Capital Circle intersection, she saw her chance and took it, abruptly turning right into the CVS parking lot. Brian lunged forward, grabbed the wheel, and tried to steer the car back onto the road, but somehow, she managed to wrest control. She maneuvered the vehicle into the parking lot and came to a halt right by the front doors of the CVS, directly in front of the security camera. She pulled on the handbrake. Her heart was racing; she felt dizzy and faint. She wanted to run screaming into the store, but Brian had one hand on her seat belt, grasping the retractor so she couldn't escape.

Denise turned around to look at him. Was he drunk, on drugs, or both?

"If you try to get away, I'll have to hurt you," said Brian. His breath smelled of alcohol. He was sweating, shaking, slurring his words. He started rambling incoherently, telling her he just wanted to talk. He wanted to know if she had a boyfriend, and when she said no, he picked up her phone and started scrolling through her photos and contacts.

"Come and sit next to me in the back," he demanded, keeping hold of her seat belt with one hand.

Denise refused. "I'll talk to you from here, but that's it," she said.

Brian kept telling her that he loved her. He begged her to call off the divorce. He'd lost Stafford, he said, and had nothing left. He was going to kill himself. "I know you still love me," he kept saying.

Denise started to sob.

"Stop crying," Brian commanded. People were walking past the car in and out of the store. She thought about signaling for help but feared Brian would shoot her. He kept repeating that he wanted to end it all.

Realizing he was desperate, Denise tried reasoning with him. She told him suicide would be a terrible mistake. He could still turn his life around, she said. He could get his whole family back if he returned to the Lord, instead of giving in to the devil. She told him she'd help him start back on the right path. She'd go to church with him and pray for forgiveness. But first, he had to get psychological help.

Her tactic worked. Brian relaxed, letting go of her seat belt, although he kept the gun in his lap. They stayed in the CVS parking lot for almost an hour. At one point, Brian appeared to wake up as if coming out of a trance.

"My God, what have I done?" he kept asking.

"You just need help," Denise reassured him. If he promised to go to rehab, she said, she'd sit down later that day to talk about their relationship. They could ask his father to act as a mediator.

Brian didn't trust her. He made her swear repeatedly that she wouldn't go to the police.

"I swear to God. I swear on my life," Denise promised him. "I'm going straight into work. I'm already late. If you don't believe me, you can call me there in fifteen minutes."

Finally, Brian agreed to let her go. She drove him back to Centennial Oak Circle, where he'd left his car. As he got out of the SUV, Denise saw him reach over into the cargo area, gather up some things, and shove them into his backpack, along with the handgun. She was horrified to see what she later described as a plastic sheet, a big bottle of bleach, and something that looked like a shovel (in fact, the "bleach" was water and the "shovel" was the magazine from the gun).

Denise's sister Deborah had been trying to call her back. She'd heard Denise blurt something out, then the phone had gone dead, and Deborah was worried. As soon as Brian's truck was out of sight, Denise called her sister and told her what had happened. She was "just hysterical," said Deborah, who promised to drive over right away. They met in front of the CVS. According to Deborah, when Denise stepped out of her car, she was so shaken up that she "actually collapsed in the parking lot."

The scene in front of CVS was the turning point in the Williams-Winchester case. By telling Deborah what Brian had just done, Denise inadvertently lit the fuse that would lead to a monumental explosion. If she hadn't spoken to her sister, it's not clear what would have happened. But Deborah, not knowing the backstory, wasn't going to let the matter drop. Her husband, David McCrainie, was a Tallahassee police officer with the Leon County Sheriff's Office. When Deborah told him what Brian had done to her sister, McCrainie, who was off work that day, insisted Denise drive to the Sheriff's Office and file a report.

She was "crying and sobbing," McCrainie later recalled. Denise told him, "Brian had been waiting in her car, put a gun to her, tried to make her drive somewhere . . ." McCrainie insisted she get a protection order against Brian before the courts closed for the weekend. Denise stayed on the phone with her brother-in-law as Deborah drove them down to the Leon County Sheriff's Office.

In fear for her life, Denise's one desire was to keep Brian away from herself and her daughter. If Mike crossed her mind, she either repressed or ignored her role in his death. In the heat of the moment, she saw herself not as a murderer but as a victim of domestic violence. She didn't stop to weigh the consequences of what she was about to do.

Note from Cheryl's Journal:

Today is Mike's birthday. Denise doesn't call.

– 4 –

A New Rock Bottom

"... the germs of fear which break out in Macbeth on the night of the murder do not develop further in *him* but in *her* ... Thus what he feared in his pangs of conscience is fulfilled in her; she becomes all remorse and he all defiance. Together they exhaust the possibilities of reaction to the crime, like two disunited parts of a single psychical individuality ..."

SIGMUND FREUD, *SOME CHARACTER-TYPES MET WITH IN PSYCHO-ANALYTICAL WORK* (1916).

At 12:50 p.m., on Friday, August 5, 2016, the day of the kidnapping, a detective named Paul Salvo took Denise to an interview room at the Leon County Sheriff's Office. He asked her to describe the incident in detail. On the police videotape, Denise looks pale and shaken. She shifts around uncomfortably in her seat. Her speech is rapid, a little choppy. As she answers Salvo's questions, she occasionally pauses to take a sip from a water bottle, then describes the kidnapping:

"I was calling my sister, and this person starts climbing out the back.

He's screaming and I'm just, like, shaking." Denise makes gestures with her hands and body, nervously replaying the scene. "And he's telling me to stop crying. That people are going to notice. I was like, 'Are you planning on, you know, ending both of our lives today?' 'Well, mine. I'm planning on ending mine.' . . . He must have said a million times, 'I want to kill myself.'"

More than once, Denise expresses concern about talking to Salvo. She's not sure she's doing the right thing. When Brian learns she's reported the incident to the police, he'll be angry, which frightens her. Even if they arrest him, he'll be free at some point, and Denise is afraid for herself and her daughter. Salvo tells her not to worry—she's done the right thing. They'll try to get Brian some help, he says. After the brief interview, he exits the room, leaving Denise alone. She is apprehensive, restless, and uneasy. She puts her head down, then sits up again and takes a sip of water. She shivers, rubs her bare arms, sobs a little.

After a short period of waiting, a smartly dressed young woman with short bleached-blond hair enters the room and identifies herself as a victims' advocate. Denise tells the woman that she's distraught. Brian will have called her office by now. When he finds out she's not there, it will "set him off again," she says. He'll be driving around looking for her, "crazy and mad," possibly suicidal. The victims' advocate tells Denise she's done the right thing by coming to the police. When they've finished taking her statement, she says, she'll take Denise to the courthouse to file for a protection order. She mentions a women's refuge that Denise and her daughter can go to, if need be. Denise hopes that won't be necessary. Left alone again, she spends time on her phone, reading and responding to texts. Again, she sobs a little. She takes off her glasses and rubs them with a Kleenex, then picks up her purse and goes to use the restroom.

When she returns, a man who introduces himself as Detective Wilkerson enters the room. He says he wants to process her car for evidence, asks a few questions about fingerprints, then asks her to sign several forms. Next, Paul Salvo comes back into the room with his supervisor, Sergeant Brian Bishop, and they ask her to run through the story again. They leave at 2:23 p.m., at which point Denise's brother-in-law David McCrainie arrives. He tells her they have a warrant for Brian's arrest, but they haven't found him yet. Denise says he's probably been to her office at FSU and discovered she hasn't been to work that day. He'll be driving around looking for her, she says. She's becoming frantic. What will happen when he finds out she's gone to the cops?

McCrainie, who makes no secret of his feelings about Brian, is unhelpful. "Hopefully he'll kill himself, so you won't have to worry about it," he says.

Unlike Salvo and Wilkerson, McCrainie doesn't sit opposite Denise but moves his chair closer to hers, on the short side of the interview desk; his position reflects his ambiguous role as both family member and police detective. For the next hour, in a tone that is both sympathetic and condescending, her brother-in-law lectures Denise about how evil and controlling Brian is and how she should have left him long ago. Her estranged husband is dangerously violent, he tells her, "a con man, a con artist." Brian wasn't planning to commit suicide, suggests McCrainie. He was going to kill her.

He then subtly changes tack, moving the conversation, implicitly, to Brian's role in Mike's death. "I know he did it, Denise, and you know exactly what I'm talking about . . . and he was going to do it again. . . . Fifteen years ago, he walked in and told you he'd done something, didn't he?" It's an assertion rather than a question, but Denise doesn't respond. In fact, in the face of her brother-in-law's badgering, she calms down a little. Alternately tearful and acquiescent, she begins to defend Brian. He's not capable of murder, she tells McCrainie. She's never seen him behave like this before. Later, McCrainie described her as "kind of in denial, as a victim would be in a traumatic event."

By the time her brother-in-law has finished with her, Denise is no longer so edgy, but she's exhausted. She's been at the police station for longer than three hours. Finally, Mike DeVaney enters the room. The heavyset detective is playing the role of bad cop, and after all the years he's spent studying and surveilling Denise and Brian from a distance, he's eager to show how much he knows. He's been waiting a long time for this moment and isn't afraid to be pushy.

DeVaney introduces himself as the "lead officer" in the "disappearance of Mike Williams." "We've never met," he tells Denise, handing her his card, "but I've literally known you, and known your family, for many, many, many, many years." He says he's "literally dissected" everything he could find about Denise and Brian. He knows the gate code of her subdivision by heart. He even remembers the day contractors came to remove her carpets—an event with dark significance, he implies.

DeVaney suggests that he knows about Denise's sexual history and that she and Kathy were "very close." Denise agrees. They're still very close, she tells him, checking her phone. "In fact, she's texting me right now."

DeVaney has something else in mind. "Apparently, you were *really* close, okay? You know what I'm talking about." He even knows about "the videos." For another half hour, he prods and probes, continuing to emphasize how much he already knows.

If DeVaney's plan is to make Denise uncomfortable, it works. Her ex-husband has just kidnapped her at gunpoint; her sister has brought her directly to the police station to file a restraining order. After three tiring hours of interrogation, she's now facing lurid insinuations about her sex life. In the face of DeVaney's apparent ambush, she tries to remain polite. She understands that he wants to talk about Mike's disappearance, she says, but she needs to focus on the current situation.

DeVaney ignores her. "Do you think he's responsible for Mike's disappearance?" he asks her of Brian.

"I do not, and I never have," Denise tells him, firmly. "I'd never have married him if I'd have thought that. I'd never have wanted so badly to have children with him. In my mind and in my heart, no."

DeVaney isn't giving up. "Where do you think Mike's buried at?" he asks.

Denise doesn't want to go any further. She's had enough. Given Brian's reckless state of mind, she emphasizes the importance of her and her daughter's safety. She reminds DeVaney that it's 3:30 p.m., and she must file for the protection order before the court closes at 5:00. She doesn't want to talk about something that happened fifteen years ago.

If at this moment Denise had told DeVaney he was right, that Brian had confessed to killing Mike, that he'd held it over her head for all these years, she might have escaped prosecution. But by this point, she believed the story she'd told herself. "Denise had repeated her lies for almost twenty years," concluded Patti Ketcham. "Mike died in a terrible accident. Mike drowned while duck hunting. Mike died at the lake." Still, however deeply repressed, memories remain. "I think, in her head, she's told herself this story so much and layered it on until it's become strong enough to make the truth really, really small and to keep it down," concluded Patti. "But in her heart, she knows. Of course she knows."

Denise isn't under arrest, and DeVaney can't hold her. Reluctantly, he ends the interview. But from his questions, it's clear he expects she'll soon be back in custody and facing charges.

After fifteen years, the couple had finally turned on each other. For good.

———

When he decided to kidnap Denise, it had never crossed Brian's mind that she might go to the cops. No doubt he assumed that a person guilty of murder would never voluntarily subject themselves to the attention of law enforcement. More than once, in the past, they'd talked—part playfully, part not—about the idea of "mutually assured destruction." As Brian put it, "If you tell on me, your world is going to fall apart. If I tell on you, my world is going to fall apart." But he'd never considered that Denise's denial might reach the stage where she truly believed she had nothing to do with Mike's murder. And if she had nothing to do with the crime, why would she be afraid of the police?

After the thwarted kidnapping, Brian was still suicidal, but not so far gone that he felt beyond help. He even took some practical steps to get treatment. He called his therapist, Ron Rickner, but Ron didn't pick up, so he called his water-skiing buddy Stephen Mnookin, an easygoing anesthesiologist who also happened to be Brian's sponsor in Sex Addicts Anonymous. Brian told Steve he'd just "hit a new rock bottom" and needed to talk as soon as possible. It was around 11 a.m. They planned to meet at noon at Village Pizza at the Village Square Shopping Center, just off Thomasville Road.

By the time he was on his way to meet Mnookin, around 11:45 a.m., Brian was starting to think that Denise wasn't going to call. He tried her office number, but she didn't pick up. At that point, realizing she must have gone to the cops, he started to panic. The roads were jam-packed with traffic that day, including what appeared to be armed vehicles and police cars. Helicopters buzzed overhead. A combination of egotism and paranoia led Brian to think the cops were already looking for him. (Later, he learned the police were out in force to oversee Vice President Joe Biden, who was visiting Tallahassee as part of his presidential campaign).

At Village Pizza, a waiter led the pair to a sidewalk table. Brian had something to eat; Mnookin ordered a Diet Coke. His friend, he said later, was "very nervous and uptight" and "extremely agitated." Brian asked for doctor-patient confidentiality, which didn't apply since Mnookin was his sponsor, not his doctor; still, Steve reassured his friend that whatever he said would stay between them. He assumed Brian was going to describe the type of shameful exploit the men had confessed to each other in the past—"something sexually crazy, with drugs." But it was worse. Far worse. Brian told Steve he'd just kidnapped his ex-wife at gunpoint, and now the police were "after him." When Steve asked why he did it, Brian said he was afraid that, as soon as his divorce from Denise was final, she was going to "say something about this guy who died . . . fifteen years ago . . ."

Steve found it difficult to follow Brian's train of thought, but he could see his friend was overwrought and suicidal. He called the Apalachee Center and Tallahassee Memorial Hospital, hoping to get Brian admitted to a psych ward immediately, but both calls went to voicemail, and Brian was reluctant; he said he'd rather talk to his dad. Mnookin thought he should see a professional. He managed to persuade his friend to at least meet with Ron Rickner, who was also Mnookin's therapist. Brian got through to Rickner on the phone and set up an appointment for 5 p.m.

Mnookin, still concerned about Brian, returned to work around 1 p.m. At 1:45, he got another call. "Steve, this is really bad," Brian told him. "We never had this conversation." Steve again assured Brian that he'd keep the information privileged. He called his friend again that evening, around 6, to see how he was doing, but Brian didn't have his phone with him.

That's because he was locked in a cell in the Leon County Detention Center. The cops had tracked him down at Winchester Financial, where he'd been arrested, placed in handcuffs, and taken downtown. He was charged with three felonies: aggravated kidnapping, domestic assault with a deadly weapon, and armed burglary.

Serious charges to be sure, but Brian had no prior record and a lot of influential friends. Most people assumed he'd soon be out on bail.

They were wrong.

Jennifer Portman, at her desk at the *Tallahassee Democrat*, was scrolling through the weekend booking report for the Leon County jail. Startled to see a name she recognized, she quickly pumped out a short article for the afternoon edition, announcing the unexpected news. "A man with ties to one of the area's most vexing unsolved crimes is in jail, accused of kidnapping his wife at gunpoint." Portman reminded readers that police investigators, who once believed alligators had eaten Mike Williams, now considered "the 31-year-old father was the victim of foul play." News of the arrest spread rapidly. Two days later, at Brian Winchester's bond hearing, the courtroom was packed with reporters, even though Brian was still in the county jail. As was customary at such hearings, he appeared before the judge via closed-circuit television.

By then, with his father's help, Brian had secured the assistance of R. Timothy Jansen, a heavyweight criminal defense attorney and former federal prosecutor. Jansen told the judge, Stephen Everett, that Brian was an upstanding citizen with no criminal record and was innocent of all charges. He was going through a difficult divorce, said Jansen, and had been arrested solely on the statement of his estranged wife, who was emotionally overwrought and not to be trusted. Brian posed no threat to community safety, Jansen insisted, and the state should release him on bond pending trial.

At this stage, Denise was still legitimately afraid of Brian. In court, she approached the stand warily and, with shaking hands, took out a preprepared witness statement. A victims' advocate accompanied her, placing a reassuring hand on her back. In a voice quivering with anxiety, Denise described her traumatic ordeal. "He shoved the gun in my rib cage, screaming profanities uncontrollably at me," she said. "I will never be the same. I can't sleep, I can't eat . . . I can't have peace because I only hear his voice screaming and cursing at me. Please don't let him out."

Judge Everett expressed sympathy for Denise. When it came to the charges, he found there was probable cause that Brian was still a threat to his ex-wife and denied bond. The defendant could reapply later, the judge informed him.

Denise certainly didn't want Brian released—at least, not right away. When she'd seen him in the rearview mirror climbing over the back seat of her car, she'd genuinely believed he was going to kill her, and she was still afraid of him. At the same time, DeVaney's interrogation had shaken her deeply, and she knew the cops would do everything they could to drive a wedge between the couple. After thinking about the situation for a few days, she appeared to realize that, by going to the police, she'd made a foolish and possibly fatal move. She couldn't undo what she'd done, but she could try to be sure things didn't get any worse. She wanted to let Brian know that she'd said nothing about the murder and didn't plan to. The week after the bond hearing, she called Kathy and asked if she'd pass along a message to Marcus Winchester.

The message was: "Tell Brian I'm not talking."

———————

Brian Winchester, suicide note to Roman Fontenot (unsent)

Roman—

Hey bro— First I want to say I am truly sorry for what I have done and any negative ways it may affect you or your family. You have been like the brother I never had and I love you so much man. I'm really

happy and jealous you are having more kids—I hope it works out.
Dude—I just couldn't take the pain and loneliness anymore. Please
know there's nothing you could have done—I have struggled with this
for years now. I'm just done bro. If at all possible, stay in touch with
my family—especially Stafford. Make sure he knows how much I love
him. Thank you for being a true friend. I know you will be angry at
me—I hope that will pass over time. We had a lot of good times—
training Chief with Michael Corrigan, almost dying in the mud at
Lake Miccosukee, and catching those trout at Rock Island.

Brian

Until his next bond hearing, set for December, Brian remained in the
Leon County Detention Center, which contained more than a thousand inmates, most of whom, like him, were waiting to go to trial.
For the first time in his life, he found himself part of a racial minority
(as with most jails in Florida, the population was around 70 percent
Black). The detention center was noisy, crowded, and stressful. The
guards were overworked and hostile, the food starchy and bland. Visits
and phone calls were monitored and restricted.

On the day of the kidnapping, Brian was at "a new rock bottom."
Now, in the county jail, he could see how stupid and shortsighted he'd
been. The divorce process had been devastating and losing Denise
and Stafford had taken a dreadful toll. But he'd still had a comfortable
home, loyal friends, a good son, and a wealthy father who loved and
supported him. Above all, he'd had his freedom. He could get up in the
morning and go water-skiing, hunting, or mountain biking. He could

take his boat out on the lake. Now the highlight of his day was walking around a prison yard. His previous "rock bottom" seemed like a long-ago pipe dream.

He knew his crime was serious—he could easily have caused Denise to crash her car—but he hadn't planned to kill anyone. Sure, he'd been reckless and self-destructive, but he was suicidal, not homicidal, driven by love and despair, not malice. True, he'd terrified Denise, but he hadn't injured her, and he'd held her for less than an hour. He had no criminal record. He had solid family and substantial community ties. Jansen, his attorney, assumed the charge would be aggravated kidnapping—typically, in a case like this, he'd have been able to make a deal for a term of probation or home detention. If they got a harsh judge who insisted on prison time, it certainly wouldn't have been more than a couple of years.

But Brian's confidence took a blow when Jansen showed him the police video of Denise's interview with Mike DeVaney. "I could see very clearly by her answers and on her face the realization that she had really screwed up," he said. He was worried the police interview had frightened her—and if she was scared, he knew, she'd want to keep him in prison at all costs. Plus, Jansen had more bad news. Two weeks after their meeting at Village Pizza, after learning about Brian's arrest, Stephen Mnookin had given in to the promptings of his conscience. He'd gone to the police and told them what Brian had confessed to him—about his fear that Denise would tell everyone about the "guy who went missing a long time ago."

Assistant State Attorney Jon Fuchs insisted on charging Brian not with aggravated kidnapping, but with armed kidnapping, which was much worse. He claimed Brian had been planning to kill Denise—that he'd brought what she believed to be a gun, a plastic sheet, and a shovel. In Florida, an armed felony gets a mandatory minimum of ten years in prison "day for day"—with no potential reduced sentence for good behavior. Even worse, armed kidnapping was a nonbondable offense, which meant that Brian couldn't be released on bail even if Denise relented. Unable to secure a plea deal, Jansen accepted a trial date of October 24, 2017.

Then came the final blow. Denise was asking for the maximum sentence: life without parole.

– 5 –

Fully and Truthfully

> "... though in Macbeth the strife of mind is greater than in his wife, the tiger spirit not so awake, and his feelings caught chiefly by contagion from her, —yet, as both were finally involved in the guilt of murder, the murderous mind of necessity is finally to be presumed in both."
>
> THOMAS DE QUINCEY,
> "ON THE KNOCKING AT THE GATE IN *MACBETH*" (1823)

By the time of Brian's kidnap attempt, Kathy Winchester, now Kathy Thomas, had moved with her new family—her husband, Rocky, the couple's two daughters, and Stafford (when he was staying there)—to a small, peaceful town in the mountains of North Carolina, where they lived quietly and modestly, far from the rumors and gossip circulating in Tallahassee. Kathy had deliberately distanced herself from her former life, but she was still Stafford's mom, and couldn't help hearing the latest news.

In early 2016, after Denise had filed for divorce, the two women had become close again. With Brian out of the picture, their friendship was revived—at least on the surface. According to law enforcement records, between May 24 and August 24, 2016, there were approximately 3,688 communications between them (texts and phone calls). After Brian's arrest, when the police in Tallahassee learned Denise was in regular contact with his ex-wife, they tried to lure Kathy back to work as a confidential informant. On September 8, she got a phone call from Special Agent Mike DeVaney; at the time, Kathy told him she didn't want to be involved. But when Denise asked her to forward the message to Marcus Winchester that she "wasn't talking," Kathy, perhaps worried that she might become implicated in the cover-up, changed her mind and once again began recording her calls with Denise.

Kathy and Denise had a lot in common. They'd both loved Mike— Denise as a wife and Kathy as a friend. They'd both been married to Brian; both had experienced his selfishness, his sexual compulsions, his capacity for violence. They both regretted their "sinful" past and wanted to detach themselves from it. Ironically, to do so, they reignited their high school bond. But although they were genuinely close, their friendship was instrumental.

Denise needed Kathy for support, comfort, advice, and the opportunity to bad-mouth Brian. She also wanted her friend to witness the strength of her faith. In her texts and conversations, she constantly referred to "the Lord." Maybe she wanted to emphasize (even if only to herself) that although she was about to be divorced, she was still an upright, respectable Baptist. In fact, she reminded Kathy that she had "Biblical grounds" for divorcing Brian, citing his addiction to porn and prostitutes. To law enforcement, Kathy described Denise as "a narcissist, vain, manipulative, and very concerned with her image." The women were friends only "on the surface," she said. But Kathy also, arguably, needed Denise. Acting as a confidential informant allowed her to reassure herself that her "bad behavior," too, was in the past; now she worked for the cops. Was it also a form of payback against the woman who stole her husband?

In her conversations with Kathy, Denise never admitted to any involvement in Mike's death, but the interview with DeVaney had rattled her. She told Kathy that if the police asked her anything about the past, she'd keep quiet. She was also concerned the police were putting pressure on Brian to talk about what had happened to Mike. But if she wasn't involved, as she claimed, why would she care?

At the Leon County jail, Brian was pacing the floor. The prison housed inmates in a series of pods, each containing around twenty men (two to a cell). The pods were observed remotely via security cameras and overseen by a duty officer. In addition to individual cells, each pod had a dayroom with a television and tables for card games and chess. The routine was monotonous, and everyone was forced together at close quarters. A lot of the inmates were mentally ill. Brian's cellmate talked to ghosts.

One of the men in Brian's pod was Wade Wilson, age twenty-three, a former personal trainer with a long criminal history. Six feet five inches tall, his muscle-bound body covered in tattoos, Wilson was an intimidating presence, but to Brian, he was one of the few men capable of rational conversation. He told Brian someone had falsely accused him of child abuse, but he'd managed to get the charges dropped and was about to get out. According to Brian, Wade told him he used to be a hit man and had people "on the streets" who would help him out. Was Brian interested in making someone "go away"? Brian didn't want to be involved in any more murders, but—according to the investigative report—he offered Wilson $10,000 "to create reasonable doubt with respect to the State's witnesses slated to testify at his upcoming trial."

Inmates plan crimes from prison all the time. With contraband cell phones, they can intimidate witnesses, organize drug deals, plot escapes, and even plan murders. But Wilson was getting out; the last thing he needed was another felony charge. What he did need was money, and Brian—wealthy, desperate, and a rookie prisoner—was an easy mark.

A few days after he got out of jail, in early February 2017, Wilson called the number Brian had given him. The man he spoke to—later identified as Brian's cousin Kevin—told Wilson to meet him in the parking lot of Pockets, a pool bar and pub in north Tallahassee. Kevin pulled up, according to Wilson, in a gold pickup truck "with tinted windows and some sort of snake or alligator skin trim," and handed him an envelope containing a thick wad of cash and fifteen to twenty pages of handwritten text. These were instructions from Brian describing what Denise and Stephen Mnookin looked like and telling Wilson where to find them.

In the instructions, Brian suggested several scenarios. Most of them involved bribing a random female FSU student. Ideas he suggested included: (1) Paying the student to tell the cops she'd been having sex and doing drugs with Denise and that Denise had told her she'd deliberately had her ex-husband put in jail; (2) paying the student to say she was into three-way sex with Denise and Mnookin, and she'd heard them talking about how they planned to get Brian arrested; (3) paying the student to say she met Mnookin at Sex Addicts Anonymous, they hooked up, and he told her he was having sex with Denise; (4) paying someone to say they were fishing in a pond near Denise's house the morning of the kidnapping and saw Denise and Brian talking to each other casually outside Denise's vehicle.

Brian had chosen the wrong fixer. Wade Wilson, he came to realize, was "a drug addict who conned me." The would-be hit man lost the instructions, spent the money on drugs, and split. The police soon rearrested him for violating his parole. Hoping for leniency, Wilson told the state attorney he had some information about Brian Winchester that might interest them. When questioned, he described the plan to suborn the state's witnesses, identified Kevin Winchester in a photographic lineup, and was released on probation to help prosecutors in their case against Brian. Predictably, he once again left town but was rearrested the following week for a traffic offense. He was hardly a reliable witness, and without a copy of the written instructions, no one could corroborate his story.

But they didn't have to. Prosecutors had been monitoring Brian's phone calls from prison. In addition to Wade Wilson, he'd also made some ridiculous plans—getting his sister Jennifer to pay off witnesses on his behalf, asking his dad to give $1,800 to one of his old hookups, a girl named Kim Adams, presumably as a bribe—none of which ever came off.

In the end, the only person Brian succeeded in discrediting was himself. In September 2017, Tim Jansen sat down with his client in the Leon County Detention Center and gave him the bad news about the taped phone calls. With attempted perjury added to his list of charges, if Brian ever had even the slightest chance of getting out of prison in the next few years, that chance was now dead and buried. Without question, he was facing a life sentence. He had nothing left to lose. The game was up. He told Jansen that if the prosecution wanted to make a deal, he was ready to talk about the death of Mike Williams.

———

On October 4, a resigned Brian Winchester signed the proffer agreement negotiated by his attorney. The terms were simple. Brian had to answer "fully and truthfully" all questions about Mike's disappearance. If any part of his confession turned out to be false, the deal was off. In exchange, the state promised him complete immunity in all charges related to Mike's death. When it came to the kidnapping case, they'd drop the attempted perjury charges and wouldn't ask for a life sentence. The trial would be postponed until December while Brian worked with prosecutors and police.

Neither side was thrilled by the terms. Brian had to plead guilty to aggravated kidnapping and burglary with a firearm, which meant he'd still be facing a minimum of ten years behind bars, possibly more. As far as the state was concerned, Brian was getting away with murder, but without the deal, he'd be facing life in prison and would have nothing to gain from confessing further crimes. Mike's murder would remain unsolved.

When news of the proffer got out, people were shocked, even disgusted. They called it a deal with the devil. "As a person who's been a member of the bar for fifty years, I've never seen anybody getting a free pass on first-degree murder," said Phil Padovano, an attorney who later worked on Denise's defense team. "Maybe they satisfied themselves by thinking that Brian was going to go to jail, but that was for a completely different crime. The bottom line is, he'll never spend a day in prison for this murder." While everyone agreed that it was essential to find out what happened to Mike, they all felt the state gave up more than was necessary.

The prosecutor in Brian's case was Jon Fuchs, a bullish forty-five-year-old assistant state attorney who looked like he'd be more at home on a farm or construction site than in a downtown office building. His associates were Tully Sparkman, who'd been on board since 2007, and a young investigator named Jason Newlin, who had no previous connection with the case.

At 2 p.m. on October 9, 2017, Brian sat down in the conference room at the state attorney's office with Tim Jansen, Jansen's associate Adam Komisar, and Special Agents Jason Newlin and Tully Sparkman. After being sworn in, he began to talk and continued for half an hour, almost without interruption. He described all the details of his affair with Denise, and how they'd planned to murder Mike. In hindsight, he said, Denise had more incentive than he did to get rid of Mike since he wasn't particularly interested in leaving his wife, and he wouldn't be getting any of the insurance money. He said he was "manipulated" in ways he wasn't aware of at the time. But he also admitted Denise didn't exactly push the idea down his throat, and although he was now tempted to "throw her under the bus," in all honesty, he couldn't do it. He wanted to be truthful and didn't want to "exaggerate her role." Neither of them spearheaded the plan, he said. It was mutual and collaborative, "pretty much fifty-fifty."

Brian's descriptions of Denise's character were revealing, although he had good reason to paint her at her worst. He portrayed her as a subtle, enigmatic character with many dimensions to her personality. "For twenty years, she's led a double life," he told investigators. On the surface, he acknowledged, Denise presented herself as "an average soccer mom . . . a professional CPA who dresses nicely, carries herself well, she's very smart." She'd reframed her past, he explained. She now claimed he'd coerced her into everything she did. "Brian was an abuser. Brian drug me down into this horrible life of sexual depravity that I never wanted any part of." But if anyone discovered the truth about Denise, her family and friends would completely disown her. "Whether it's drug use . . . sex with prostitutes, whether it's sexual activities with animals . . . sexually she's off the charts." He added that Denise had been talking about adopting a baby from China; he felt "that woman should not be in contact with a Chinese baby."

It's unclear whether Brian was exaggerating for effect or if these really were the kinds of "perverse acts" that Denise claimed he'd forced her to perform. Of course, Brian himself was no saint. When asked in a deposition what kinds of sexual services he'd paid prostitutes for, he replied, "It would be easier to say what I haven't paid them for." Later, when asked for further specifics about Denise's "secret life," he was hesitant and vague. He admitted her drug use was "pretty minimal," and all she ever did was smoke pot from time to time. He couldn't name anyone who could corroborate his claims about "off-the-charts" sexual behavior except for a friend of Denise's with whom they once had a threesome and who liked to "hang out and party."

Whether or not Brian was embellishing, the fact that a person has a strong sexual appetite or engages in threesomes is not a criminal offense. Still, as Brian pointed out, it certainly didn't fit Denise's "Sister Christian" persona.

Nine days later, for the first time in sixteen months, Brian, in handcuffs, left the county jail. As usual for Tallahassee in October, the temperature was in the 80s; patchy clouds brought relief from the sun. Brian rode in a squad car with Jason Newlin, Tully Sparkman, and Adam Komisar. Following them, like a funeral procession, was a convoy of cops from the state attorney's office. The mood in the car was strained and tense. Brian was on edge.

Sitting up front, he directed the driver along the route of his past life. Down North Meridian Road, where Denise used to live. Past North Florida Christian High School, where it all began. Past North Florida Baptist Church. Past Rhoden Cove Road, where he'd met up with Denise when she had second thoughts about the murder. (Why hadn't he listened to her?) Past the Maclay School, which his son had attended as a child. Past the couple's "dream home" on Miller Landing Road, sitting empty.

Four miles north of the Maclay School, Brian instructed the driver to turn left on Gardner Road, a two-mile lane bordered by longleaf pine flats, palms, and magnolia trees. The road ended in an unpaved track that led to a boat launching area, Gardner Landing, on the southeast shore of Carr Lake. The small cove was surrounded by trees and thick undergrowth. Long grass covered the shoreline. The lake, thick with reeds and bulrushes, looked like a cornfield. Although easily accessed, it was a primitive swamp, isolated and silent, miles from human habitation.

"This is it," said Brian. The driver stopped the car and pulled on the brake.

They were here to dig up Mike's body.

———

According to Jason Newlin, who rode in the car with him, Brian had been "uptight" on the way to the lake, but on the way back to the prison, he seemed more relaxed and acknowledged the confession had been a "relief." He was returned to Wakulla Correctional Facility while investigators began to dig.

It was a strange, sad echo of the search on Lake Seminole seventeen years earlier, only this time there was no speculation about what had happened to Mike, only a grim, dark certainty. The excavation lasted six days and went on for sixteen hours a day; it involved equipment and personnel from the Department of Public Works, a team of cadaver dogs, and at least thirty people (police told curious onlookers that the dig was a "training exercise"). Normally, crime scene investigators would use ground-penetrating radar to locate the site of a dead body, but in this case, the body had obviously sunk beneath the water, which meant radar would have been useless. There was virtually no scent for cadaver dogs to pick up; when they indicated, the traces were so faint that the dogs' handlers couldn't provide a definite location. A construction crew from Leon County Public Works built a cofferdam—a temporary barrier—made from black plastic sheets supported by metal stakes; sections of the lakebed, three to four feet deep, were gradually pumped dry. State officials called a tree-removal company to clear enough space for a hydraulic backhoe. The hoe scooped buckets of thick, swampy mud from the lakebed and dumped them on makeshift plywood tables, then crime scene officers sifted it meticulously using rakes and shovels. It was nasty work. Sometimes eels or water moccasins would jump out from the mud, angry at having their homes invaded.

On the sixth day, the hydraulic backhoe hit up against a canvas tarp around three feet down. The operator turned off the engine and officers carefully surrounded the area. The tarp had shifted and twisted over the years, spilling some of its contents. A hunting boot was found, along with knee and femur bones. A spinal cord was discovered nearby, then a pelvic bone, partly clad in a pair of red boxer shorts. Two men put a sheet underneath the tarp, lifted the contents to shore, and placed them on a wooden table. The muddy shroud was opened; the contents laid bare. Bones, rags, fragments of clothing. A foot in a thick blue sock. A skull riddled with shotgun pellets. Two gloves full of finger bones.

On a left-hand finger, a gold wedding ring, perfectly intact.

– 6 –

We Are Not Murderers

"Who is so safe as we? where none can do
Treason to us, except one of us two."

JOHN DONNE, "THE ANNIVERSARY" (1601)

Cheryl Williams was in shock. Three men in suits stood on her doorstep. One of them was the state attorney Jack Campbell. The others were Special Agents Tully Sparkman and Mike DeVaney. Good news, they said. Her seventeen-year search to find her son was over. Mike's body had been found.

But to Cheryl, now sixty-eight, this was anything but good news. Until that moment, she'd still believed Mike was alive. At first, she couldn't understand what the officers were telling her.

"Are you saying my son is dead?"

"I'm afraid so, ma'am," said Campbell.

The men told her all about Brian's confession but insisted she keep the news strictly confidential. That was easy enough—Cheryl, stricken with grief, had no desire to talk. It took her weeks to realize the bad news had to be part of God's plan. "It had to be done this way," she concluded. "If I'd thought Michael was dead, I wouldn't have had the heart to fight." From that point on, she embarked on the second part of her quest: for justice.

The prosecutors asked Cheryl to keep quiet because they didn't want the news to reach Denise. They knew their decision to grant Brian complete immunity would be controversial, and they'd be under enormous pressure from the public and the media to hold someone accountable. When it came to Denise, they were determined to get a conviction.

But seventeen years had passed. There was no evidence left, nothing to prove that Denise had any involvement in the crime. It wasn't easy even to prove she'd had an affair. The couple had been meticulous, cautious, and mindful about cell phone records and credit card receipts. There was no paper trail. Even Brian, a sucker for souvenirs, could come up with nothing but a pile of ticket stubs for rock concerts the couple had been to in their early twenties:

Fuel at the Moon on October 21, 1999.
Buckcherry at Floyd's Music Store on July 3, 2001.
U2 at the Ice Palace Arena in Tampa on December 1, 2001.
Battery, a Metallica tribute band, on April 27, 2002.

There were also a couple of undated love letters and a receipt for a necklace bearing the name Meridian. It was hardly enough to carry a murder charge.

With no concrete evidence connecting Denise to the crime, investigators set out to provide their own. Initially, they came up with a clumsy ploy described in the homicide file as "the parking lot bump" (a "bump" is police jargon for a "controlled contact" between the subject of an investigation and a confidential source or undercover agent). Agent William Mickler approached Richard Wooten, chief security officer at the Doak S. Campbell Stadium, where Denise worked, and explained that, as part of a police ploy, a law enforcement agent in disguise would be approaching Denise in the parking lot. She might call security and file a complaint, said Mickler. If she did, he told Wooten to pretend to take the complaint seriously and proceed with the usual steps.

The "bump" took place on Monday, October 30, 2017. When Denise arrived for work that morning, she was approached in the parking lot by a person she later described to Kathy as a "homeless guy." He addressed her by name. "Hey, Denise," he said. "My name's Chuck. I've been serving time with Brian." "Chuck" tried to hand her a letter, purportedly from her ex-husband, but she yelled at him to leave her alone, ran into the stadium, and went directly to the security office to file a complaint. Two days later, she found a note from "Chuck" on the windshield of her car. It said, "Denise, sorry I scared you the other day. I just wanted to talk. I was in jail with Brian and he told me everything. I need money to get out of Florida and back to Missouri." He provided a telephone number, then added: "DO NOT GO TO POLICE OR I WILL CALL THE NEWSPAPER." Denise immediately turned over the note to Sergeant Wooten. After that, she installed a camera in her car, and when walking through the parking lot, always activated the video recorder and personal alarm on her phone.

Her nerves must have been on edge, especially in December, when Jennifer Portman's yearly article about Mike's disappearance came out. Portman was now the *Tallahassee Democrat*'s news director, and on December 16, 2017, the seventeenth anniversary of Mike's death, her annual article contained an ominous twist. She mentioned "the denouement of a related drama that I and others interested in the Mike Williams mystery have been closely following." After revealing that Brian had recently pled "no contest" to kidnapping and armed burglary, Portman suggested that, as he was "facing a long stay in prison," if Brian knew anything about what had happened to Mike Williams, "now might be a good time to talk."

Portman didn't know it yet, but Brian was singing like a canary.

Three days later, on Tuesday, December 19, 2017, Brian Winchester went to court for sentencing in the kidnapping case. He knew he was facing a mandatory ten-year minimum for the use of a firearm, but Jansen warned him to prepare for the worst. The presentencing investigative report recommended a maximum of fifteen years. More bad news: The judge in the case was James "Hangman" Hankinson, a hardheaded former state and federal prosecutor with an uncompromising attitude and a reputation for handing out tough sentences.

Brian and his attorney had done everything possible to plead for mitigation. Brian, by hand, had written a thirteen-page letter apologizing for his actions and describing his troubled childhood and struggle with various addictions. With his father's help, he'd also managed to accumulate more than forty letters of support from friends, family, clients of Winchester Financial, fellow congregants, and other members of the community, including a retired federal law enforcement officer, a pastor, a Baptist minister, a retired U.S. Army colonel, three medical doctors, and a veterinarian. All vouched for Brian as a gentle, moral, God-fearing family man and asked the judge to be lenient in his sentencing.

The hearing took place in the Leon County Courthouse, in a formal, high-ceilinged room with old-fashioned wooden benches and a polished parquet floor. Brian, handcuffed and wearing a dark green prison jumpsuit, sat between his two attorneys, tightly clutching a manila envelope bulging with documents. Tim Jansen reiterated to Judge Hankinson that his client had been desperate and suicidal on the day of the kidnapping but had no intention of harming Denise. After all, Jansen pointed out, Brian had written ten suicide notes, including one to his ex-wife, which suggested he meant to leave her alive. On top of all his client's other problems, his mother, Patricia, a strong force in his life, had passed away in November; Brian had been in the county jail and hadn't been permitted to attend the funeral. Testifying as character witnesses were his father, Marcus, and his uncle Mark (his father's twin brother), two grim, balding older versions of Brian.

Next, Denise stepped forward. Wearing jeans, sandals, and a black sweater, she looked frail and vulnerable. Her hair was tied back in a low ponytail. She put on a pair of black-framed glasses and read her statement in a quavering voice while a victims' advocate, standing by her side, rubbed her back gently. Denise explained that she'd been diagnosed with PTSD and "extreme anxiety" since the kidnapping and begged the judge to impose the maximum sentence. "It comes down to my life or his," she concluded, on the verge of tears. "And I'm asking you to choose mine."

While Denise was testifying, Brian had his head lowered, but when Jon Fuchs asked the judge to impose a sentence of forty-five years, he sat up and stared in horror. As part of the plea deal, Fuchs had agreed not to request a life sentence. Brian was now forty-seven. A forty-five-year sentence was life in all but name. He'd been betrayed.

The judge asked him to stand.

"I sentence you to twenty years in the Department of Corrections," said Hankinson. He went on to explain further details of the sentence but Brian, still stunned, didn't hear him.

The judge asked if he had any questions.

"You're giving me twenty years?" asked Brian.

"Twenty years, a credit of five hundred and two days, followed by fifteen years' probation," confirmed Hankinson. "Good luck to you, sir."

———

"The remains of Mike Williams, the 31-year-old real estate appraiser murdered 17 years ago, were found in northern Leon County off Meridian Road on the eastern shore of Carr Lake, an extension of Lake Jackson, sources confirmed Thursday," wrote Jennifer Portman in the *Tallahassee Democrat* on December 22, 2017, three days after Brian's sentencing. "His body was found at the end of dead-end Gardner Road, about five miles away from the home where he grew up and where his mother still lives."

Another article appeared on January 24, 2018, making front-page news: "Fears About Williams Case Drove Kidnapping." From court records, Portman had unearthed the police interview with Stephen Mnookin. "Anesthesiologist Dr. Stephen Mnookin said he went to lunch with Brian Winchester hours after the Aug. 5, 2016, incident involving Denise Merrell Williams," wrote Portman. "Mnookin said a nervous Winchester told him the police were 'after him' and kept contacting him."

Amid all the gossip and rumor, Denise held her head up high. On the surface, she maintained her polished façade, but privately she was shaken by the discovery of Mike's body and upset by Portman's recent articles. At 2:31 p.m. on January 24, she sent Kathy a text referring to Portman's article in that morning's edition of the *Democrat* quoting Stephen Mnookin. "I expect dr. steve to sue her," Denise texted. "Shes an idiot . . . Reading out right lies is maddening." She went on to speculate, "J portman is writing a book abt all this as her retirement plan depends on a great story." But Denise's faith kept her strong, she told Kathy. "As the shit storm brews I really have an inner confidence that i am right where the Lord wants me to be and it brings me to a calm peaceful place." She also mentioned her new Hello Fresh meal delivery plan—she was "cooking hello fresh steak tonite." Kathy wondered what would happen to Mike's unearthed remains, adding, "Send me a picture of the steak."

Two weeks later, on February 9, at 8:39 p.m., at the prompting of investigators, Kathy texted Denise and told her she'd received a "witness subpoena" and was "freaking out." Denise's response was wary—she may have begun to suspect that Kathy was working with the police. She advised her to take her attorney along when she gave the statement. Kathy appeared distraught. She was worried about details coming out about the past. She could lose her family, she said. "If I lie I'm screwed and if I tell the truth I'm screwed."

"They r looking for a murderer!!" Denise reminded her. "And whoever or whatever might have happened, we have the peace to know we are not murderers. Peace from the good Lord." Her advice to Kathy was to pray. "The devil is taking hold telling you these lies. Dont let the damn devil win. This is a spiritual war."

The next day, Kathy took part in a recorded "controlled call" with Denise. She pretended to be troubled about the subpoena and followed a "loose script" designed by the investigators. At their instigation, she made up a story about something that happened to her sixteen years ago. After the incident with Chuck Bunker in Atlanta, she told Denise, Brian had called her at work, crying, and he'd confessed to killing Mike.

On the recording, Kathy is plausibly upset, occasionally sobbing. Denise remains guarded. Hesitant and circumspect, she admits nothing. She no longer trusts Kathy; she obviously suspects the call is being recorded and is unwilling to talk openly.

Kathy, flustered and agitated, tells Denise she's terrified of being placed under oath because she will have to admit what she knows.

"And what do you know?" asks her friend, cagily.

Kathy tells her the story about Brian coming back from Atlanta and calling her at work. "And he told me about what happened to Mike," she concludes.

But Denise isn't biting. "Well, I would love to know what happened to Mike," she responds. "They said they found his remains and that he was beaten or that he was shot."

"Brian told me that y'all planned it," Kathy tells her.

"Planned *what*?" asks Denise.

Kathy said that after Brian confessed to her, Marcus Winchester came by her workplace in the afternoon and warned her that she'd have to take what she knew "to the grave."

Denise appears to be confused. "Wait, wait, wait. So, Mike . . ."

"Apparently, Brian told Marcus that he had talked to me," explains Kathy. "Marcus went on to tell me how my life would be ruined, how I would never be able to start over if Stafford's life was ruined, if . . ."

"So Marcus knew?" asks Denise. "And when you said Brian . . . you're talking about me and Brian? Or Marcus? Or who?"

"*You and Brian*," Kathy insisted.

On the call, Denise sounds baffled, slightly bemused, and a little indignant. "And that Marcus is involved? I mean, obviously, if he came and talked to you . . . What in the world? . . . But yeah, that's pretty major, especially with Marcus involved."

The rest is inconclusive. Kathy sobs a lot, anxious about all the "stupid shit" that will come out at trial. She's afraid her husband will leave her when he learns about her past. Rocky, she says, is good and honest. "Not like us."

That was their last conversation. Denise, as she'd told Brian, "wasn't talking." She went about her life as usual for the next three months, having minimal contact with Kathy. Meanwhile, quietly and discreetly, the prosecutors were building their case. With Brian's confession, the phone calls with Kathy, and the notes kept by Cheryl, they finally had probable cause to make an arrest.

On May 8, 2018, a warm, cloudy day after a morning of thunderstorms, Officers Kimberly Tyus and Richard Wooten of the FSU Police approached Denise in her office. They told her she was under arrest and led her through the parking lot to a waiting police car. The moment was caught on camera. Denise's hands are cuffed behind her back, and Officer Tyus has a tight hold on her upper right arm. She's wearing black-framed glasses, a matching blue-and-purple blouse and skirt, footless olive-green tights, and flip-flops. Her wavy blond hair is clipped up at the front, away from her face. She walks silently, her head down, avoiding Portman's questions. As one observer put it, she had "the dead-eyed look of someone who knows the party is over." At the police car, Officer Tyus pats her down, helps her into the back seat, fastens her seat belt, then slams the passenger door.

The spiritual war was over, and the devil had won.

− ACT IV −

What's Done in the Dark

"For my mouth shall speak truth."

PROVERBS 8:7

S tate of Florida v. Denise Williams opened in Tallahassee's Leon County Courthouse on December 11, 2018, just seven months after Denise's arrest. This was unusually fast. High-profile murder cases normally take years to reach trial. But in this case, there was almost no incriminating evidence against Denise, so neither defense nor prosecution needed to conduct investigations, file for discovery, or schedule expert witnesses. Everything hinged on Brian's confession.

The charges against Denise were first-degree murder, conspiracy to commit first-degree murder, and accessory after the fact in the death of Jerry Michael Williams. Originally, she was also charged with three counts of insurance fraud, but these had been dropped as part of a settlement made with Cheryl and Nick Williams. According to this agreement, all Denise's former assets would be given to Anslee, the victim's benefactor. But there was one provision: Anslee couldn't use any of the assets to help pay her mother's legal fees, any costs associated with the trial, or any ongoing appeals.

When prosecutors began their opening arguments, Denise had been in the women's section of the Leon County jail for six months. Brian, who'd been incarcerated for more than two years, was still in the Wakulla Correctional Institute in Crawfordsville, half an hour south of Tallahassee. Once again, the judge was James Hankinson, age sixty-five, who retired shortly after the trial concluded.

The jurors were evenly split in race and gender: six men and six women; six white and six Black. When it came to age, there was less diversity: Both defense and prosecution favored younger jurors, perhaps assuming they'd be more open-minded. Of the twelve selected, two were in their late teens, and three were in their twenties.

All twelve claimed they'd never heard of the Mike Williams case, which seems unusual, given the publicity in the *Tallahassee Democrat* and Cheryl's prominent billboard displays. But, as Judge Hankinson later explained, "my experience picking many juries in high-profile cases both as a prosecutor and a judge, is that most people pay no attention to the news." Moreover, this wasn't the kind of case that could be "contaminated" by publicity, since there were no extraneous facts.

All twelve jurors were Tallahassee locals apart from a retired corporate vice president who'd recently moved to the area to be closer to his wife's family. James Karabasz, age seventy-six, had served on juries before, had some legal knowledge, and, being from out of town, was completely unfamiliar with the case. One of the defense attorneys described him as "the perfect juror."

Before the trial began, the jurors were taken to the jury room and asked to nominate a foreperson. Karabasz and three others all volunteered for the position, so they decided to draw lots. The winner was eighteen-year-old Kierra Idlett, a recent high school graduate who'd been thrilled when she was chosen for the jury because she thought she'd be getting $15 per hour (rather than $15 a day), an improvement on her usual wage (making sandwiches at Firehouse Subs). Idlett was "perfectly pleasant," said Karabasz, but he thought she had "absolutely no leadership skills." Like all juries, the group of citizens represented a cross-section of the local community. Still, Karabasz felt that many of the younger jurors lacked the appropriate temperament for such a serious undertaking.

Using her ample savings, Denise had hired Ethan Way, a hard-hitting criminal defense attorney with a graying Amish-style beard and an office full of big-game trophies. A few months before the trial, Way decided to bring another attorney on board as second chair. This was Philip Padovano, age seventy, a retired circuit court judge who'd presided over several high-profile death-penalty cases; Way chose Padovano because of his expertise in appellate work. His mannerly, old-fashioned demeanor also made a valuable counterbalance to Way's uncompromising style.

Denise, seated at the defense table, looked drained and tired. She wore glasses with transparent plastic frames. Her formerly thick hair now fell limply to her shoulders, half yellow, half mousy brown. She dressed modestly, usually in a light-colored blouse and cardigan. A group of her supporters sat in the front row—her three sisters, other family members, friends, work colleagues, and church congregants.

In general, the more family support a defendant has during a trial, the better the chance of a favorable verdict. If a jury sees the alleged perpetrator as a real human being, with people who love, respect, and rely on them, they'll be less likely to convict. But people also notice if supporters are absent. Some observed that none of Denise's male relatives showed up in court. "Denise has grown adult nephews," commented Patti Ketcham. "They weren't there. Not one of the sisters' spouses, not one of the brothers-in-law attended."

Another notable absentee was Anslee, now eighteen. Perhaps, like Cheryl, Kathy, and other key players in the case, she'd been subpoenaed as a possible witness and wasn't allowed in the courtroom. It's also possible that Denise, understandably, didn't want to subject her daughter to the storm of publicity generated by the trial. Florida is well-known for its liberal Sunshine Laws, which grant widespread access to state records and legal proceedings. For *Florida v. Denise Williams*, there was a "pool" camera shared among the *Tallahassee Democrat*, various other newspapers, and the online legal network Law and Crime, where the coverage was live-streamed (and has since been viewed more than 6 million times). The Associated Press, a national wire service, distributed stories about the case, and articles appeared in newspapers as far away as Australia and the United Kingdom.

On social media, too, the trial was followed with bustling excitement. *Florida v. Denise Williams* was one of those cases that acts like a magnet, galvanizing the emotions of strangers. These onlookers were the trial's Greek chorus, providing an unfiltered stream of opinions on social media and in comment forums such as the Live Chat streamed by the Law and Crime Network's YouTube Channel during its coverage of the courtroom proceedings.

————

Although court junkies and true-crime fans love to follow courtroom proceedings in the media, the number of trials live-streamed is vastly disproportionate to the number that occur. The same is true in films and literature; a nail-biting trial makes a thrilling climax to a crime story, but trials are increasingly a thing of the past. Today, only 2 percent of federal criminal cases go to trial; for state cases, it's closer to 4 percent.

There are lots of reasons for this, but in a nutshell, the system is broken beyond repair. Courts are so overwhelmed by legal cases they'll find any means to lighten the load. Criminal trials are cumbersome; they're expensive for the state, and even more so for the accused, who, if they're not eligible for a public defender, may well be facing bankruptcy. Lawyers' fees are often prohibitive to the ordinary person; many defendants emerge from criminal trials deeply in debt, even if they win the case.

Mandatory minimum sentences also give prosecutors a powerful tool to induce guilty pleas: If someone takes a plea instead of going to trial, they can get less than the minimum, but if they go to trial and are found guilty, they may very well get more. As well, prosecutors will often "overcharge" defendants, piling charge on top of charge until a plea seems like the only option. This reliance on plea bargaining has dreadful consequences; worst of all, it creates incentives for the innocent to plead guilty, leading to a disproportionate number of people with criminal records. A prison sentence is stigmatizing, and when a person can't get work or pay rent, they often turn to crime. Thus, the circle goes around.

Even when cases do come to trial, the proceedings are usually uneventful, often tedious even to those involved. The most compelling trials have their tiresome stretches: dull witnesses called in to establish facts of evidence, lengthy openings and closings, long explanations of scientific processes, bureaucratic interruptions. But *Florida v. Denise Williams* was transfixing, even though there were no shocking outbursts, no compelling props, and no grandstanding lawyers. The focus was solely on witness testimony. Information emerged often inadvertently, in a tone of voice, choice of phrase, a moment's hesitation, or a too-ready response.

The court was packed, the atmosphere tense, and the room haunted by the victim's presence. No one could escape the specter of Mike Williams, whose untimely and tragic death had magnified his status. As Jon Fuchs took the stand, Mike's boyish face, projected on a screen, beamed down on the proceedings like that of a cheerful saint. In his absence, Mike seemed vital and immortal. Later, when Fuchs projected a photograph of his remains, it was difficult to connect this pile of old brown bones with Mike's grinning, bright-eyed face.

In his opening statement, Jon Fuchs made the case into a tidy narrative with none of the tangents or contradictions of real life. Denise, he said, was a woman who wanted everything—sex, murder, money, and sole custody of her daughter. She was a manipulator motivated by love and greed. It was an open-and-shut case of good versus evil. Of course, this is what trial attorneys must do—simplify and streamline to make their case clear. But it was precisely the tangents and contradictions that made this case so compelling: strange drama, secret passion, holy faith, guilty secrets. In Fuchs's telling, it was about as exciting as a high school statistics class.

Fuchs was an experienced prosecutor—he'd recently been lead counsel in the Henry Segura quadruple murder case—but although he may have been dynamic behind the scenes, he had little public charisma. He kept walking away from the microphone, turning his back on the jury, mumbling, repeating himself, and swallowing his words ("Is the prosecutor chewing tobacco?" wondered one observer). A lead prosecutor doesn't have to be a showman, but Fuchs sucked the life out of the room. His long-winded and monotonous presentation was accompanied by an unimaginative PowerPoint slideshow consisting primarily of bullet points. By the time he'd finished his opening statement, jurors were openly yawning.

Philip Padovano, for the defense, was smoother and more articulate, but his story was equally simple and clear-cut. Brian was a sociopath who killed Mike of his own volition in order to marry Denise, his lust object and lifelong obsession. Denise was a kind, gentle, righteous woman who was horrified to discover that she'd married her first husband's murderer. Brian, angry that Denise had asked for a life sentence on the kidnapping charge, had stewed for two years in prison, concocting an elaborate series of lies in revenge.

The first witness took the stand. Alton Ranew, now retired from the Fish and Wildlife Commission, described the disappearance of Mike Williams in December 2000, and the extensive search on Lake

Seminole. His memory was remarkable, his testimony clear and concise. Two other witnesses confirmed Ranew's account of the meticulous investigation.

Next, Special Agents Tully Sparkman and Michael DeVaney described the case from the perspective of law enforcement. DeVaney seemed to welcome the opportunity. After Brian's confession and Denise's arrest, the police had faced extensive public criticism—not uncommon in high-profile cases—compounded by plenty of second-guessing and hindsight bias. Commenters on social media claimed that everyone in the community had always known Brian and Denise had killed Mike Williams. People accused the police of incompetence and laziness for blaming the murder on alligators.

But if the alligators were scapegoats, so were the police, whose ability to intervene had been frustratingly limited. As Sparkman and DeVaney explained, they'd been discreetly observing Denise and Brian for almost twenty years, but with no concrete evidence of a crime, all they could do was follow the proceedings from a distance, hoping for a break in the case. And when it came, they seized it.

———

Angela Stafford, who'd worked as an assistant at Ketcham Appraisals, looked very uncomfortable on the stand, especially when Jon Fuchs asked her about an event that had happened fourteen years earlier, in 2004. This was the night when she went drinking at a gay bar with Brian and they later went back to his place to hook up. Angela confessed they were "in the middle of intimacy" when Denise stormed into Brian's bedroom. "She saw us and ran out," said Angela. "Brian got up and put on a pair of pants and ran out after her." Her embarrassment made her testimony plausible. It seemed to confirm Brian had been involved with Denise while still married to Kathy.

Angela's testimony was characteristic of the trial's atmosphere: a blend of shame, schadenfreude, and voyeurism. It was mesmerizing. Online, commenters described it as "juicy as fuck." "Pretty hot stuff." "All the dirty laundry is being exposed." "I've never seen so much scum and so many perverts all in one place before." "I am having a hard time trying to keep up with who cheated on who and who knew about the murder." "What's done in the dark will always come to light." "What a bunch of weirdos and evil people." "This is better than any soap opera. I'm munching popcorn—riveted."

One after another, Brian and Denise's former high school friends— now respectable, conservative citizens approaching middle age—were forced to face the phantoms of their younger selves and answer questions about long-ago sexual capers. At one point, Jon Fuchs wanted to enter a set of photographs into evidence. Ethan Way objected strenuously, arguing that the images were irrelevant and "highly prejudicial." The state wanted to "inflame the jury," he fumed, and "to appeal to a prurient interest." He said the pictures showed "two women in what may be described as compromising conditions." The judge took the pictures and glanced at them. Unimpressed, he withheld nine, and admitted the rest.

They were photographs from the old days, taken in Panama City when the two couples were still tight. Denise and Kathy, both topless, posed suggestively on a hotel room bed. In one picture, Brian's image was reflected in a mirror behind them, holding the camera. The images didn't prove Brian and Denise were having an affair while Mike was still alive; all they proved was that Brian had taken risqué pictures of Kathy and Denise. Perhaps Fuchs wanted to suggest that if Denise was the type of person who fooled around with her best friend in front of her best friend's husband, it was also likely she'd had an extramarital affair. They certainly weren't evidence of murder, nor were they offered as such.

Kathy Thomas, too, looked uneasy on the stand. Twenty years had passed since the topless frolics in Panama City. Now forty-seven, Kathy was a modest, quiet mother of three. Dressed in a black blouse, gray wool cardigan, and glasses, she looked like a small-town librarian. She was popular among the court watchers, who described her online as "a sweet and composed woman," "quite genuine and adorable," "wholesome," "a good girl," "a smart girl." Swiveling nervously from side to side in her seat, she admitted she'd always suspected Brian and Denise were having an affair. She described finding the receipt for the "Meridian" necklace, and explained how, over the last fifteen years, she'd worked sporadically as an undercover agent for law enforcement.

Fuchs next played the recorded phone call in which Kathy told Denise the fabricated story about Brian coming to see her at work and confessing to the murder. Since Denise didn't testify, this was the only time jurors got to hear her voice. The courtroom was silent; everyone listened intently. Denise kept her eyes downcast, making notes on a legal pad.

Jon Fuchs made much of the tape and Denise's failure to react when Kathy told her Brian had confessed to murdering Mike. If Denise was innocent, Fuchs argued, wouldn't she have been more indignant? Instead, she calmly tells Kathy the police and the State Attorney's Office have been planting lies about everyone. "What they've been doing is, they've been lying to me, and they've been lying to them," she tells Kathy ("them" referring to Brian and Marcus). "They're playing everybody against each other . . . they can say whatever they want to say."

Kathy was a convincing witness, and although the phone call had little weight—at least in legal terms—her evidence had cumulative value. More than anything else, it gave the jury more insight into the two couples, and the kind of lives they used to lead. There was an ironic moment during the phone call when Kathy expressed concern—surely not feigned—that, should the case go to trial, "then everything . . . you know, all the stupid shit we ever did would come out—and everybody would know."

———

Ward Schwoob, the crime scene investigator who supervised the exhumation of Mike's body, led the jury through the excavation process. He coolly described the unearthing of the tarp and discovery of the bones and remnants of clothing. So little remained of Mike's body that the autopsy report was less than a single page.

When the state called Cheryl Williams, a great hush fell over the room. She was the opposite of a diva; nonetheless, her entrance was showstopping. After a moment's delay, the courtroom doors opened and Jon Fuchs emerged, pushing Mike's wheelchair-bound mother slowly through the room. Cheryl smiled serenely, like Cleopatra sailing by on her barge. Her hair was tied in her trademark gray pigtails.

She wore a black dress and matching long-sleeved jacket; a wedding ring was prominently displayed on a chain around her neck. When the bailiff pushed her wheelchair into the witness box, she was so low down that only the top part of her face was visible. Fuchs lowered the microphone to make things easier, but the witness still seemed a little at sea. When the clerk asked her to introduce herself to the jury, Cheryl turned, nodded, and smiled at them sweetly, not realizing she was being asked to give her name. But once the questioning began, it became clear that, despite her age and physical frailty, her mind was intact and her memory superlative.

Cheryl was a profoundly sympathetic witness, even more so when she acknowledged how much she'd loved Denise. In response to the prosecutor's questions, she described the day her son went missing on Lake Seminole and her unrelenting quest to find out what had happened to him. Especially moving was her testimony that, after she'd pushed the police to open an investigation into Mike's death, Denise refused to let her have any contact with Anslee.

When it came to cross-examination, Philip Padovano was judiciously gentle. "The sympathy is always with the witness, not the lawyer," Padovano said later. "I was cautious with her, and I was very polite to her while trying to bring out the points I wanted to make." Padovano pointed out that when Denise decided to prevent Anslee from seeing her grandmother, Mike had been declared dead, a memorial had taken place, and Anslee had been told her father wasn't coming home. Given those circumstances, he suggested, it must have been tough for Denise and Anslee "to see missing posters and billboards and things such as that." If Denise was innocent, and her mother-in-law was accusing her of being involved in a murder, "it would be logical for her to be upset," he suggested. Cheryl conceded that this was true.

Thanks to her tireless search for justice, Mike's mother was the story's heroine. Newspapers described how she'd spent years walking up and down the side of the road with Mike's photograph on a sign; how she'd saved for months to pay for billboards above the highway. In the press, she was "inspirational," "impressive," "amazing," a "bulldog-spirited grandmother" who was "saintly" in her devotion. Without Cheryl's constant pressure, everyone said, Mike's murderers would never have been brought to justice.

Certainly, it was Cheryl's persistence that forced law enforcement to reopen the investigation, and it was Jennifer Portman's dedication to the case that kept it in the public eye. But the truth is plain: If Brian and Denise hadn't turned on each other, the crime would have remained unsolved.

I Loaded My Gun

"For there is nothing hid, which shall not be manifested; neither was any thing kept secret, but that it should come abroad."

MARK 4:22

After lunch on Tuesday, December 11, the state's star witness, led by a deputy, emerged through a door on the left of the judge's bench. The court reporter swore him in. Bound by transport restraints—wrist and ankle cuffs attached to a chain around his waist—Brian Winchester wore a short-sleeved blue prison jumpsuit over a white T-shirt. At forty-eight, he was still strong and vital, with a full head of dark blond hair, but his face was gaunt and drawn, his eyes dark, his mouth narrow. He was on the stand for an hour and forty-five minutes. The following morning, Wednesday, December 12, he continued testifying for another hour and a half. His testimony was "compelled"—in other words, he was testifying against his will. If the state discovered he was telling anything but the truth, they would cancel the deal and charge him with first-degree murder.

Brian may have gone over his testimony in his head, but he couldn't have been prepared for the ordeal he was about to endure. For the most part, he was composed and articulate, but from time to time, he hesitated, sighed, and tried to repress his emotions. Sometimes he failed; on one occasion, he broke down completely, put his head in his hands, and began to sob, causing the judge to call for a break in proceedings.

A guard removed Brian's handcuffs; Jon Fuchs asked a couple of questions, then gave him the floor. His virtually uninterrupted account was spontaneous, personal, and heartfelt, unfettered by the orderly language of the law. He'd described the murder a year earlier in private, as part of the proffer negotiation; now he was telling the story in public for the first time, in front of Denise, his father, Mike's family and friends, a courtroom full of spectators, and the national media.

His testimony was mesmerizing.

On the evening of Friday, December 15, 2000, Mike Williams went to ring Christmas bells with the Salvation Army as part of his volunteer work for the Rotary Club. That night, Brian took his wife out and made sure she had plenty to drink. "I wanted Kathy to be as drunk as possible because I wanted her to sleep in late the next morning," he said. They went to Floyd's Music Store on the Tennessee Strip to see Vast, an alternative rock band from Seattle. Brian's plan worked. "She went to sleep hard."

He'd arranged to go duck hunting with Mike at Lake Seminole very early the following day, around 4 a.m., reminding him to bring his waders. Unbeknownst to Mike, Brian had also made plans to go duck hunting at 6 a.m. that same morning with his father-in-law, Jimmy Aldredge—this would be his alibi. Denise was going to stay at home with the baby, making several calls from the landline in case she needed to prove her whereabouts.

Brian and Mike met at a gas station on Thomasville Road, northwest of the city. Brian said he'd discovered a "secret special hunting spot" at the lake; he added that Mike wouldn't be able to call him during the drive because his phone was dead (in fact, he'd turned it off so there'd be no record of any calls). Brian was driving a white Chevy Suburban. Mike, in his Ford Bronco, pulled the boat behind him. The sixty-mile drive to Lake Seminole took almost an hour. It was still dark; the sun wouldn't be up for three or four hours. Mist and dew were beginning to rise over the fields and shale hills on either side of the road. They turned north at Sneads and drove up Route 271, past Three Rivers State Park, to a boat landing on the west side of the lake, a small cove abutting a series of inlets and islands.

Fog shrouded the Spanish moss and a haze hung over the lake. Brian suggested the men save time by putting on their waders before they launched Mike's boat, a large, motor-powered canoe. He was starting to worry about time. The drive and preparations had taken longer than he'd anticipated, and he didn't want to be late meeting Jimmy Aldredge. The two friends set out on the lake, and Brian, at the rudder, guided the boat to an area a couple hundred yards from the landing, where the water was deep.

From his seat in front, he said something to Mike about a problem with the motor, asking him to come over and check it out. "I got him to stand up," said Brian. "And when he did, I pushed him in the water."

For five long seconds, there was silence in the courtroom. Brian gave a heavy sigh and his face clenched up as if he were about to burst into tears, but he recovered his equilibrium, and after a few more dreadful seconds of silence, he went on. Until then, he'd been facing his audience; now he stared blankly at a point in front of him. His voice trembled.

"So," he continued, "he was in the water, and he was, like, struggling." He wriggled his shoulders to depict his friend's movements. "And the motor of the boat was still running. And I pulled off, just a little bit, to get, kind of, away from him so that he couldn't reach back into the boat." He made a gesture with his hand indicating distance. "And—I didn't know it at the time—I didn't know if he was trying to swim, or"—Brian shook his head—"didn't know what was going on, but what I came to find out, or eventually realized was, he was taking the waders and the jacket off."

"I think I forgot to tell you about this before," he added, addressing the prosecutor, "but I remember now. That area of the lake had a lot of snags and dead trees that came up out of the water." His face clenched and grimaced; his mouth quivered. "And he swam over to one of the stumps," he said. "And he held on to it."

No one breathed. After a moment, Brian went on, blinking rapidly. He shook his head as he spoke, trying to negate the horrible scene his words described. "And he was panicking," he said. "And I was panicking. And none of this was going the way I thought it was going to go." He sighed deeply and shook his head slowly from side to side. "And

I didn't . . . I didn't know what to do." He shrugged his shoulders. He swallowed. "But, uh . . ." He sniffed. He licked his lips. He shook his head again. "He was . . . he started to yell."

Brian looked down, shaking his head, then looked up. His tongue bulged in his right cheek as if refusing to speak. His neck muscles were taut; he was going through a frightful inner struggle.

"And I didn't know . . . I didn't know . . . I didn't know how to get out of that situation." His voice began to break. "And so," and he gestured with an upturned palm, "I had my gun in the boat." Four seconds of dead silence. Brian looked down. "And, uh. So. I loaded my gun. And I just . . ." He made a turning motion with his finger. "I made one or two circles around." He sniffed. He shook his head from side to side. "And I ended up circling closer towards him." He lifted his left hand to his forehead, wiped away some sweat, then moved it forward in a gliding motion, describing the boat's progress. "And he was in the water." He reached out with a grasping gesture, imitating Mike clinging desperately to the stump of a tree. "And as I passed by," said Brian, making the two-fingers-together gesture representing a gun, "I shot him."

He closed his eyes and looked down.

"Where did you shoot him?" asked Fuchs.

"In the head."

———

The lake was black. The gunfire made a flash in the darkness. Brian closed his eyes and kept them closed for a few seconds. He was a good shot; he knew he'd hit Mike because the yelling had stopped, but he didn't want to see. Everything was silent except for the boat motor, throbbing quietly. Brian took the rudder, circled back around, and drove the boat nearer to Mike's body. He didn't look too closely. He didn't need to. His friend was dead.

If things had gone to plan, when Mike's body surfaced in the lake, everyone would have assumed he'd had a boating accident and drowned. But a shot to the head was a different matter. No question: This was a murder. He couldn't leave the body in the lake.

Gritting his teeth, he reached down into murky darkness and grabbed hold of one of Mike's feet, then, with his other hand, turned the rudder and headed back to the shoreline, dragging the body behind him. He was in a rush now, eager to get off the lake before the sun came up. It wasn't easy to drive the boat and drag the body at the same time. He got to shore as soon as he could, steering the boat to the closest ramp, half a mile from the landing where the men had parked their vehicles.

He let go of Mike's body, cut the motor, climbed out of the boat, and pulled it a short distance up the ramp. He then took a deep breath, took hold of both of Mike's feet, dragged him out of the water, and left his body on the ramp, half-submerged but resting on solid ground. Then, trying to suppress his panic, he ran half a mile back down the road to the landing where the men had parked their vehicles, unlocked his Chevy Suburban, climbed in, drove back to his boat and Mike's body, reversed his truck down the ramp to the edge of the lake, and lowered the tailgate.

Mike was the same height as Brian and a little heavier, maybe 180 pounds. Plus, he was soaking wet. It wasn't easy, and it wasn't pretty, but he had to make it happen. He had no choice. Brian was in shock. He could feel the adrenaline pumping through his veins. Still, the struggle was dreadful. He lifted the body and propped it against the back of the Chevy, then climbed into the passenger compartment. He lowered the back seats, crawled into the cargo area, then reached down and dragged his friend's wet, bloodied corpse up into the back of the truck. For a moment, he thought he wouldn't be able to do it. He forced his body to work harder than ever before. He tried not to look at Mike's face, but he couldn't help catching a glimpse. It was shot to pieces.

He kept telling himself there was nothing else he could have done.

Brian trained Labrador retrievers as a hobby; there was a large dog crate in the back of his Suburban. He managed to wedge the upper part of Mike's body into the crate, which held it in place and contained the bleeding, then climbed out of the trunk and slammed the tailgate. The back windows of the Chevy were dirty. From the outside, unless you looked closely, it just looked like a dog crate and a pile of old clothes in the back of a truck.

Before leaving, he started the engine of Mike's boat and pushed it out on the water. He then climbed back into his vehicle and set off toward Tallahassee. The exertion had left him sweaty, and his clothes were stained with dirt. Nothing had gone the way he'd planned. Now he was driving down Route 271 with his best friend's corpse in the back of his Chevy.

He needed to haul ass as fast as possible to meet up with his father-in-law before it got too late. The sun was coming up. He hit the gas and shot straight through Sneads, but before he reached Route 90, he came to a red stoplight. Opposite him, a car pulled up. A state patrol car. When the light turned green, Brian barely moved until the cops were out of sight; even then, he was so spooked he was afraid to break the speed limit. He couldn't call Jimmy to let him know he'd been delayed because he didn't want to leave a record of his location. His phone was still turned off. It was almost 6:30 now. He was half an hour late, with another half hour's drive to go.

Instinctively, he kept his mind on the immediate tasks ahead of him—it stopped him from thinking about what had just happened. He had to bury the body. Before that, he had to go and buy a shovel, a tarp, and what else? Weights? Bleach?

He'd arranged to meet Jimmy Aldredge in the T.J.Maxx parking lot at Carriage Gate, a suburban shopping mall just outside Tallahassee, but by the time Brian pulled up, his father-in-law was long gone. He knew he'd be seeing Jimmy later that day at his in-laws' Christmas get-together in Cairo, but he thought he should call and apologize anyway, to be on the safe side. He decided to drive back to his home in nearby Killearn Lakes, call Jimmy from the landline, and say he'd overslept. If Kathy was still asleep, he could slip back into bed and pretend he'd just woken up. Getting rid of the body was urgent. But first, he needed an alibi.

He parked the truck in his driveway where the neighbors couldn't see it, unlocked the door, and slipped inside. Kathy, thank God, was still sleeping off her hangover. He removed his dirty clothes and slipped into bed next to his wife, then made a loud performance of waking up and cursing at himself for oversleeping. Kathy mumbled something and turned over. Brian called his father-in-law from the landline and apologized for missing their appointment, speaking in a loud voice so Kathy would hear. He'd overslept, he told Jimmy, then he'd lost the key to his friend's boat, which he'd been planning for them to use to go hunting. See you this afternoon in Cairo, he said. At the Christmas party.

He started to get dressed, saying something to Kathy about going out with the dogs.

Leaning down to tie his shoelaces, Brian suddenly wondered—if he prayed hard enough, could he start the day over?

If he got down on his knees, could he ask God to turn back time?

He said a prayer. That he would leave the house and his truck would be empty.

But God wasn't listening. His truck was in the driveway by the house, where he'd left it half an hour ago.

And there was blood dripping from the tailgate.

———

He ran into the garage, turned on the wall faucet, unrolled the hose, and washed the blood off the driveway and the back of the truck. He opened the tailgate and, keeping his eyes averted, shoved Mike's body farther into the dog crate to stop the blood from leaking out. The corpse had spent enough time in the water that most of the blood had been washed away, but there was still a constant trickle. He had to get rid of the body right away. Time was running out.

From his home in Killearn Lakes, Brian headed south. Kathy had registered his presence, so at least he had an alibi. Good. Now he had to bury the body, and fast. But to do so, he needed tools. There was no other way: He had to go to Walmart. He drove to Thomasville Road, pulled into the Walmart parking lot, and found an isolated space, far from other vehicles. It was inconceivable, but he had to leave his truck there. The Chevy looked inconspicuous, he thought—there was no more blood. The trickle was being contained by the dog crate, and the sides of the vehicle were clean.

He clicked the lock and walked toward the store, trying to repress the thought that kept struggling to make its way into his head: My best friend's dead body is wedged in a dog cage in the back of my truck, and I'm in Walmart, shopping for a shovel.

Inside the store, he got a cart and tried to be speedy but casual. He had to think on his feet, loading up with everything he'd need. A weather-resistant tarp, 10 by 20 inches. A set of cast-iron barbells. A heavy-duty, long-handled spade.

As he was heading toward the checkout, someone called his name.

He turned. It was Mike Phillips, an old buddy from North Florida Christian High. Brian hadn't seen him for a while. Mike asked Brian what he was up to. Brian said he was working for his dad. As he was speaking, he suddenly remembered something. Mike Phillips was now an agent with the Florida Department of Law Enforcement.

Brian was kind of pressed for time, he said. Good to see you, man.

A couple of weeks later, when word spread that Mike Williams had gone missing, Phillips misremembered the time of their encounter. He assumed Brian had been in a rush because he was anxious about his missing buddy.

And in a way, he was right.

At the checkout, Brian felt himself starting to sweat. When someone buys a tarp, weights, and a shovel, it doesn't take Sherlock Holmes to figure out there's something shady going on. But the cashier smiled and wished him a blessed day. (Too late for that.) She asked him if he needed any help loading his purchases, but he said he was good. It was a lot to carry, but he sure as hell wasn't going to let anybody else get near his truck. He dumped everything on the rear passenger seat and headed south, taking a right on Ox Bottom Road. There were plenty of lakes around Tallahassee. Next to the water, the soil would be damp and easier to dig. If he was lucky, he might find a convenient gator hole—he could sink the body into the mud. Brian knew the lakes well—he was a water-skier, as well as a fisherman and a duck hunter. He could think of a lot of places that were isolated, but none were accessible by vehicle. The only place that came to mind was Gardner Road, a long stretch of highway that led to a boat ramp on the edge of Carr Lake. It wasn't ideal, but it would do.

Gardner Road was a left-hand turn off Meridian, about seven miles from his house in Killearn Lakes. The lane petered out after about two miles into a rough dirt track leading to the boat ramp. Brian figured it was remote enough that he was unlikely to be interrupted. He drove up to the lake's edge, got out of the truck, and started looking around for a gator hole. He'd planned to weigh the body down and sink it into the mud, but he was out of luck—it had been a mild winter; the lake was low, even dried up in places. There were no gator holes. Even worse, when he managed to dislodge Mike's body from the dog crate, he realized there was no way he could move it—the body was just too heavy, and he was utterly exhausted. He had no choice but to bury it in the lakebed itself, in a trough across from the boat ramp, out of view of the road. Hopefully, it would be completely submerged by the time the water rose in spring.

Burying the body was a nightmare. Brian's nerves were shattered; he was worried about the time; he knew Kathy would be looking for him. They were supposed to be driving up to Cairo that afternoon, with Stafford. Summoning all his strength, he unrolled the tarp, pulled Mike's corpse out of the back of the car, then rolled up the ghastly bundle and dragged it over to the lake, into the underbrush of winter grape and hickory saplings. The earth was waterlogged and swampy; digging the hole was an unpleasant task and seemed to take forever. At least the mosquitos and horseflies were dormant for the winter, but Brian somehow dislodged a nest of fire ants and got bitten all over. Then, just when he'd managed to kill the last of the ants and was about to roll Mike's body into the hole, he heard a vehicle coming down the dirt track.

Jesus. He dropped his shovel. Mike's body was still wrapped in the tarp. Hidden by the underbrush, it was barely visible. Brian walked back to the road, trying to look as if he was just taking a morning stroll. A truck was pulling up with a boat attached to the rear axle. A man in a hunting cap got out, walked around to the back, and started to detach the boat. He noticed Brian and nodded. They made small talk about hunting. The man told Brian he liked to shoot deer on the shoreline from his boat. Brian got the sense he was a game warden or forest ranger, maybe because of the hat, or just because he seemed familiar with the area. Brian wished him good luck in his hunting. The stranger launched his vessel. Brian returned to his labor.

The hole was deep enough, he decided. He wrapped the weights in the tarp along with the body, rolled it down the side of the lakebed into the makeshift grave, then shoveled dirt and mud on top until it was completely covered. He smoothed the ground with the shovel, trying to make it look undisturbed.

It was a crude, hasty, spur-of-the-moment burial. But Mike's body lay undiscovered for the next seventeen years.

———

It was the middle of the afternoon. Brian was drained, overwhelmed, and covered in painful ant bites, but he had to keep moving. Kathy must have been calling him to find out where he was, but his phone was still turned off, and he didn't stop to check his messages. He didn't want to leave a trace. Anyway, there wasn't time.

His truck was inconspicuous from the outside, but the cargo compartment was a mess and there was blood all over the dog crate. He needed to clean it out somewhere he wouldn't be seen. He drove to his parents' house. Assuming they were out, he parked behind the garage, turned on the faucet, opened the back of the Chevy, and triggered the hose. Pretty quickly, he realized it was no good—there was too much blood, and the stains were too deep. He needed to find a pressure washer. He got back in his truck and drove to a few gas stations, but none of them had what he needed; finally, someone directed him to a pay-and-spray on the other side of town. Luckily, it wasn't too busy, and after twenty minutes of forceful cleaning, he'd washed out the dog crate and got rid of the stains.

At last, he drove home to shower and change. The ant bites had left marks all over his legs—he hoped Kathy wouldn't notice. To his relief, his wife and son had left for Cairo without him; the half-hour drive gave him time to decompress and get his story straight. The first person he ran into when he got to Kathy's grandmother's house was Jimmy Aldredge, who told him he was in trouble with his wife for being late. Brian repeated the story about losing the key to his friend's boat. He repeated it again to Kathy. Apart from showing up late, his behavior at the Christmas get-together raised no red flags.

There was no feeling of exhilaration, no relief, no sense of achievement in pulling off the plan, no excitement about the prospect of finally having Denise all to himself. None of it was how he'd imagined it would be. All he could think about was the shock and horror of what he'd done. He regretted the murder right away. It weighed on him every day of his life.

– 3 –

She Was in My Head

"... neither is the man without the woman, neither the woman without the man ..."

1 CORINTHIANS 11:11

People are murdered because they are loved, because they were once loved, or because they stand in the way of love. When a person kills another out of the blue, if they're not mentally ill, we assume they must be in the grip of some great passion: rage, desire, jealousy, greed, or lust for revenge.

Most of us don't commit murder, even though we might sometimes want to, because our fear of the consequences outweighs the impulse or the desire of the moment. It seems impossible to believe that two otherwise rational, God-fearing people would decide to kill someone rather than contemplate divorce. But it happens all the time. People aren't reasonable. God-fearing people sometimes least of all.

———

Although the lovers had planned Mike's death together, Brian explained in court that they'd always talked about it cagily, in terms of an "accident" and "the will of God." They'd never used words like "killing" or "murder." Afterward, he realized they'd been daydreaming, thinking in soft focus. They hadn't imagined Mike struggling to get out of his waders, clinging to a tree stump, screaming for help.

Without the slightest attempt to verify the truth of the "duck hunters' myth" that "if you fall overboard with your waders, you're going to sink really quickly and drown," the lovers had made it a central feature of their plan. Brian hadn't discussed the theory with other duck hunters. Had he done so, he would have learned that the new neoprene-style waders don't increase a duck hunter's risk of drowning, except in the circumstances that, after falling overboard, they start to flail and panic.

If pushing Mike into the water was a test, it failed. God, it seems, did not want Mike to die—so now what? Neither Brian nor Denise had stopped to consider what would happen next. Were things supposed to go on as before, with Mike knowing his best friend had just tried to murder him? "I was panicking," admitted Brian, describing the scene. ". . . I had gotten myself into a situation I couldn't get out of . . . I didn't feel like there was any way I could explain what I had done." In hindsight, he realized they'd never expected Mike to "pass the test." He also saw he'd been completely unprepared for the dread and terror of the murder. He didn't tell Denise what had happened because it was unspeakable, and because he was ashamed.

On Tuesday, in court, Brian had been emotionally unstable, but on Wednesday morning he seemed poised, confident, and unruffled. When faced with cross-questioning, he remained polite, always addressing Ethan Way as "sir," but he was ready to negate and contradict, sometimes emphatically.

Way, emphasizing that Brian had been given a sweet deal, asked him to affirm to the jury that he would "one day walk out of the Florida Prison system."

"If I survive it," he mordantly replied.

Way asked Brian about his trip to Arkansas with Mike, when his friend was complaining about his job and his marriage, and how he wanted to leave Tallahassee and move out west. Brian could have encouraged Mike to leave town, suggested Way. But "instead, you killed him."

"That's what *we* did, yes," insisted Brian.

Way tried again. "When you shot Mike Williams at Lake Seminole with a twelve-gauge shotgun, was Denise Williams standing there with you?"

"No, she wasn't," said Brian, calmly. "She was in my head."

Way walked Brian through the murder again, making him describe the crime in gut-wrenching detail. He also brought up Brian's proposed deal with Wade Wilson to perjure the state's witnesses. He reminded the jury that the only evidence to implicate Denise was "the word of a murderer and a convicted felon." He claimed Denise knew nothing about the crime. But he didn't clear up one of the case's most significant inconsistencies.

The day before the murder, Mike told his wife he was planning to go hunting early the next morning with Brian Winchester. Later, Denise told everyone that Brian had called late at night to cancel, but Mike said he planned to go anyway, on his own.

For Brian to have acted on his own, as the defense argued, he'd somehow have to have known Mike was going hunting alone, waited outside Denise's house, secretly followed Mike to the lake, ambushed him, shot him, and pushed his boat into the water. Then, instead of weighing down the body and sinking it in the lake, or burying it in an isolated place near Lake Seminole, he'd had to have loaded it into his truck and driven all the way back to Tallahassee to bury it at a different lake closer to town.

If there were no duck-hunting plans, why wouldn't Brian have ambushed Mike as he left home—in his garage, say, or at Ketcham Appraisals when he went to pick up his gun, or in the woods nearby? Why risk the sixty-mile drive with a corpse in the car?

To some, the shotgun cap found in Mike's skull suggested that he was killed from much closer than Brian described. Perhaps Brian somehow lured Mike out to Carr Lake, people speculated, to kill and bury him there. But if so, he'd have to have buried the body then driven Mike's car and boat out to Lake Seminole, leaving them there to be found. And how would he have gotten back to Tallahassee? He'd have needed an accomplice. Someone whose identity Brian would have been willing to protect even to the tune of a twenty-year prison sentence. Someone perfectly willing to sit back and watch Denise face life in prison for a crime she didn't commit.

The defense claimed that Brian and Denise had never had any romantic or sexual involvement while Mike was alive, and the prosecution had a hard time proving otherwise. While they'd enjoyed taking risks, the lovers had been careful to cover their tracks. Plus, eighteen years is a long time; things get lost or discarded; people forget. There were no texts or cell phone records, no Google search histories, no Facebook status updates, no pictures posted on Instagram.

The state offered a few ghostly relics, but they didn't amount to much: the concert stubs, the necklace receipt, two movie tickets for *The Virgin Suicides*. The photographs from Panama City, made much of by the press, showed that Brian liked watching his wife get it on with another woman, but nothing more. The most damaging testimony was Angela Stafford's description of Denise walking into Brian's bedroom in the middle of the night, but this happened after Mike's death when Denise was a widow, and Brian separated from Kathy.

Nonetheless, logic dictates that Brian was telling the truth. Why, while married with an infant son, would he choose to murder Mike simply because he was "obsessed" with Denise, with no evidence that she returned his feelings or ever would? Why would he sell Mike a million-dollar insurance policy knowing Denise would collect on it after the murder? As a wealthy widow, wouldn't she find a more eligible suitor than her best friend's ex-husband? Especially when her best friend was always griping about how selfish and useless he was.

Certain details in Brian's account had the ring of truth. The cop car on the way back from the lake. The blood in the driveway. Running into Mike Phillips at Walmart. The fire ants. The game warden. The power washer. He told the story to law enforcement officers on two occasions a year apart, then again during the trial; he omitted nothing. His account of Mike's death is congruent with how the body was found—in hunting gear, with shotgun pellets in the skull. The boat, cap, jacket, and waders were found in Lake Seminole. Also consistent with Brian's story are witness accounts from the morning of the murder: gunshots out on the lake and a man running down Three Rivers Park Road in the predawn hours.

But it was Brian's demeanor on the stand that weighed most heavily in the jury's deliberations. As he described the murder, it was clear: Something broke through the surface. The mask was finally lifted, and he faced the hard truth. In the witness box, he could no longer resort to the lies, falsehoods, and deceptions that had become second nature to him over the last eighteen years. The shocking details of the murder made the testimony difficult to listen to, and it was very hard to watch a man sobbing in public. Still, few questioned the integrity of Brian's emotions. Juror number 1, Joslyn Bynum, who was twenty-three at the time of the trial, felt Brian was honest and credible. "His testimony was imperative to the case since Denise decided not to testify," she said. "He owned up to what he did."

The chorus of viewers watching the trial on YouTube concurred. In the comments, people described Brian's testimony as "emotional," "dramatic," and "incredible." The majority believed him. "I've never seen a more genuinely remorseful testimony," wrote one. A second called it "compelling watching and listening." Others agreed: "I believe everything this man said." "This is the most honest painful confession I have ever watched . . ." "You can tell that Brian feels pure remorse . . . for what he did. This entire thing has been eating him up alive for decades." "This confession is captivating. It is the anatomy of a murder in real time." "Imagine having to live with this for 17 years."

There was something else that seemed to confirm Brian was telling the truth, and that was Denise's demeanor in the courtroom. If she'd truly had nothing to do with the crime, this would have been the very first time she'd learned that Mike hadn't been eaten by alligators but murdered by her ex-husband. Yet when Brian described shooting Mike in the face and hauling his bloody corpse into the back of his truck, Denise seemed unmoved. To those watching the trial online, this clinched it. Denise was "the alligator everyone was searching for." "Pure evil." "Clearly a sociopath." "Cold-hearted." "One cold-blooded woman."

Emotionally, people respond in different ways. Some don't wear their hearts on their sleeves. In moments of intense stress, most people show their feelings—they shake, burst into tears, or go weak at the knees. But others are different: They may go numb, laugh nervously, or enter a state of denial, appearing detached and aloof.

No question: Denise's stoicism in the courtroom should not have been held against her. Who knows why she didn't display any emotion? Maybe she'd already been prepared for Brian's testimony. Maybe her attorneys had gently broken the news to her beforehand. Maybe she'd resolved to keep calm for her daughter's sake, or the sake of her family and friends in the courtroom. Maybe she'd prayed to God for strength. Maybe she'd taken a couple of Valium. The defense attorney Phil Padovano gave Denise a practice cross-examination; he said, "I made her cry in about three minutes." To Padovano, Denise wasn't hardhearted; she was simply a "formal" and "buttoned-down" kind of person, unaccustomed to letting her feelings show.

———

When Judge Hankinson told the jury they'd been selected for a high-profile murder case, Joslyn Bynum couldn't help getting excited. "It felt surreal," she recalled. "It was like something you'd see in a movie or an episode of *Criminal Minds*."

Deliberations took eight hours, which, although it doesn't sound long, is a lot longer than usual—for trials involving major crimes, the average jury deliberation time is between two and three hours and can be as short as eleven minutes. And while juries are told emphatically not to start deliberating until they've heard all the evidence, this is asking the impossible. It goes against human nature. We evaluate people constantly, even if we're not conscious of it. Juries start judging the defendant from the moment they're sworn in, if not earlier. They may not always admit it—they may not even be aware of it—but it's what happens in the courtroom, not the jury room, that leads to the verdict. Jurors change their minds, of course, but you can only change your mind if it's already made up.

Why else would juries typically take a vote right after the trial, if not to see what people already thought? In *Florida v. Denise Williams*, as usual, jury proceedings began with a brief show of hands. "I would say at least half of us walked into the deliberation room with our minds made up," recalled Bynum. "We knew Denise was guilty." Still, the jurors took their duties very seriously. They knew gut instinct wasn't enough. Bynum looked forward to deliberating. "I didn't want to put someone in jail without absolutely being sure."

According to the brief show of hands, at least eight of the twelve jurors agreed with Bynum. They concurred on two things: Brian's confession was highly plausible, and Denise showed "no emotion at all." The remaining time was spent trying to convince the holdouts. Using a whiteboard, each juror presented their arguments, explaining how they'd come to their conclusion. Bynum remembered discussions about "affairs" and "swinging," but she didn't believe the more lurid aspects of the case played a part in the jury's decision.

James Karabasz was the final holdout. His argument was this: Even if Brian was telling the truth about Denise (and he had every reason to throw her to the wolves), all she agreed to was that Brian would push Mike out of the boat as a "test of God's will." After that point, Brian acted as a free agent. He couldn't confer with Denise in the moment and didn't tell her what he'd done after the fact. All she ever learned was that Mike didn't survive the "accident." For all she knew, his body had been lost in the lake. It might very well have been eaten by alligators.

This, Karabasz felt, was a long way from first-degree murder. Criminal conspiracy, at the most. For the sake of his fellow jurors, he asked the judge to clarify their instructions. "If the defendant helped another person or persons commit the crime of first-degree murder," they were told, "the defendant is a principal and must be treated as if she had done all the things the other person or persons had done." Karabasz was finally persuaded: If they found Denise guilty of conspiracy to commit murder, they also had to find her guilty of murder in the first degree.

Still, that night he found it hard to sleep.

———

The jury returned to the courtroom.

Everyone held their breath. Some looked down and closed their eyes. Others began to pray. Judge Hankinson admonished the onlookers: Outbursts of emotion would not be tolerated. He waited for a moment, then asked the jury foreperson to step forward.

There were three charges: Conspiracy to commit first-degree murder, first-degree murder, and accessory after the fact.

The verdict: guilty, guilty, guilty.

—————

In November 2020, the Florida First District Court of Appeal overturned Denise's murder conviction. "The State, according to the Appeal Court, failed to prove that Denise acted as a principal to first-degree murder," the Appeal Court decided. "Her only ostensibly culpable conduct . . . did not constitute commanding or impelling Brian to commit the murder . . . or the assisting or encouraging of Brian at the time he was actually committing the offense."

Denise was no longer guilty of first-degree murder, and as a result, her life sentence was overturned. But she was still guilty of conspiracy to commit first-degree murder, and although there was no need for another trial, she did need to be resentenced. This took place in Leon County Courtroom 3-A at 9 a.m. on September 9, 2021. The court was closed to press and public, but the proceedings were filmed, and footage was made available to the media. The witnesses read preprepared statements, and no questioning was allowed.

At the time of her resentencing, Denise had been in prison for three years and four months. She was serving her sentence at the Florida Women's Reception Center, twelve miles north of Ocala and a three-hour drive from Tallahassee. The prison is set back on a road lined with palmetto and Norway spruce in a landscape of farms, churches, ranches, equestrian centers, and dog breeders. It's a long way from her former life.

By this time, both Brian and Denise had been in prison long enough to accept the situation, and to adapt. Most of us view the prospect of incarceration—quite rightly—with horror, but the truth is, people get used to all kinds of restrictions. A situation that seems intolerable will, in time, become bearable, then manageable, then, finally, taken for granted. What hurts most is the sudden precipitous change, the shock of the plunge.

———

"Hangman" Hankinson retired in 2018; Judge Kevin Carroll had taken his place. For the conspiracy charge, the lowest possible sentence would be twenty-one months, which would mean that, given the time she'd already served, Denise could be released immediately. If things didn't go in her favor, her thirty-year conspiracy sentence would remain unchanged.

Denise's three sisters, Deborah, Darla, and Deanna, testified as character witnesses. They stood before the judge together, and Deanna read a statement prepared by all three. They described Denise as "generous, positive, gracious, compassionate, hardworking, and humble." They loved her, were proud of her, and were eager for her to come home. When she was released, they said, she planned to help continue working with women in the Florida prison system.

The next character witness was Denise's longtime friend and coworker Carla Daniels. She described Denise as "one of the kindest, most genuine people that I know," someone who was dedicated to helping others in the church and community. According to Carla, Denise made loving connections with those less fortunate, raising her daughter to be humble and God-fearing, just like herself. The way the state attorney and the media had depicted her, said Carla, was "laughable."

Denise herself took the stand next. When she'd appeared in court two years earlier, her hair had been blond and shoulder-length, like that of her sisters, although the blond had been growing out. Now her hair was completely brown and hung almost to her waist. She wore prison blues, a standard-issue mask (the hearing occurred during the coronavirus pandemic), and plain, round glasses. While far from glamorous and perhaps a little too thin, she was still attractive, in a stern and simple way. She read her statement quickly, in a low voice broken by sniffs and stifled sobs. At moments, she was overcome with emotion and needed to pause and get ahold of herself. "I have never and would never want anyone to be murdered, not even the people that want this for me," she began. But she was, she confessed, "guilty of great moral failure at a time in my life when I chose to make a reckless decision that affected everyone around me, and for that, I am truly sorry."

Nothing she could do would bring Mike back, said Denise, adding, "If I could trade my life for his right now, then I would." As that was impossible, she said, she had been "striving every day to turn this nightmare into something good." She said the years away from family and friends had shown her many things about herself that had been hard to face. In the past, while she served God and gave to charity, she admitted, "I only gave out of my excess, and I only served others when it was convenient for me." Three years in prison had opened her eyes to her "selfishness and pride." She expressed deep penitence and said she had a new mission: to help "each precious lady that I've met in prison." To this end, she said, she'd started a GED prep class and directed educational seminars. If the judge reduced her sentence to the minimum of twenty-one months, she promised to continue her prison ministry from the outside.

Next, with her attorney Baja Harrison by her side, Denise's daughter, Anslee, addressed the judge. In media coverage of the proceedings, her image was pixelated by the camera, as is a right for members of a victim's family in Florida. Anslee read her statement rapidly, like her mother, only her voice was louder and more confident. This was strictly a sentencing hearing—the court had already decided the facts of the case—still, Anslee wanted the judge to know that "there is no way my mother would conspire with Brian to kill my father." She said her mother had done everything in her power to keep Mike's memory alive.

After her mother married Brian, said Anslee, she saw how dominating he was, how he often acted independently, on the spur of the moment, paying no attention to what she or her mother felt. Anslee said that prison was taking a great "physical and emotional toll" on her mother, which made her "deeply concerned." She presented the two of them, mother and daughter, as united in victimhood against Brian. She asked Judge Carroll to "please consider the lowest sentence of twenty-one months so that she can come home, and we can begin to heal together from the pain he caused us."

Cheryl was the only witness for the prosecution. There was a slight struggle to get her wheelchair through the door, and to attach her microphone. She wore a knee-length black skirt, blue orthopedic socks, a paisley-print blouse, blue cardigan, and a blue polka-dot mask. As she began her statement, she put on a pair of heavy-framed black glasses.

Her voice amplified by the microphone, Cheryl reminded the judge that Denise had plotted with Brian to kill her husband because although she didn't want to remain married, she didn't want to get divorced either, as "a divorce would ruin her social reputation." In addition, she didn't want to share custody of Anslee, and "she wanted to collect a five-hundred-thousand-dollar life insurance policy before it lapsed." The bereft mother described her agony when Mike went missing, her unending search, her struggle for publicity and to keep the investigation open while also working full-time. She described holding her sign on Sunday in front of the local churches "whose ministers would cuss me out and tell me to leave."

"Judge Carroll," said Cheryl. "My granddaughter was raised by two murderers while being denied the love and support of her father's family." She said the coroner had told her that "Mike didn't suffer when he died." At this point, her voice rose and cracked, becoming a desperate wail. "What about the time he was trying to get out of his waders in the freezing waters of Lake Seminole?" she cried. "What about the time he's clinging to a stump in the dark, knowing his best friend, whom he loved, is going to kill him? Mike suffered horribly. For the rest of my life, at night, when I try to go to sleep, I will see my son clinging to a stump . . . I will hear him screaming for help . . . It will haunt me forever."

Cheryl said Denise didn't deserve any mercy. She hadn't shown any mercy to Mike. "For seventeen years," she reminded the judge, "Denise traveled the world spending Mike's insurance money while his dead body was crammed into a muddy hole under Lake Carr." In the interests of justice, said Cheryl, Denise should serve "every minute of her thirty-year sentence for conspiracy to commit murder." Her sobs echoed down the hallway long after she'd been wheeled out of court.

After a few moments of coughing and paper-shuffling, Jon Fuchs took the stand. After Cheryl's plaintive eloquence, Fuchs, once again, seemed clumsy and heavy-handed. He mumbled, getting names mixed up, tying himself grammatically in knots. He replayed long segments of Denise's phone call with Kathy. He repeated Brian's confession. He described Mike's death. He evoked Denise's old "party name," Meridian, arguing that this was her secret self, her alter ego. Those who claimed Denise was a "devoted mother" had "clearly never met Meridian." It was "Meridian," not Denise, who had carefully plotted to murder Anslee's father, then cut off all contact with her father's family, telling her daughter that Cheryl was "crazy." During her statement, Denise had wept. "There's a term called 'crocodile tears,'" said Fuchs. "I think, in this case, 'alligator tears' would be a more appropriate wording." The first time she heard what had happened to Mike, Fuchs wondered, "Where were the tears then?"

As he drew to the end of his address, Fuchs shifted uncomfortably from foot to foot, putting his hands in his pockets, then taking them out again and leaning on the stand. He quoted from "a book called *The New Land*": "I see no evil because love is blind." Love may be blind, but the trial jury was not blind, Fuchs reminded the judge. Everyone had seen photographic evidence of "Meridian having a threesome with her co-conspirator and his wife." The person standing in court before them was not Denise Williams, insisted Fuchs, but "Meridian." He asked the judge to "sentence Ms. Williams—Meridian—to thirty years in the Department of Corrections."

Philip Padovano, on behalf of the defense, had the last word. As he'd done at trial, Padovano appeared polished, delicate, and genteel, especially in contrast with the bluff, lumbering Jon Fuchs. The state attorney, said Padovano, seemed to be implying that the crime of conspiracy was committed not by Denise but "by somebody else—somebody named Meridian." Throughout Fuchs's speech, Padovano said he was sitting there, "and I'm thinking, 'Why is he saying that?'" Finally, it dawned on him: Fuchs had to make Denise out to be a monster for her to get the sentence he thought she deserved. In fact, argued Padovano, anyone who looked at Denise's record would see that she was a gentle, generous person, not a "monster," and a sentence of thirty years "isn't even remotely justifiable." Padovano asked the judge to "get beyond the fantasy" and to see Denise for what she truly was.

He reminded the judge that the jury had convicted Denise of conspiracy on the word of Brian Winchester, the man who committed the murder, and nothing more—and the state had given Brian complete immunity. As a result, Denise was the only person whose punishment could satisfy Cheryl Williams's grief, "and that's not fair." He said that the Court of Appeals had affirmed that, even if Brian was telling the absolute truth, Denise had very little involvement in the crime. He pointed to Denise's excellent work in the Department of Corrections, where she'd been teaching Bible studies, helping to set up a GED program, and giving piano lessons to fellow inmates. Padovano reminded the court that the legislature had established minimum sentence guidelines for appropriate circumstances, and what case could be more suitable than this?

But sentences don't always meet the intention of the legislature. In this case, even before Cheryl's desperate plea, there was no possibility of a lesser sentence. As Padovano recognized, someone had to pay for the death of Mike Williams and redeem his mother's grief. Judge Carroll said he'd read all the letters from Denise's family and friends and the letters from Cheryl and the Williams family. He said it was "a sad case, a tragedy," but didn't find it appropriate that Denise's punishment should be reduced, and he judged that she should serve her original thirty-year sentence.

She'll be eligible for release in May 2047, at the age of seventy-seven.

– 4 –

The Eve Factor

"And the Lord God said unto the woman, What is this that thou hast done? And the woman said, The serpent beguiled me, and I did eat."

GENESIS 3:13

After the trial, people in Tallahassee made it clear that the murder of Mike Williams had always been an open secret. But if "everybody knew" Brian and Denise had killed Mike, why were the lovers allowed to go about their lives undisturbed for almost seventeen years? Blame was cast in all directions, but in truth, the community itself bore responsibility: the hypocrisy of social rituals, the shield of religion, the veneer of civility, people's reluctance to get involved.

But civil procedures have their benefits; if the community covered up the crime, it also brought the perpetrators to justice. Brian and Denise turned on each other, in part, because they could feel the local pressure building, especially after the airing of *Disappeared* in 2011. Cheryl's refusal to let go, Jennifer Portman's investigative journalism, Mike DeVaney's detective work, and the stress of divorce proceedings caused Brian's defenses to shatter, leading to his final breakdown.

―――――

A trial is a performance—a public drama of indictment, defense, deliberation, and sentencing. Whatever a jury might claim and despite the legal fiction of "objectivity," the verdict comes down to a matter of sympathy. Some people are simply more likable than others. This is why defendants are discouraged from taking the stand, especially in high-profile murder cases; when they do, instead of the facts of the case, the jury—although they may try not to—can't help judging the defendant's attitude, demeanor, choice of words, even hairstyle and fashion choices.

An apology, too, is a performance. Most of the people who witnessed Brian's confession instinctively believed his remorse and contrition, although some were unconvinced; they thought he was just a talented actor. Either way, Brian wasn't on trial, so the state had nothing to lose by putting him on the stand. A confession, by its very nature, is a renunciation of lying and deceit. By admitting his guilt, Brian accepted responsibility for his crime; he had a conscience, it seemed, and a sense of right and wrong. His fits of weeping restored his humanity, making him seem vulnerable and exposed. The murder, he confessed, was committed for reasons of greed and passion. But as he described the circumstances of his affair, his marriage, his relationship with his father, and the psychological pressures that weighed on him, the crime came to seem less of an isolated act.

Denise, on the other hand, remained a blank slate. Those watching the trial never got to know her the way they got to know Brian. Instead of a real person with a conscience and a human heart, she became an archetype, a force of evil. Ethan Way concluded, "The jurors were looking at my client's lifestyle and appearance and not the facts," and if the comments on social media reflected feelings in the jury room, he was right. People noted gleefully that her dark roots were showing now that she couldn't dye her hair, as if her true malice was creeping out beneath her disguise. There was a lot of gossip about threesomes, adultery, and strippers. Denise was stigmatized for being sexually impassioned, even insatiable; at the same time, she was also condemned for her coldness, her heart of stone.

After his client was found guilty, Denise's attorney Ethan Way explained: "There is an ingrained concept I call the 'Eve Factor.' When a man and woman face a crime together and one is thought to be the mastermind, it is generally the 'Eve' who tempts the 'Adam.'" Adulterous relationships aren't unusual, nor, unfortunately, are murders that grow out of them. When lovers plot to kill the wife's husband, or the husband's wife, although the woman might help plan the murder, it's almost always the man who carries it out. But the woman is punished equally, if not more so, and unlike her co-conspirator, she's publicly sex shamed. She's scorned, ridiculed, and condemned, described as a Black Widow, a Jezebel, or a Delilah. Examples are easy to find.

————

It's commonplace murders, not grotesque or bizarre ones, that hit the public nerve. The Winchester-Williams case exemplified a kind of thrilling hubris: adulterous Baptist lovers beat a murder rap, collect on the insurance, but can't escape each other. People love a tale of outrage and scandal; they love to witness the unmasking of those who haven't practiced what they preach. It's a wish-fulfillment fantasy: Accomplices turn on each other. A mother, despite gossiping naysayers, never stops fighting to find her missing son. Murder will out, however long it takes. And when the case comes to trial, the adversarial nature of proceedings panders to public interest. Complex situations are reduced to simple terms: the binaries of victim or villain, good or evil, guilty or innocent.

Setting, too, added spice to the story. The passion, greed, deception, and fraud unfolded in Tallahassee's manicured subdivisions: Killearn Lakes, Foxcroft, Midyette Plantation, Royal Oaks. This is first-generation suburbia, an ecosystem of oak-shaded brick-and-mortar homes, cul-de-sacs, beltways, megachurches, outlet malls, and big box stores—clean, prosperous, exclusive, safe, and repressed. It's a "great place to raise a family." But let's not forget—most murders take place at home.

Domestic crimes are both unspeakable and banal, motivated by sharper versions of everyday emotions: desire, envy, anger, greed. Mike's murder took place in the context of ordinary domestic relations, and people eagerly consumed the details. The full trial was posted on YouTube, giving millions of strangers access to intimate letters, phone calls, and photographs. They saw and heard details of secret encounters. By studying the homicide file, which was posted online, people could peer into Brian's and Denise's private lives: orthodonture bills, shopping at CVS, home meal kits, soccer practice, reality television, family vacations—the same ordinary middle-class lives led by the true-crime fans, primarily female, who eagerly follow cases online.

It's easy to assume that familiarity robs a story of its intrinsic interest, but the contrary is true—events are uniquely engrossing when they're closer to home. The more alike we are, the more hypersensitive we become to tiny differences. There was a vast outpouring of sympathy for Cheryl, but was it possible that many of those following the case recognized themselves, albeit unconsciously, in Brian or Denise? We don't want to accept how similar we are to someone who's done something reprehensible, so we exaggerate minor distinctions to separate ourselves from them. We try to find an otherness to disguise our sameness.

The public judged—and harshly. Brian and Denise were trashy and ugly; their story was lurid and tawdry, a cheap tabloid scandal. It was also a guilty pleasure. People loved the inside scoop, the intimate glimpse into the couple's "dirty little secrets" ("this case is so full of drama . . . it feels like I'm watching a soap opera"). They enjoyed gossiping about Brian and Denise's "out-in-the-open affair," "countless acts of adultery, hanging out in strip clubs," "wild partying, concert-going, bar-hopping," "mutual guilt, partying, and make-up sex." Outside the state, the Florida setting was titillating. The alligators made a great punch line.

According to press and public, Denise was the main antagonist: rapacious, devious, and sinister. She betrayed her loyal, hardworking husband to indulge her "off-the-chart" sexual desires. She entangled the weakling Brian in her evil web; she lured him away from gentle, home-loving Kathy. Perverse and sexually aggressive, she used female trickery to gain wealth, freedom, and independence; she was the archetypal "femme fatale" ("Black Widow Liked Threesomes and Murder," declared the *Toronto Sun*). Although the pair were considered equally elemental and cold-blooded in their pursuit of money, power, and community status, it was Denise, according to press and public, who opened Pandora's box, unleashing sorrow and grief into the Tallahassee suburbs.

————

When a crime comes to light after almost twenty years, it supports the belief that "murder will out." In fact, the current "clearance rate" for homicide (to use the FBI's terminology) is around 50 percent, and this only includes reported murders. It doesn't include cases where the murder is successfully disguised as an accident, or when the victim "goes missing" and never comes home. Most murders, it's fair to say, are never solved. And while Brian and Denise were brought to justice, how many other couples lie together in bed at night with the shadow of a murder in their hearts—a weight, perhaps, that gets a little lighter every day?

In a high-profile murder case, the public learns everything about the perpetrator—their habits, choices, tendencies, predilections. Everyone looks for explanations and confirmations; they want to imagine that this person, who seems on the outside just like them, is secretly a "psychopath" or "narcissist." In this way, ordinary people are sensationalized, made glamorous and fantastic, forced into roles that match the public's expectations. Making people into archetypes is how we distance ourselves from them, renouncing our similarities and connections. But in truth, those who commit terrible crimes have ambivalent emotions and complex relationships like anyone else; they change over time; they're tangled up with family, community, sex, religion, and the wider world.

A murder is a crash at the intersection of two lives, splitting them open at the seams, laying them bare for analysis and speculation. Yet for all this poking and probing, we remain in the dark, trying to convince ourselves this horrible event is an aberration. We don't want to admit that people who commit murder are just like the rest of us. But there is no "rest of us." There's just us.

Notes

v *I have heard*: William Shakespeare, *Hamlet*, Arden edition (Bloomsbury, 2006), 278.

1.
The Four of Us

3 *"I am now"*: John Muir, *A Thousand Mile Walk to the Gulf* (1867) (Houghton Mifflin, 1916), 93.

4 *land speculators and desperadoes*: Edward Waldo Emerson and Waldo Emerson Forbes, eds., *Journals of Ralph Waldo Emerson 1820–1872*, with Annotations, 10 vols. (Houghton Mifflin, 1909–1914), II, 149–90.

4 *"a small town with big pants on"*: See "engineergraves," "What was growing up in Tallahassee like?" Reddit.com forum, www.reddit.com/r/Tallahassee /comments/klh4ri/what_was_growing_up_in_tallahassee_like/ (accessed May 3, 2022).

4 *"slumbrous, voluptuous"*: Edward King, *The Great South*, ed. W. Magruder Drake and Robert R. Jones (Baton Rouge, 1972), 380–81.

4 *pine, hickory, and magnolias*: Andre F. Clewell, "Prior Prevalence of Short-leaf Pine-Oak-Hickory Woodlands in the Tallahassee Red Hills," *Castanea* 78, No. 4 (December 2013), 266–76.

5 *misogynistic gunman . . . fatally*: The gunman, who committed suicide after the attack, was Scott Paul Beierle, age forty. See Chas Danner, "What

to Know About the Tallahassee Yoga Studio Attack," *New York*, November 2018, nymag.com/intelligencer/2018/11/what-to-know-about-the-talla hassee-yoga-studio-attack.html (accessed November 20, 2022).

5 *over child support payments:* A jury found Segura guilty of the 2010 murders of Brandi Peters and her three children, one of whom was also Segura's son. As in the Winchester-Williams case, his trial was presided over by Judge James Hankinson, and the prosecutor was Jon Fuchs. After a 2017 mistrial, nine years after the murders, Segura received a life sentence in 2019. See *Segura v. State of Florida*, case no. 1D19-4266, Nov. 3, 2021 (rejected appeal). www.1dca.org/content/download/801247/opin ion/194266_DC05_11032021_140442_i.pdf.

5 *periodontist brother:* Markel was killed in a murder-for-hire in 2014, motivated by child custody issues following his divorce. The case is still ongoing. Charlie Adelson (Markel's ex-wife's brother) was arrested in 2022 and charged with first-degree murder, conspiracy to commit murder, and solicitation of murder, but has not yet been tried.

5 *the couple's swimming pool:* This story was also covered by Jennifer Portman, whose investigations helped reopen the Winchester/Williams case. See Jennifer Portman, "Frasch Murder Investigation Reveals Couple's Volatile Relationship," *Tallahassee Democrat*, February 21, 2015, p. 1.

5 *Ted Bundy . . . killing two:* "Ted Bundy and His Tallahassee Reign of Terror," *Tallahassee Democrat*, January 23, 2019.

5 *badly fitting door:* Stephen J. Whitfield, "Florida's Fudged Identity," *Florida Historical Quarterly* 71, no. 4 (April 1993), 413–35.

6 *pink and white balloons:* Descriptions of Brian, Denise, Kathy, and Mike are taken from their photographs in the 1988 North Florida Christian High School Yearbook, pp. 14, 19, 23, and 224.

6 *"homosexuality, lesbianism . . . action":* Quotes taken from North Florida Christian High School 2016–17 Middle School High School Planner and Student Handbook. See quotes posted online at www.reddit.com/r/Tal lahassee/comments/ewsdi6/check_out_north_florida_christian_anti lgbt/.

7 *"very strong" belief in God*: Details of churchgoing, from phone interview with Cheryl Williams, April 9, 2022.

9 *commuting to class*: Mike, a C-grade student, spent a year at Florida A&M University in Tallahassee before transferring to FSU. Phone interview with Cheryl Williams, April 9, 2022.

9 *autocratic leadership . . . power*: See Coralie Buxant and Vassilis Saroglou, "Feeling Good, but Lacking Autonomy: Closed-Mindedness on Social and Moral Issues in New Religious Movements," *Journal of Religion and Health* 47, no. 1 (March 2008), 20.

10 *widespread paranoia*: James C. Hefley, *The Truth in Crisis: The Conservative Resurgence in the Southern Baptist Convention*, vol. 6 (Hannibal Books, 2008).

11 *covering up the abuse*: For full details of the Baptist church sexual abuse scandal, see Robert Downen et al., "Abuse of Faith," *Houston Chronicle*, February 10, 2019, www.houstonchronicle.com/news/investigations/abuse-of-faith/ (accessed November 21, 2022).

12 *Cake and lemonade*: Deposition of Katherine Anne Thomas, August 22, 2018, 9:30 a.m., Waynesville, N.C., case no. 2018-CF-001592, *Florida v. Denise Williams*, Circuit Court of the Second Judicial Court, Leon County, Florida, 29, 48.

14 *"He's just got to work"*: Details about Mike's work habits and relationship with money from interview with Clay and Patti Ketcham at Ketcham Appraisals in Tallahassee, July 22, 2022.

14 *"He worked almost twenty-four hours a day"*: Interview with Clay and Patti Ketcham, December 4, 2006, p. 2, Jerry Michael Williams Homicide FDLE Case Number TL-1-0102. Investigators Derrick Wester and Donnie Branch, case no. 00121624.

14 *set her nerves on edge*: Cheryl Williams submitted all her notes and journals about Mike's disappearance to FDLE; these are contained in the homicide file. This is from a document entitled "Personal History," p. 1 (these documents are hereafter referred to as "personal history," and "correspondence and notes"). See Jerry Michael Williams Homicide FDLE Case Number TL-1-0102.

15 *"It wasn't uncommon"*: Details about Mike's work habits and relationship with money from interview with Clay and Patti Ketcham at Ketcham Appraisals in Tallahassee, July 22, 2022.

2.
Alligators in the Winter

17 *"This is the law"*: Leviticus 11:46. King James Version.

17 *12:30 p.m.*: Although only an hour from Tallahassee, Sneads is in the Central Time Zone, but for the sake of ease and consistency, Eastern Time is used throughout.

17 *Once before . . . happened again*: Details of Mike's disappearance taken from Jerry Michael Williams Homicide FDLE Case Number TL-1-0102. Investigators Derrick Wester and Donnie Branch, case no. 00-121624, Interview with Deanna Lamb, October 5, 2005, pp. 3–4.

20 *unreasonable risks*: Cheryl and Nick Williams, Howard Drew, and other friends and family members insisted that Mike was always careful to follow safety procedures, but Clay Ketcham told investigators, "It's not unlike Mike to take risks out hunting and fishing, I mean he, we've seen him go thirty miles offshore by himself in four- or five-foot seas uh, grouper fishing." Others said they'd known Mike to stand up in the boat to take a trick shot. See Jerry Michael Williams Homicide FDLE Case Number TL-1-0102. Investigators Derrick Wester and Donnie Branch, case no. 001-21624, Interview with Clay and Patti Ketcham, 10.04.06, p. 3.

20 *"a friendly conversation"*: Cheryl Williams, "Personal History," p. 7. Jerry Michael Williams Homicide, FDLE Case Number TL-1-0102. JCSO box, "correspondence and notes."

21 *"bitterly cold"*: This quotation is taken from Scott Dungey's testimony, *Florida v. Denise Williams*, Circuit Court of the Second Judicial Court, Leon County, Florida, Transcript of Jury Trial, volume 1 (December 11, 2018), p. 89.

25 *struggled to remove it*: Details from Jerry Michael Williams Homicide

FDLE Case Number TL-1-0102. Kansas City Life Insurance File. Petition for Presumptive Death Certificate, p. 226.

25 *Hurricanes come out of nowhere*: No doubt partly because of its many lakes, Florida has far more boating-related fatalities than any other state. See Curry Pajcic, "Florida Leads Nation in Boating Accidents and Fatalities," Pajcic & Pajcic Law firm blog, August 20, 2022, www.pajcic.com/florida-leads-na tion-in-boating-accidents-and-fatalities/ (accessed November 20, 2022). Statistics on boating accidents available from the Florida Fish and Wildlife Conservation Commission. The 2021 numbers are available at myfwc.com /media/29126/2021-basr-trends.pdf (accessed November 21, 2022).

25 *a thirty-four-year-old duck hunter*: The victim was John Mark Slappey. "Search Continues for Missing Duck Hunter on Lake Seminole," WALB News 10, December 29, 2009, www.walb.com/story/11716659/search -continues-for-missing-duck-hunter-on-lake-seminole/ (accessed No-vember 20, 2022).

25 *hydrilla and fishing line*: Willie Matthew, fifty-six, was found underwater, wrapped in fishing line and hydrilla. "Investigation into Lake Semi-nole Death Underway," WALB News 10, May 1, 2017, www.walb.com /story/35298814/investigation-into-lake-seminole-death-underway/ (ac-cessed November 20, 2022).

26 *kept them on the leash*: See Cotton States Insurance File, Montgomery County Search and Rescue Summary of Search Operations, May 6, 2001, Lake Seminole Florida, p. 33. Jerry Michael Williams Homicide FDLE Case Number TL-1-0102.

26 *"submerged alligator"*: Ibid.

27 *"hunting jacket"*: Special Agents Cesar Salandha and Diana Hunter, taped interview with Charles English, March 4, 2008, pp. 13–14. Jerry Michael Williams Homicide FDLE Case Number TL-1-0102.

28 *"a lot of information"*: Investigators Derrick Wester and Donnie Branch, case no. 00-121624, interview with Deanna Lamb, October 5, 2005, p. 22. See Jerry Michael Williams Homicide FDLE Case Number TL-1-0102.

28 *nonfatal attacks . . . January*: Statistics taken from Ricky Langley, "Alligator Attacks on Humans in the United States," *Wilderness and Environmental Medicine* 16 (3), 119–24.

3.
Your Son Is in the Lake

29 *"Almost without exception"*: Gary Haupt, "Drowning Investigations," *FBI Law Enforcement Bulletin* 75, issue 2 (February 2006), 20.

29 *"You have to bring him home"*: Deposition of Cheryl Williams, August 9, 2018, 11:30 a.m., Leon County Courthouse, Tallahassee, FL, case no. 2018-CF-001592, *Florida v. Denise Williams*, Circuit Court of the Second Judicial Court, Leon County, Florida, p. 5.

30 *"every hole"*: Cheryl Williams, "Personal History," p. 2. Jerry Michael Williams Homicide FDLE Case Number TL-1-0102. JCSO box, "correspondence and notes."

31 *"Alligators did not eat your son!"*: Ibid., JCSO box, "correspondence and notes." Cheryl Williams, "Missing Information from 2001," pp. 31–32.

32 *"I have a mother"*: Cheryl Williams, "Missing Information from 2001," pp. 31–32.

32 *"It would kill the alligator"*: Ibid.

32 *August 5, 2001*: Tony Bridges, "Missing People Not Lost Causes," *Tallahassee Democrat*, August 5, 2001, p. 1. Later, Cheryl's case was taken up by Jennifer Portman at the *Democrat*.

32 *"knowing who he is"*: Cheryl Williams, cited in ibid.

33 *her journal*: Cheryl Williams, "Personal History," p. 10.

34 *"she is dating"*: Ibid., pp. 23–24.

35 *"could look legally"*: Cheryl Williams, "Missing Information from 2001," pp. 2–5. Jerry Michael Williams Homicide FDLE Case Number TL-1-0102, JCSO box, "correspondence and notes."

36 *"THANK YOU"*: Ibid., p. 5. Capitals in original.

37 *"I looked everywhere—nothing"*: Ibid.

37 *"that he's okay?"*: Ibid., p. 15.

37 *bothering Denise at work*: Ibid., p. 11.

4.
Persons of Interest

39 *" 'Had a husband once' "*: Raymond Chandler, *The Big Sleep & Farewell My Lovely* (Modern Library, 1995), 314.

39 *at a stoplight*: Cheryl Williams, "correspondence and notes," p. 19.

39 *"what prison is like?"*: Ibid.

40 *in a fancy hotel*: Ibid.

40 *"what you want me to know"*: Cheryl Williams, "correspondence and notes," February 26, 2004.

41 *"You are not crazy"*: Ibid.

42 *"said something earlier"*: Ibid., p. 22.

42 *"She's too thin!"*: Ibid., p. 43.

42 *"Get Denise to eat"*: Ibid., p. 45.

42 *"to survive it"*: Ibid., p. 47.

43 *going duck hunting*: Interview with Clay and Patti Ketcham, Ketcham Appraisals, Tallahassee, July 22, 2022.

44 *"advice of the experts"*: Sworn statement of Cheryl Ann Williams, May 30, 2018, case no. 2018-CF-001592, *State vs. Denise Williams*, Circuit Court of the Second Judicial Court, Leon County, Florida, p. 1.

45 *"Not even Denise's makeup"*: Cheryl Williams, "Diary notes, 2004," p. 35. Jerry Michael Williams Homicide FDLE Case Number TL-1-0102. JCSO box, "correspondence and notes."

45 *went to the lake alone*: Cheryl Williams, "Diary notes, 2004," p. 35–36. JCSO box, "correspondence and notes."

47 *"spoke of it again"*: Jerry Michael Williams Homicide FDLE Case Number TL-1-0102. Investigators Derrick Wester and Donnie Branch, case no. 00121624, interview with Deanna Lamb, October 5, 2005, p. 52.

48 *for lunch*: Ibid., p. 27.

48 *metal detector*: Ibid.

50 *"an overwhelming compulsion"*: Ibid.

51 *on December 21*: Deposition of Denise Williams, December 22, 2004, *Florida v. Denise Williams*, Circuit Court of the Second Judicial Court, Leon County, Florida, p. 4.

51 *"sorry for her"*: Ibid., p. 26.

1.
David and Bathsheba

55 *"Hell could have"*: James M. Cain, *The Postman Always Rings Twice, Double Indemnity, Mildred Pierce and Selected Stories* (Everyman's Library, Random House: 1941), 41.

55 *"had grown up"*: Quotes taken from deposition of Katherine Anne Thomas, August 22, 2018, 9:30 a.m., Waynesville, N.C., case no. 2018-CF-001592, *Florida v. Denise Williams*, Circuit Court of the Second Judicial Court, Leon County, Florida, p. 35.

56 *"To Meridian"*: Details of the foursome's "wild years" in their early twenties are taken from Katherine Anne Thomas's witness testimony, *Florida v. Denise Williams*, Circuit Court of the Second Judicial Court, Leon County, Florida, Transcript of Jury Trial, vol. 5 (December 13, 2018), p. 561.

56 *"ready to have kids"*: Deposition of Katherine Anne Thomas, August 22, 2018, 9:30 a.m., Waynesville, N.C., case no. 2018-CF-001592, *Florida v. Denise Williams*, Circuit Court of the Second Judicial Court, Leon County, Florida, p. 37.

56 *thought about little else*: Jerry Michael Williams Homicide FDLE Case Number TL-1-0102, Brian Winchester, notes, p. 38. After Brian's arrest in 2017, his notes, journals, and emails were all subpoenaed by the prosecution and are contained in the homicide file. These documents are hereafter referred to as "Brian Winchester, notes."

56 *looked at porn daily*: Ibid., p. 38.

57 *"what sex should've been"*: Ibid.

57 *"two of us"*: Brian Winchester, testimony, *Florida v. Denise Williams*, Circuit Court of the Second Judicial Court, Leon County, Florida, Transcript of Jury Trial, vol. 2 (December 11, 2018), pp. 201–202.

58 *"her and I"*: All details of Brian and Denise's hookups given here, see ibid., p. 203.

59 *"down the drainage ditch"*: Ibid., p. 205.

59 *"forbidden sexual activities"*: Ibid.

60 *Brian would recall*: Ibid., vol. 3 (December 12, 2018), p. 281.

60 *release of self-control*: For research on the correlation between moral behavior and sexual experience, see Caroline Rigo, Filip Uzarevic, and Vassilis Saroglou, "Make Love and Lose Your Religion and Virtue: Recalling Sexual Experiences Undermines Spiritual Intentions and Moral Behavior," *Journal for the Scientific Study of Religion* 55, no. 1 (March 2016), 29.

61 *"I had it pretty good"*: Office of the State Attorney, Circuit Court of the Second Judicial Court, Leon County, Florida. Proffer of Brian Winchester, 2016, case no. CF 02265. Transcript of recorded interview, Leon County Jail, October 12, 2017, p. 59.

61 *"between [Mike and Denise]"*: Patti Ketcham. Interview with Clay and Patti Ketcham, Ketcham Appraisals, Tallahassee, July 22, 2022.

61 *"kept her juices flowing"*: Ibid.

61 *"worse and worse"*: Brian Winchester, testimony, *Florida v. Denise Williams*, Circuit Court of the Second Judicial Court, Leon County, Florida, Transcript of Jury Trial, vol. 2 (December 11, 2018), p. 212.

62 *"we could be together"*: Ibid., p. 214.

62 *"Warren and Johnnie"*: Interview with Cheryl Williams, February 4, 2022.

62 *"she did not want to get divorced"*: Brian Winchester, testimony, *Florida v. Denise Williams*, Circuit Court of the Second Judicial Court, Leon County, Florida, Transcript of Jury Trial, vol. 2 (December 11, 2018), p. 214.

62 *"rich widow than a poor divorcée"*: Ibid., p. 216.

63 *consequences of divorce*: For 2019, a typical year, statistics about homicide victims drawn from the 2019 FBI Report "Crime in the United States: Expanded Homicide Statistics." In 50 percent of murders, the victim-

offender relationship is unknown; it is likely that many of these victims were in a relationship of some kind with the perpetrator, since the vast majority of homicides occur in the home. Details available at ucr.fbi.gov /crime-in-the-u.s/2019/crime-in-the-u.s.-2019/topic-pages/expanded -homicide (accessed November 21, 2022).

63 *"what was going on"*: Office of the State Attorney, Circuit Court of the Second Judicial Court, Leon County, Florida. Proffer of Brian Winchester, 2016, case number CF 02265. Transcript of recorded interview, Leon County Jail, October 12, 2017, pp. 5–6.

64 *"scenarios that were discussed"*: Ibid., p. 7.

65 *"happened to him"*: *Florida v. Denise Williams*, Circuit Court of the Second Judicial Court, Leon County, Florida, Transcript of Jury Trial, vol. 2 (December 11, 2018), p. 211.

65 *"who need no repentance"*: Luke 15:7, New King James Version. "Parable of the Lost Sheep."

66 *a wise and respected king*: 2 Samuel chapter 11 recounts how King David saw Bathsheba bathing on her roof, summoned her, and got her pregnant. He then contrived to kill Bathsheba's husband, Uriah, and married her. The story is often used to justify ethical failings, especially in religious people. For more details, see Dean C. Ludwig and Clinton O. Longenecker, "The Bathsheba Syndrome: The Ethical Failure of Successful Leaders," *Journal of Business Ethics* 12, no. 4 (1993), 265–73. See also David Janzen, "The Condemnation of David's 'Taking' in 2 Samuel 12:1–14," *Journal of Biblical Literature* 131, no. 2 (2012), 209–20.

66 *"God was going to forgive us"*: *Florida v. Denise Williams*, Circuit Court of the Second Judicial Court, Leon County, Florida, Transcript of Jury Trial, vol. 2 (December 11, 2018), p. 298.

67 *"we were put under"*: Ibid.

67 *"wishy-washy about"*: Office of the State Attorney, Circuit Court of the Second Judicial Court, Leon County, Florida. Proffer of Brian Winchester, 2016, case no. CF 02265. Transcript of second recorded interview, Wakulla Correctional Institute, February 8, 2018, pp. 11–12.

2.
Double Indemnity

69 *"When a man takes out"*: James M. Cain, *The Postman Always Rings Twice, Double Indemnity, Mildred Pierce and Selected Stories* (Everyman's Library, Random House: 1941), 164. Very few media accounts drew connections between the Winchester-Williams case and *Double Indemnity*, with the exception of a widely circulated AP Press wire account by Gary Fineout, "Witness Details How He Killed Lover's Husband for Insurance," December 11, 2018 ("With a plot that echoes a well-known Hollywood masterpiece . . ."), apnews.com/article/3f931d32aabb44e882e82f5972006816 (accessed November 21, 2022). See also Matthew T. Mangino, "A Florida Murder Trial, Life Imitating Art," *Erie Times-News*, December 14, 2018. Mangino wrote: "As Winchester calmly testified in detail about the events leading up to Mike Williams' death, I thought this story—although diabolical—is made for the big screen. Then it struck me—this movie has already been made [. . .] Had Denise Williams and Brian Winchester watched 'Double Indemnity' they might have thought twice about their ill-fated plan." www.goerie.com /story/opinion/columns/2018/12/14/matthew-t-mangino-florida-murder /6627770007/ (accessed November 21, 2020).

69 *self-destructive perversity*: For more on the subject of *Double Indemnity*, see W. M. Frohock, "The Tabloid Tragedy of James M. Cain," *Southwest Review* 34, no. 4 (Autumn 1949), 380–86; Christopher Orr, "Cain, Naturalism and Noir," *Film Criticism*, Fall 2000, 47–64.

70 *"chances to do it"*: For anecdote about printer's error, see Roy Hoopes, *Cain: The Biography of James M. Cain* (Southern Illinois University Press, 1987), 258. See also V. Penelope Pelizzon and Nancy M. West, "Multiple Indemnity: Film Noir, James M. Cain, and Adaptations of a Tabloid Case," *Narrative* 13, no. 3 (October 2005), 211–37; David M. Fine, "James M. Cain and the Los Angeles Novel," *American Studies* 20, no. 1 (Spring 1979), 25–34.

70 *"make himself rich"*: Anecdote recounted in Hoopes, p. 258. See also

John T. Irwin, "Beating the Boss: Cain's *Double Indemnity*," *American Literary History* 14, no. 2 (Summer 2002), 255–83.

71 *children, or their estate*: This is, in fact, what happened in the Denise Williams case; Mike's daughter, Anslee, was the beneficiary of the couple's estate. Information about life insurance payouts is from Douglas R. Richmond, "Investing with the Grim Reaper: Insurable Interest and Assignment in Life Insurance," *Tort Trial & Insurance Practice Law Journal* 47.2 (Winter 2012), 659.

71 *death by fire*: Information here is drawn from Michael Clarke, "Insurance Fraud," *British Journal of Criminology* 29.1 (Winter 1989), 3, n. 3.

72 *failing to cancel their policy*: Ben Kinglee and Louise Tanner, "Life Insurance as a Motive for Murder," *Tort & Insurance Law Journal* 29, no. 4 (Summer 1994), 5–6.

72 *you'll be kidnapped*: Information from Gideon Parchomovsky and Peter Siegelman, "The Paradox of Insurance" (2020), *Faculty Scholarship at Penn Law* 2158, p. 6; for information about life insurance in relation to the novel of James M. Cain, see Frederick Whiting, "Playing Against Type: Statistical Personhood, Depth Narrative, and the Business of Genre in James M. Cain's 'Double Indemnity,'" *Journal of Narrative Theory* 36, no. 2 (Summer 2006), 190–222.

72 *"icing on the cake"*: Brian Williams testimony, *Florida v. Denise Williams*, Circuit Court of the Second Judicial Court, Leon County, Florida, Transcript of Jury Trial, vol. 3 (December 12, 2018), p. 339.

73 *"will be doubled"*: Deposition of Marcus Winchester, August 9, 2018, 9:45 a.m., Leon County Courthouse, case no. 2018-CF-001592, *Florida v. Denise Williams*, Circuit Court of the Second Judicial Court, Leon County, Florida, p. 13.

74 *"Accidental Drowning"*: Insurance documents, Jerry Michael Williams Homicide FDLE Case Number TL-1-0102. Kansas City Life Research Service Bureau, Inc., Jerry M. Williams Contestable Death Claim Investigation Interim Report, p. 3.

74 *"eager widow ready to cash in on her life insurance"*: Testimony of Brian Winchester, *Florida v. Denise Williams*, Circuit Court of the Second Judicial Court, Leon County, Florida, vol. 2 (December 11, 2018), p. 245.

75 *"very tense and upset"*: Jerry Michael Williams Homicide FDLE Case Number TL-1-0102. Insurance documents. Kansas City Life memo, p. 7.

76 *tricky position for a while*: Telephone interview with Clay Ketcham, April 6, 2022.

77 *"under the guidelines"*: Brian Winchester, Jerry Michael Williams Homicide FDLE Case Number TL-1-0102. Special Agents Michael Devaney and William Mickler, case no. 00121624. Phone conversations of Kathy Thomas and Brian Winchester, p. 38.

78 *"like a pauper"*: Investigators Derrick Wester and Donnie Branch, case no. 00121624, interview with Deanna Lamb, October 5, 2005, p. 40.

78 *commented Brian sardonically*: Deposition of Brian Winchester, Volume 1, September 24, 2018, *Florida v. Denise Williams*, Circuit Court of the Second Judicial Court, Leon County, Florida, p. 70.

79 *"They all used the same phrase"*: Telephone interview with Clay Ketcham, April 6, 2022.

79 *"saith the Lord"*: Romans 12:19, King James Version.

80 *cheating and stealing*: Information drawn from Jingqiu Chen, Thomas Li-Ping Tang, and Ningyu Tang, "Temptation, Monetary Intelligence (Love of Money), and Environmental Context on Unethical Intentions and Cheating," *Journal of Business Ethics* 123, no. 2 (August 2014), 213.

80 *keep information to themselves*: Information about money habits from Adrian Furnham, Sophie von Stumm, and Mark Fenton-O'Creevy, "Sex Differences in Money Pathology in the General Population," *Social Indicators Research* 123, no. 3 (September [II] 2015), 702.

3.
Spiritual Awakening

82 *"all the time"*: James Cain, *The Postman Always Rings Twice, Double Indemnity, Mildred Pierce and Selected Stories* (Everyman's Library, Random House: 1941), 119.

83 *"It's hate"*: Quotation from ibid., 99.

84 *Board of Administration*: *Florida v. Denise Williams*, Circuit Court of the Second Judicial Court, Leon County, Florida, Transcript of Jury Trial, vol. 1 (December 11, 2018), p. 64. During Denise's murder trial, her defense attorney Philip Padovano announced in his opening statement that the jury would be hearing from Mr. Bunker, but he was never called to the stand.

84 *"flirty at work"*: Deposition of Katherine Anne Thomas, August 22, 2018, 9:30 a.m., Waynesville, N.C., case no. 2018-CF-001592, *Florida v. Denise Williams*, Circuit Court of the Second Judicial Court, Leon County, Florida, p. 77.

84 *"to be with her"*: Brian Winchester, testimony. *Florida v. Denise Williams*, Circuit Court of the Second Judicial Court, Leon County, Florida, Transcript of Jury Trial, vol. 2 (December 11, 2018), p. 252.

84 *"get her back or kill myself"*: Brian Winchester, notes, p. 38; Jerry Michael Williams Homicide FDLE Case Number TL-1-0102.

84 *"holding his hand"*: Ibid.

84 *"into traffic"*: Ibid.

85 *"but other men"*: Office of the State Attorney, Circuit Court of the Second Judicial Court, Leon County, Florida. Proffer of Brian Winchester, 2016, case no. CF 02265. Transcript of second recorded interview, Wakulla Correctional Institute, February 8, 2018, p. 7.

85 *"spiritual awakening or conversion"*: Brian Winchester, testimony. *Florida v. Denise Williams*, Circuit Court of the Second Judicial Court, Leon County, Florida, Transcript of Jury Trial, vol. 2 (December 11, 2018), p. 252.

85 *it hit home*: Jerry Michael Williams Homicide FDLE Case Number TL-1-0102. Brian Winchester, notes, p. 39.

87 *"he was in charge"*: Deposition of Charles "Chuck" Bunker, October 3, 2018, 2:30 p.m., Leon County Courthouse, Room 311, case no. 2018-CF-001592, *Florida v. Denise Williams*, Circuit Court of the Second Judicial Court, Leon County, Florida, p. 21.

87 *"get all upset"*: Deposition of Katherine Anne Thomas, August 22, 2018,

9:30 a.m., Waynesville, N.C., case no. 2018-CF-001592, *Florida v. Denise Williams*, Circuit Court of the Second Judicial Court, Leon County, Florida, p. 79.

88 *"ex-husband Brian Winchester"*: Jerry Michael Williams Homicide, FDLE Case Number TL-1-0102. Anonymous letter, postmarked August 10, 2003, Tallahassee.

88 *"will be around when this happens"*: Ibid.

89 *his long-dead marriage to Kathy*: *Florida v. Denise Williams*, Circuit Court of the Second Judicial Court, Leon County, Florida, Transcript of Jury Trial, vol. 2 (December 11, 2018), p. 254.

89 *a "white trash" thing to do*: Deposition of Katherine Anne Thomas, August 22, 2018, 9:30 a.m., Waynesville, N.C., case no. 2018-CF-001592, *State vs. Denise Williams*, Circuit Court of the Second Judicial Court, Leon County, Florida, pp. 68–69.

90 *file for divorce*: Ibid., 52.

90 *sobbing uncontrollably*: Ibid., 64.

93 *"ran out after her"*: *Florida v. Denise Williams*, Circuit Court of the Second Judicial Court, Leon County, Fl., Transcript of Jury Trial, vol. 3 (December 12, 2018), p. 384.

94 *his girlfriend, Erin*: *State of Florida v. Brian Winchester*, Circuit Court of the Second Judicial Court, Leon County, Florida, case no. 2016-CF-2265, Felony Division. Letters of Support, p. 51, letter from Erin L. Fontenot.

94 *"leading a double life"*: Deposition of Katherine Anne Thomas, August 22, 2018, 9:30 a.m., Waynesville, N.C., case no. 2018-CF-001592, *Florida v. Denise Williams*, Circuit Court of the Second Judicial Court, Leon County, Florida, p. 65.

4.
Good Christian People

95 *"are silent"*: Friedrich Nietzsche, *Beyond Good and Evil*, trans. Helen Zimmern, ch. 1, p. 39 (T.N. Coulis, 1907).

96 *"find out what happened?"*: Telephone interview with Clay Ketcham, April 6, 2022.

96 *traditional Baptist doctrines*: Information drawn from email correspondence with Jo Godfrey and Pastor Paul Gilbert, Four Oaks Church, Tallahassee, July 12, 2022, www.fouroakschurch.com/our-beliefs (accessed November 21, 2022).

97 *shadow of its opposite*: See Andrew Strathern and Pamela J. Stewart Strathern, "The Affirmative Powers of Denial," *Journal of Ritual Studies* (2013), 97.

97 *"a little milk in it . . ."*: Love letter from Denise contained in homicide file. See Jerry Michael Williams Homicide FDLE Case Number TL-1-0102, "Brian Notes," p. 35.

98 *"man like any other"*: Georges Simenon, *Maigret's Childhood Friend*, trans. Shaun Whiteside (Penguin Random House, 2020), 22.

98 *from Brian to Denise*: Jerry Michael Williams Homicide FDLE Case Number TL-1-0102. Investigators Derrick Wester and Donnie Branch, case no. 00121624. Letter from Brian Winchester, "Fifty Things I Love About Denise."

99 *"don't need to talk to her"*: Deposition of Katherine Anne Thomas, August 22, 2018, 9:30 a.m., Waynesville, N.C., case no. 2018-CF-001592, *Florida v. Denise Williams*, Circuit Court of the Second Judicial Court, Leon County, Florida, pp. 19–20.

101 *"regardless of the outcome"*: Jerry Michael Williams Homicide FDLE Case Number TL-1-0102. Investigator Ronald Branch, email from Kathy Thomas, October 13, 2005.

102 *musician Chris Tomlin*: *Florida v. Brian Winchester*, Circuit Court of the Second Judicial Court, Leon County, Florida, case no. 2016-CF-2265, Felony Division. Letters of Support, p. 51, letter from Erin L. Fontenot.

103 *abiding love*: *Florida v. Brian Winchester*, Circuit Court of the Second Judicial Court, Leon County, Florida, case no. 2016-CF-2265, Felony Division. Letters of Support, p. 51, letter from Erin L. Fontenot.

103 *group prayer before hunting*: *Florida v. Brian Winchester*, Circuit Court of the Second Judicial Court, Leon County, Florida, case no. 2016-

CF-2265, Felony Division. Letters of Support, p. 45, letter from Jerry Ford, MD.

103 *"merciful ending"*: Ibid.

105 *"a parenting lesson"*: Jerry Michael Williams Homicide FDLE Case Number TL-1-0102. Special Agents Michael DeVaney and William Mickler, case no. 00121624. Recorded phone conversations between Kathy Thomas and Brian Winchester, p. 7.

105 *"you don't know them"*: Here, Brian may be referring to what he called the "horribly dysfunctional things" that occurred in his childhood, which he described in a journal entry entitled "Rigorous Honesty," included in the homicide file. "Rigorous Honesty" was a Christian therapy program Brian was involved in. His account describes alcoholism and sexual abuse in his extended family, as well as his sex and porn addiction. See Jerry Michael Williams Homicide FDLE Case Number TL-1-0102, "Brian Notes," p. 35.

106 *"letting Anslee see Cheryl"*: Jerry Michael Williams Homicide FDLE Case Number TL-1-0102. Special Agents Michael DeVaney and William Mickler, case no. 00121624. Recorded phone conversations between Kathy Thomas and Brian Winchester, pp. 8–10.

106 *"I don't think she's a Christian, Kathy"*: Ibid.

107 *partners in crime*: *Florida v. Denise Williams*, Circuit Court of the Second Judicial Court, Leon County, Florida, Transcript of Jury Trial, vol. 3 (December 12, 2018), p. 291.

107 *go over their alibis*: Office of the State Attorney, Circuit Court of the Second Judicial Court, Leon County, Florida. Proffer of Brian Winchester, 2016, case number CF 02265. Transcript of recorded interview, Part 2, Wakulla Correctional Institution, February 8, 2018, p. 11.

108 *"watched or monitored"*: *Florida v. Denise Williams*, Circuit Court of the Second Judicial Court, Leon County, Florida, Transcript of Jury Trial, vol. 3 (December 12, 2018), p. 249.

108 *"live in denial"*: Ibid.

1.
Venal Foul Play

111 *"Foul whisperings are"*: William Shakespeare, *Macbeth, The Annotated Shakespeare* (Yale University Press, 2005), 144.

111 *"He's Been Missing"*: Jennifer Portman, "Tomorrow Makes 2,556 Days He's Been Missing," *Tallahassee Democrat*, December 15, 2007, pp. 1, 11A.

112 *"in peace"*: Ibid., p. 11A.

112 *August 8*: Jennifer Portman, "Divers Search for Missing Hunter," *Tallahassee Democrat*, August 8, 2007, p. 1.

112 *"New Look at Disappearance"*: Jennifer Portman, "Insurance Investigators Take New Look at Disappearance," *Tallahassee Democrat*, February 27, 2008, pp. 1, 6A (internal documents from Cotton States refer to Mike's disappearance as the "death claim alligator case").

112 *Mike's death*: Jerry Michael Williams Homicide FDLE Case Number TL-1-0102. Cotton States Insurance documents, November 6, 2001, p. 80.

113 *in Kentucky*: Tallahassee Regional Operations Center, Jerry Michael Williams Homicide FDLE Case Number TL-1-0102. JCSO box, correspondence and notes. Email to Derrick Wester from Carrie Cox, March 14, 2008, p. 54. Ms. Cox seemed ambivalent about her involvement in the case. Despite offering her services to the police and self-publishing a book on the subject (*Alligator Alibi*, published in 2019 on Lulu.com but no longer available), she signed off, "Please do not tell the media about me. I have three little boys I have to protect. I do not think the PTA needs to know that I talk to dead people on the side."

114 *bottom of the page*: Jennifer Portman, "Eight Years Later, Still No Trace of Missing Hunter," *Tallahassee Democrat*, December 16, 2008, pp. 1, 2A.

115 *eye to possible prosecution*: *Florida v. Denise Williams*, Circuit Court of the Second Judicial Court, Leon County, Florida, Transcript of Jury Trial, vol. 2 (December 11, 2018), p. 60.

116 *"police suspect foul play"*: "Mystery on Lake Seminole," *Disappeared*, In-

vestigation Discovery. Episode 10, Season 4. Aired at 10 p.m. on Monday, November 28, 2011. Episode is available on various streaming networks, including Apple TV+. See IMDB, /www.imdb.com/title/tt2321204/ (accessed October 3, 2021).

119 *"does not want anyone to find"*: All comments are taken from Websleuths forum. "Jerry Mike Williams, 31, Tallahassee, 16 Dec 2000," www.web sleuths.com/forums/threads/fl-jerry-mike-williams-31-tallahassee-16-dec -2000-wife-arrested-in-2017.57462/page-2, and www.websleuths.com /forums/threads/fl-jerry-mike-williams-31-tallahassee-16-dec-2000-wife -arrested-in-2017.57462/ (accessed October 2, 2021). Comments quoted: "Bree03872," November 28, 2011 ("This case SCREAMS of MURDER!"); "JaneDoe 91" January 3, 2012 ("My mom and I"); "littlegreycells31," November 30, 2011 ("I don't mean to prejudge people"); "Missing Budweiser," November 29, 2011 (*"Disappeared* sure made it look like"); "jjbomber" ("What I am puzzled about"); "noZme" January 3, 2012 ("these are prominent families"); "Meraxes" January 12, 2015, ("This case infuriates me!"). Comment from forensic psychologist "Tuba" ("venal foul play") at www.websleuths .com/forums/threads/forensic-astrology-case-briefings-only-1.79041/page -11#post-4533231 and also i481.photobucket.com/albums/rr172/Caustic Salt/DuckHunterVanishes001.jpg (accessed November 21, 2022). Grammar and spelling consistent with original comments.

121 *"dedicated to hating me"*: If such Facebook pages existed, they're no longer extant. Tallahassee Regional Operations Center, Jerry Michael Williams Homicide FDLE Case Number TL-1-0102, Brian Winchester, "Notes," 2012, p. 58.

121 *"anything about it"*: Ibid.

121 *"burst it open"*: Sigmund Freud, "Repression" (1915), in *The Standard Edition of the Complete Psychological Works of Sigmund Freud*, vol. 14 (Hogarth Press, 1953), 146, 149.

121 *"a hell within him"*: Quotation from Thomas De Quincey, "On the Knocking at the Gate in *Macbeth*," first published in the *London Magazine*, October 1823. Reproduced in De Quincey, *On Murder* (Oxford World's Classics, Oxford University Press, 2009), 5.

2.
You Will Answer to God

123 *"I had killed a man"*: James M. Cain, *The Postman Always Rings Twice, Double Indemnity, Mildred Pierce and Selected Stories* (Everyman's Library, Random House), 158.

124 *"into that house"*: Office of the State Attorney, Circuit Court of the Second Judicial Court, Leon County, Florida. Proffer of Brian Winchester, 2016, case number CF 02265. Transcript of recorded interview, Leon County Jail, October 12, 2017, p. 19.

125 *"I am seeking help with it"*: All quotations are from Tallahassee Regional Operations Center, Jerry Michael Williams Homicide FDLE Case Number TL-1-0102, Brian Winchester, "Notes," 2012, pp. 1–2.

125 *"Brian never worked"*: Deposition of Katherine Anne Thomas, August 22, 2018, 9:30 a.m., Waynesville, N.C., case no. 2018-CF-001592, *Florida v. Denise Williams*, Circuit Court of the Second Judicial Court, Leon County, Florida, p. 93.

126 *"between the two of them"*: Ibid.

126 *"I did it on purpose"*: Tallahassee Regional Operations Center, Jerry Michael Williams Homicide FDLE Case Number TL-1-0102, Brian Winchester, "Notes," November 5, 2012, 4.

127 *"hookers and everything else"*: Ibid., p. 97.

129 *"everything she did"*: Cain, *The Postman Always Rings Twice, Double Indemnity, Mildred Pierce and Selected Stories*, 219.

129 *"her relationship with you"*: All quotations are from Tallahassee Regional Operations Center, Jerry Michael Williams Homicide FDLE Case Number TL-1-0102, Brian Winchester, "Letters," p. 35.

129 *"ANSLEE"*: Tallahassee Regional Operations Center, Jerry Michael Williams Homicide FDLE Case Number TL-1-0102, Brian Winchester, "Notes," 2012, pp. 1–2.

129 *"fake, spoiled"*: Ibid., pp. 3–4.

129 *"clothes, shoes" everywhere*: If Brian's description is accurate, the state of the house suggests Denise, too, may have been having problems with emotional self-control.

131 *networks of donors*: Quotes in this paragraph taken from Reddit, "lapsed pastor AMA." See www.reddit.com/r/AMA/comments/vlm93y/i_was_an _ordained_pastor_in_a_large_evangelical/ (accessed November 21, 2022).

131 *Bible on their cell phones*: Description and information gleaned from attendance at 9 a.m. service at Celebration Baptist Church, Tallahassee, Sunday, July 24, 2022.

132 *"pain through sex"*: Tallahassee Regional Operations Center, Jerry Michael Williams Homicide FDLE Case Number TL-1-0102, Brian Winchester, "Notes," 2012, p. 40.

132 *"health and healing"*: Tallahassee Regional Operations Center, Jerry Michael Williams Homicide FDLE Case Number TL-1-0102, Brian Winchester, "Letters," 2012, p. 24.

133 *payments to Kathy*: Ibid., pp. 25–26.

133 *emails and texts*: Ibid., "Notes," p. 64.

133 *"God is so good!!"*: Ibid., pp. 64–84.

134 *"I miss Denise"*: Ibid., p. 27.

134 *"for this decision"*: Ibid., "Letters," p. 17.

3.
Enjoy Your Riches and Your Daughter

135 *"I had killed a man"*: James Cain, *The Postman Always Rings Twice, Double Indemnity, Mildred Pierce and Selected Stories* (Everyman's Library, Random House), 43.

135 *"I was so ashamed"*: Tallahassee Regional Operations Center, Jerry Michael Williams Homicide FDLE Case Number TL-1-0102, Brian Winchester, "Notes," February 11, 2014, p. 10.

135 *"abnormal and abusive"*: Ibid., p. 13.

135 *"trauma victim"*: Ibid., p. 15.

136 *"abused wives conference"*: Brian's wording. Office of the State Attorney, Circuit Court of the Second Judicial Court, Leon County, Florida. Proffer of Brian Winchester, 2016, case no. CF 02265. Transcript of recorded interview, Leon County Jail, October 12, 2017, Part 2, p. 92.

136 *"as a victim"*: Ibid., p. 45.

136 *anything she wanted*: Tallahassee Regional Operations Center, Jerry Michael Williams Homicide FDLE Case Number TL-1-0102, Brian Winchester, "Notes," February 11, 2014, p. 32.

136 *"where it might lead"*: Office of the State Attorney, Circuit Court of the Second Judicial Court, Leon County, Florida. Proffer of Brian Winchester, 2016, case no. CF 02265. Transcript of recorded interview, Leon County Jail, October 12, 2017, p. 31.

137 *"was wearing a wire"*: Office of the State Attorney, Circuit Court of the Second Judicial Court, Leon County, Florida. Proffer of Brian Winchester, 2016, case no. CF 02265. Transcript of recorded interview, Leon County Jail, October 12, 2017, Part 2, p. 25.

137 *Brian in his journal*: Tallahassee Regional Operations Center, Jerry Michael Williams Homicide FDLE Case Number TL-1-0102, Brian Winchester, "Notes," February 11, 2014, p. 10.

137 *"like she was 'acting'"*: Tallahassee Regional Operations Center, Jerry Michael Williams Homicide FDLE Case Number TL-1-0102, Brian Winchester, "Letters," 2013, p. 9.

138 *he confessed*: Office of the State Attorney, Circuit Court of the Second Judicial Court, Leon County, Florida. Proffer of Brian Winchester, 2016, case no. CF 02265. Transcript of recorded interview, Leon County Jail, October 12, 2017, Part 2, p. 45.

139 *Brian admitted*: Tallahassee Regional Operations Center, Jerry Michael Williams Homicide FDLE Case Number TL-1-0102, Brian Winchester, "Letter to Judge," p. 3.

139 *"when things got rough"*: Ibid., p. 4.

140 *"financially and emotionally"*: Office of the State Attorney, Circuit Court of the Second Judicial Court, Leon County, Florida. Proffer of Brian Winchester, 2016, case no. CF 02265. Transcript of recorded interview, Leon County Jail, October 12, 2017, Part 2, p. 7.

141 *"I lost everything"*: Tallahassee Regional Operations Center, Jerry Michael Williams Homicide FDLE Case Number TL-1-0102, Brian Winchester, "Letter to Judge," p. 4.

142 *"anything came up"*: Office of the State Attorney, Circuit Court of the Second Judicial Court, Leon County, Florida. Proffer of Brian Winchester, 2016, case no. CF 02265. Transcript of recorded interview, Leon County Jail, October 12, 2017, Part 2, p. 24.

142 *"in the bank"*: Ibid., p. 18.

142 *"of her saying anything"*: Ibid., p. 23.

142 *"anything to talk about"*: Ibid., p. 36.

143 *"I was a wreck"*: Deposition of Brian Winchester (September 24, 2018), *Florida v. Brian Winchester*, Circuit Court of the Second Judicial Court, Leon County, Florida, p. 56.

143 *sporting goods store*: It's not clear what happened to the Beretta Brian had in his bedroom; Roman Fontenot denied lending him a gun.

144 *then got "plastered"*: Deposition of Brian Winchester (September 24, 2018), *Florida v. Brian Winchester*, Circuit Court of the Second Judicial Court, Leon County, Florida, p. 5.

147 *She was "just hysterical"*: Description of kidnapping from Brian and Denise's police interviews, and deposition of Deborah McCrainie (September 19, 2017), *Florida v. Brian Winchester*, Circuit Court of the Second Judicial Court, Leon County, Florida, p. 7.

148 *"he was going to kill her"*: Deposition of David McCrainie (September 20, 2017), *Florida v. Brian Winchester*, Circuit Court of the Second Judicial Court, Leon County, Florida, p. 7.

4.
A New Rock Bottom

149 *"individuality"*: Sigmund Freud, "Some Character-Types Met with in Psycho-analytical Work" (1916), *The Standard Edition of the Complete Psychological Works of Sigmund Freud*, vol. 14 (Hogarth Press, 1953), p. 25.

149 *can't remember the house number*: This is rather difficult to explain, unless it's simply an indication of Denise's extreme anxiety. After all, 2695 Miller Landing Road was the "dream home" the couple had spent years looking for, and months negotiating to buy. Perhaps Denise had simply let go of the past.

150 *"'I want to kill myself'"*: Denise Williams police interview, Leon County Sheriff's Office, August 5, 2016. Uploaded online by the *Tallahassee Democrat*, June 1, 2018. See Jennifer Portman, "On the Day She Was Kidnapped, Interrogators Grilled Denise on Mike Williams' Disappearance," www.tallahassee.com/story/news/2018/06/01/after-kidnapping-cops-grilled-denise-mike-williams-disappearance/656786002/ (accessed November 21, 2022). The full interview has been uploaded to YouTube by James Wasczewski's "Deep Dive True Crime" channel. See "Full Interrogation of Denise Williams, Who Married the Murderer of Her First Husband Mike Williams," www.youtube.com/watch?v=PsnuyP4excE. See also deposition of David McCrainie (September 20, 2017), *Florida v. Brian Winchester*, Circuit Court of the Second Judicial Court, Leon County, Florida, p. 7.

151 *police detective*: Ibid. There is some later debate, in the court transcript and in McCrainie's deposition, about whether his interview with Denise was "official" or "off the record."

151 *"a con artist"*: Denise Williams police interview, Leon County Sheriff's Office, August 5, 2016.

152 *"didn't he?"*: Ibid.

152 *"in a traumatic event"*: Deposition of David McCrainie (September 20, 2017), *Florida v. Brian Winchester*, Circuit Court of the Second Judicial Court, Leon County, Florida, p. 15.

154 *"Mike died at the lake"*: Patti Ketcham. Interview with Clay and Patti Ketcham, Ketcham Appraisals, Tallahassee, July 2, 2022.

154 *"Of course she knows"*: Ibid.

154 *"going to fall apart"*: Office of the State Attorney, Circuit Court of the Second Judicial Court, Leon County, Florida. Proffer of Brian Winchester, 2016, case no. CF 02265. Transcript of recorded interview, Leon County Jail, October 12, 2017, p. 19.

155 *"extremely agitated"*: Deposition of Dr. Stephen Mnookin (September 19, 2017), *Florida v. Brian Winchester*, Circuit Court of the Second Judicial Court, Leon County, Florida, p. 11.

156 *"this guy who died"*: Jennifer Portman, "Fears Over Mike Williams Case Drove 2016 Kidnapping," *Tallahassee Democrat*, January 24, 2018, p. 1.

158 *"Please don't let him out"*: Denise's testimony, Brian Winchester Bond Hearing, August 10, 2016, Leon County Courthouse, Tallahassee, Florida.

160 *"she had really screwed up"*: Deposition of Brian Winchester (September 24, 2018), *Florida v. Brian Winchester*, Circuit Court of the Second Judicial Court, Leon County, Florida, p. 45.

5.
Fully and Truthfully

162 *"presumed in both"*: Thomas De Quincey, "On the Knocking at the Gate in *Macbeth*," first published in the *London Magazine*, October 1823. Reproduced in De Quincey, *On Murder* (Oxford World's Classics, Oxford University Press, 2009), 5.

164 *talked to ghosts*: Deposition of Brian Winchester (September 24, 2018), *Florida v. Brian Winchester*, Circuit Court of the Second Judicial Court, Leon County, Florida, p. 22.

165 *who would help him out*: Ibid.

165 *"his upcoming trial"*: Agent William Mickler, FDLE Investigate Report on Wade Wilson report, case no. TL-73-2691, July 6, 2017, p. 2.

165 *"alligator skin trim"*: Ibid.

166 *"who conned me"*: Deposition of Brian Winchester (September 24, 2018), *Florida v. Brian Winchester*, Circuit Court of the Second Judicial Court, Leon County, Florida, p. 48.

166 *for a traffic offense*: Wilson was soon to be in far more trouble than this. On November 19, 2019, the state charged Wade Wilson with the murders of two women in Cape Coral. In October 2020, Wilson, age twenty-six, and his cellmate, Joseph Katz, age thirty, were charged with attempted escape and criminal mischief after trying to escape from prison. The court documents said a note had been passed between Wilson and another inmate, who were allegedly connected via a white supremacy gang known as "The Unforgiven." Wade Wilson claims the public defender's case files were hacked in April 2021, which destroyed attorney-client privilege, "making this case unviable for prosecution." Information about Wade Williams from Jeff Burlew, "Former Tallahassee Man with Link to Mike Williams Case Charged in Two Lee County Murders," *Tallahassee Democrat*, December 13, 2019, www.tallahassee.com/story/news/local/2019/12/13/former-tallahassee-man-link-mike-williams-case-charged-two-lee-county-murders/4401641002/ (accessed September 14, 2022).

166 *some ridiculous plans*: Neither Brian's sister, father, nor Kim Adams was ever involved in any bribery and were never charged with any wrongdoing in the case.

168 *"for this murder"*: Zoom interview with Philip Padovano, June 31, 2022.

168 *aware of at the time*: Office of the State Attorney, Circuit Court of the Second Judicial Court, Leon County, Florida. Proffer of Brian Winchester, 2016, case no. CF 02265. Transcript of recorded interview, Leon County Jail, Part 2, October 12, 2017, p. 59.

169 *"exaggerate her role"*: Office of the State Attorney, Circuit Court of the Second Judicial Court, Leon County, Florida. Proffer of Brian Winchester, 2016, case no. CF 02265. Transcript of recorded interview, Leon County Jail, Part 1, October 9, 2017, p. 49.

169 *"pretty much fifty-fifty"*: Ibid., p. 31. Among the revelations: Brian didn't plant Mike's jacket and waders in the lake. These items had become the case's most significant red herring. When a fisherman discovered them six months after Mike's disappearance, people became suspicious. If Mike had been torn apart by alligators, why were his jacket and waders so pristine? Why hadn't they been discovered during the thorough search for his body? Why weren't they covered in algae? How could the flashlight still be functional? Brian thought the items didn't sink to the bottom of the lake because they got caught in the hydrilla. The cold temperature, he suggested, prevented algae from forming. He wasn't surprised no one found them during the "extensive searches" for Mike's body. "I was there for the 'extensive searches,'" he reminded the investigators sardonically, "and . . . you're talking about a bunch of good old boys . . . in fifteen feet of water . . . using poles to poke." Ibid.

169 *"she's off the charts"*: The rumor about "sex with animals" was one of the case's red herrings, like the discovery of Mike's jacket and waders in the lake. There's no evidence that Denise had ever had "sex with animals," although there's a strange moment during Brian's deposition when, in the middle of asking questions about the murder, Denise's defense attorney Ethan Way suddenly changes the subject, and seemingly out of nowhere, the following dialogue occurs:

Q: Do you have any pets or did you have any pets as a child?
A: Yes.
Q: What were the names of your pets?
A: Which ones?
Q: Well, let me just jump right to the question. Did you ever name a pet after Denise?
A: Yes.
Q: What pet was that?
A: It was a dog.
Q: And when did you have that dog?

A: Like elementary school age, I think. I don't think I actually named it after her. I think I had the idea or thought of it.

Perhaps Way thought this implied that Denise liked "sex with animals," but it could equally imply that Brian was obsessed with her from an early age. However irrelevant to the facts of the case, Denise's sexuality became a significant issue to the public and the prosecution. Clay Ketcham said an investigator told his wife, Patti, that he'd worked for ten or fifteen years at the state attorney's office and had seen "a lot of pictures of sex stuff." The investigator allegedly told Patti, "What that girl did is beyond anything I've ever seen. And we have photographic evidence. She's just a nasty girl." (Clay and Patti Ketcham, interview, Tallahassee, July 22, 2022.)

169 *"Chinese baby"*: Office of the State Attorney, Circuit Court of the Second Judicial Court, Leon County, Florida. Proffer of Brian Winchester, 2016, case no. CF 02265. Transcript of recorded interview, Leon County Jail, Part 2, October 12, 2017, p. 43.

169 *"paid them for"*: Deposition of Brian Winchester (September 24, 2018), *Florida v. Brian Winchester*, Circuit Court of the Second Judicial Court, Leon County, Florida, p. 79.

171 *the confession had been a "relief"*: Testimony of Jason Newlin, *Florida v. Denise Williams*, Circuit Court of the Second Judicial Court, Leon County, Florida, Transcript of Jury Trial, vol. IV (December 12, 2018), p. 408.

6.
We Are Not Murderers

174 *"had the heart to fight"*: Cit. in Jennifer Portman, "Mike Williams' Remains Located in Leon County," *Tallahassee Democrat*, December 24, 2017, 2A.

176 *"time to talk"*: Jennifer Portman, "Mike Williams: Missing for 17 Years, and Counting," *Tallahassee Democrat*, December 16, 2017, 1, 5A.

178 *"his mother still lives"*: Jennifer Portman, "Mike Williams' Remains Located in Leon County," *Tallahassee Democrat*, December 24, 2017, 2A.

182 *"the party is over"*: See www.tigerdroppings.com/rant/o-t-lounge/milf -arrested-for-husbands-murder-17-years-later/76660196/, "cleeveclever," posted on May 9, 2018 (accessed September 15, 2022).

1.
What's Done in the Dark

185 *"shall speak truth"*: Proverbs 8:7, King James Version.

186 *any ongoing appeals*: According to an article by Jennifer Portman published in the *Tallahassee Democrat* on July 16, 2019, the assets given to Anslee included four pieces of Tallahassee real estate valued at about $877,000, including her home on Centennial Oak Circle, purchased by her parents when she was a baby. Assistant State Attorney Jon Fuchs had no comment on the total dollar figure, though Cheryl Williams said it was about $1.4 million. See Jennifer Portman, "Denise Williams Insurance Fraud Case Dropped, Daughter Gets All Assets," *Tallahassee Democrat*, July 16, 2019, www.tallahassee.com/story/news/2019/07/16 /mike-williams-daughter-awarded-all-assets/1742234001/. A pressing question came to the surface in connection with the assets: Could Anslee be Brian's biological daughter? When Brian was asked this question during his 2018 deposition, he said that although Denise had been "on and off the pill" between 1997 and 2000, and they had used condoms "some of the time," nonetheless, he was "ninety-nine percent sure" that Anslee was Mike's daughter just because everyone agrees her "appearance looks like Mike." (Office of the State Attorney, Circuit Court of the Second Judicial Court, Leon County, Florida. Proffer of Brian Winchester, 2016, case no. CF 02265. Transcript of recorded interview, Leon County Jail, October 9, 2017, Part 1, p. 74.)

186 *"no attention to the news"*: James Hankinson, email interview, April 23, 2022.

187 *"the perfect juror"*: Comment recounted by James Karabasz to James Waczewski, a Tallahassee attorney who, under the name "Mentour Lawyer," maintains a Youtube channel ("Deep Dive True Crime") devoted to cover-

ing local court cases and high-profile crimes. His interview with Karabasz is available at www.youtube.com/watch?v=K2BwspwpNk0.

187 *"a serious undertaking"*: Ibid.

188 *"brothers-in-law attended"*: Interview with Clay and Patti Ketcham, Ketcham Appraisals, Tallahassee, July 22, 2022.

188 *allowed in the courtroom*: No potential witness is ever sure they'll actually be called. It all depends on the way things are going in court. Clay Ketcham had no idea why the state didn't call him as a witness; he believes it was possible that the defense attorneys "didn't want my presence in the courtroom" as "a legal strategy," although he had no idea what this strategy could have been (phone interview, April 6, 2022).

189 *closer to 4 percent*: Statistics are taken from Table C-4 of the Annual Reports of the Administrative Office of the U.S. Courts, cited by Jeffrey Q. Smith and Grant R. McQueen, "Going, Going, but Not Quite Gone: Trials Continue to Decline in Federal and State Courts. Does It Matter?" *Judicature* 101, no. 4 (Winter 2017), p. 15, judicature.duke.edu /articles/going-going-but-not-quite-gone-trials-continue-to-decline -in-federal-and-state-courts-does-it-matter/ (accessed November 14, 2022).

190 *the circle goes around*: See "The Truth About Trials," *The Marshall Project*, issue 5, www.themarshallproject.org/2020/11/04/the-truth-about-trials (accessed November 22, 2022).

191 *wondered one observer*: See Fuchs's testimony at www.youtube.com /watch?v=BSFLqUrVCTE. Comment from "Ralph Stewart" ("Chewing tobacco"); to be fair, other commenters found Fuchs efficient and professional.

191 *jurors were openly yawning*: Fuchs declined a request to be interviewed for this book.

193 *"ran out after her"*: *Florida v. Denise Williams*, Circuit Court of the Second Judicial Court, Leon County, Florida, Transcript of Jury Trial, vol. 4 (December 11, 2018), p. 384.

193 *"one place before"*: Comments taken from www.youtube.com/watch ?v=ICTsFCD1fcw&t=594s "Shar Crum" ("juicy as fuck"); "James Smith"

("Pretty hot stuff"); "Unconstructed Belle" ("so much scum"). "Dirty laundry" from "whatever5575" from https://youtube.com/watch?v=ICTs FCD1fcw), "Denise Williams Love Triangle Trial Day 2, Part 4, Angela Stafford Jason Newlin Testify."

193 *I'm munching popcorn—riveted*": Comments taken from www.youtube .com/watch?v=a_giR3lzPT0&t=3622s: "Foxibot" ("having a hard time"); "Me" ("bunch of weirdos"); "Ladykflo" ("munching popcorn").

193 *"prurient interest"*: *Florida v. Denise Williams*, Circuit Court of the Second Judicial Court, Leon County, Florida, Transcript of Jury Trial, vol. 3 (December 11, 2018), p. 320.

194 *"a smart girl"* Comments take from www.youtube.com/watch?v=a _giR3lzPT0&t=3622s: "KisoTKev Kisovev" ("sweet and composed"); "JsnYnk20" ("genuine and adorable"); "ddub wizbo" ("wholesome"); "barbara allison" ("good girl"); "vknaga" ("sweet girl").

195 *a single page*: *Florida v. Denise Williams*, Circuit Court of the Second Judicial Court, Leon County, Florida, Transcript of Jury Trial, vol. 4 (December 11, 2018), p. 16.

196 *"wanted to make"*: Zoom interview with Philip Padovano, March 31, 2022.

197 *"for her to be upset"*: *Florida v. Denise Williams*, Circuit Court of the Second Judicial Court, Leon County, Florida, Transcript of Jury Trial, vol. 4 (December 11, 2018), p. 523.

2.

I Loaded My Gun

198 *"come abroad"*: Mark 4:22, King James Version.

3.

She Was in My Head

212 *"without the man . . ."*: 1 Corinthians 11:11, King James Version.

213 *"killing"* or *"murder"*: This reluctance continued; even on the stand, Brian

spoke about the crime in the passive voice (e.g., "The plan was for his death to occur, but not for it to occur in the way that it did").

213 *"quickly and drown"*: *Florida v. Denise Williams*, Circuit Court of the Second Judicial Court, Leon County, Florida, Transcript of Jury Trial, vol. 1 (December 11, 2018), p. 226.

213 *flail and panic*: "Water in your waders isn't any heavier than water outside your waders and won't drag you down like a rock. In fact, neoprene is buoyant (ever notice how easy it is to pick your feet up while wearing waders in the water?) and won't create much if any resistance while trying to swim in them. I would be willing to bet you that most hunter deaths attributed to waders are actually the result of panicking." See comment by "Duck Dawg," January 3, 2012, www.duckhuntingchat.com/threads/no-waders-in-the-boat.176280/.

213 *"what I had done"*: Deposition of Brian Winchester (September 24, 2018), *Florida v. Brian Winchester*, Circuit Court of the Second Judicial Court, Leon County, Florida, p. 17.

215 *to be found*: During Brian's deposition, after he described burying Mike's body at Carr Lake, Ethan Way asked him, "So, you didn't shoot him there and then drive his truck, trailer, and boat out to Lake Seminole and have someone come and pick you up there?"

215 *needed an accomplice*: This is a popular theory. It's been suggested that Brian's well-connected father, Marcus (or perhaps his cousin Kevin), is the most likely candidate. Clay Ketcham indicated that the prosecutors, too, might have suspected that Brian wasn't telling the truth but had no motive for investigating alternative scenarios. "They probably didn't want to allocate any more resources to the case," Clay speculated. "They probably thought, 'We have a confessed murderer, so we've got the killer of Mike Williams. The story is over, whether Brian's telling the truth or not. There's no way for us to prove it.' So there it sits. I just don't think it played out the way he portrayed it." Interview with Clay and Patti Ketcham, Ketcham Appraisals, Tallahassee, July 22, 2022.

217 *"to what he did"*: Joslyn Bynum, email interview, August 17, 2022.

217 *The chorus of viewers*: Brian's trial testimony is available on YouTube: www.youtube.com/watch?v=GouoClh_gVk&list=PLoW1SIeAWaWYBY aZ8jw07pbOYrTPRsOEE&index (accessed August 17, 2022). Comments: "=77700Purplexity" ("emotional"); "Grounded Gameplay" ("dramatic . . . incredible"); "Glenda Pospisil" ("remorseful testimony"); "Dmichael100" ("compelling watching and listening"); "Nancy C Kawimbe" ("I believe everything . . ."); "James Ryan" ("painful confession"); "Dr. Voodoo" ("You can tell . . ."); "Marc Broussard" ("anatomy of a murder"); "HoneyBoner29" ("Imagine having to live with this for 17 years").

218 *"One cold-blooded woman"*: Comments posted at www.youtube.com /watch?v=6KsVr9GuD_Y. "Anisha Annu Rary" ("the alligator"); "Joe Tamburello" ("pure evil"); "LadySandraisaBolton" ("clearly a sociopath"); "Goose" ("cold-hearted"); "Tammy Vaughan" ("one cold-blooded woman").

218 *her feelings show*: Zoom interview with Philip Padovano, June 31, 2022.

219 *"Criminal Minds"*: Joslyn Bynum, email interview, Wednesday, August 17, 2022.

219 *as short as eleven minutes*: Statistics taken from Thomas L. Brunell, "Factors Affecting the Length of Time a Jury Deliberates: Case Characteristics and Jury Composition," *Review of Law & Economics*, January 2009, 15. www.researchgate.net/profile/Thomas-Brunell/publication/46556298 _Factors_Affecting_the_Length_of_Time_a_Jury_Deliberates_Case _Characteristics_and_Jury_Composition/links/09e4150e18892d1e76 000000/Factors-Affecting-the-Length-of-Time-a-Jury-Deliberates-Case -Characteristics-and-Jury-Composition.pdf (accessed November 17, 2022).

219 *"without absolutely being sure"*: Joslyn Bynum, email interview, August 17, 2022.

219 *"no emotion at all"*: Ibid.

220 *"persons had done"*: Jury Instructions, *Florida v. Denise Williams*, Circuit

Court of the Second Judicial Court, Leon County, Florida, Transcript of Jury Trial, vol. 7 (December 14, 2018), p. 865.

221 *Denise's murder conviction*: First District Court of Appeal, State of Florida, case no. 1D19-498, *Denise Williams v. State of Florida*, November 25, 2020.

221 *"first-degree murder"*: Ibid., p. 6.

221 *"committing the offense"*: Ibid., p. 12.

222 *Hankinson retired*: The Honorable James C. Hankinson died from a brain tumor on July 6, 2023.

223 *"truly sorry"*: Most likely, the "reckless decision" Denise referred to was getting married to Brian; it seems unlikely she'd finally admitted that she'd encouraged him to murder Mike.

226 *"The New Land"*: Fuchs didn't name the author, but presumably he was referring to *The New Land* by Ljupka Cvetanova (Makform, 2013), a self-published collection of aphorisms. The aphorisms are quoted ubiquitously online, but the book itself is elusive.

4.
The Eve Factor

229 *"I did eat"*: Genesis 3:13, King James Version.

230 *"lying and deceit"*: For the performative nature of confessions, see M. Hepworth and B. Turner, "Confession, Guilt and Responsibility," *British Journal of Law and Society* 6, no. 2 (Winter 1979), 222.

231 *"the 'Eve' who tempts the 'Adam'"*: Ethan Way, email interview, March 31, 2022.

232 *was posted online*: Until mid-August 2022, all the documents in the case were made available by Steven B. Epstein, author of the first book about the case, *Evil at Lake Seminole* (Black Lyon Publishing, 2020), at the now obsolete website www.evilatlakeseminole.com (last accessed August 8, 2022).

233 *a great punch line*: All comments taken from YouTube trial footage, www

.youtube.com/watch?v=-t96WR1I3qM&t=19s: "Colonel Reb" ("dirty little secrets"); "Suzanne Marie" ("so full of drama"); "Bugsea" ("out-in-the-
open affair"); "Jon Blackstone" ("countless acts"); "Lee Primeaux" ("wild
partying"); "Beaux Day Shush" ("mutual guilt").

235 *the wider world*: It's been said that "if you want to see the face of a murderer,
just look in the mirror." The line is used by Gary Indiana in the Preface to
Three Month Fever (Quartet, 1999), his superb book on Andrew Cunanan.
Indiana attributes it to Gore Vidal, but the exact provenance is unknown.

About the Author

Mikita Brottman is a writer and psychoanalyst living in Baltimore, Maryland. Her most recent book, *An Unexplained Death*, was shortlisted for the Gold Dagger award for nonfiction by the Crime Writers Association of the UK. She has a D.Phil from Oxford University and is a professor of literature at the Maryland Institute College of Art.